Ultimate Questions

Ultimate Questions

An Anthology of Modern Russian Religious Thought

Edited and with an Introduction by

Alexander Schmemann

ST. VLADIMIR'S SEMINARY PRESS
Crestwood, New York 10707
1977

Scriptural quotations in the selections from Florensky and Bulgakov have, in most instances, been translated directly from their Russian texts by the Rev. Ashcleigh E. Moorhouse. Otherwise, the *Revised Standard Version of the Bible* has been followed.

ISBN 0-913836-46-X

Printed in Great Britain

Acknowledgments

GRATEFUL ACKNOWLEDGMENT is made to the following copyright
holders for permission to include in this anthology excerpts from
the books listed:

Geoffrey Bles Ltd., London, for the chapter "Ethics of Creativity,"
from *The Destiny of Man* by N. A. Berdyaev, translated by
Natalie Duddington (1955).

Mrs. Helen N. Fedotov, for *Khristianin v revolyutsii* by G. P.
Fedotov (Paris, 1957).

St. Sergius Brotherhood, Paris, for *Radost tserkovnaya* by S. N.
Bulgakov (Paris, 1938).

Student Christian Movement Press Ltd., London, for a chapter
from *A Solovyov Anthology*, edited by S. L. Frank (1950).

Vladimir Weidlé for his *Zadacha Rossii* (New York: Chekhov Publishing House, 1956).

Contents

Ultimate Questions

Introduction

THE AIM of this anthology is to give to those who are studying Russia, her history, literature, and religious life, at least a general idea of that area of Russian culture which Russians usually define as "religious philosophy." This word combination may confuse Western readers, since in the West theology and philosophy are usually strictly separated, as are the areas of religion and culture themselves. The authors presented here are quite unlike one another in background, education, and manner of life. With very few exceptions they are all outside the world of official theology or academic philosophy—a former officer of the hussars, a librarian, a writer, a journalist. One thing, however, they all share: the centrality of the religious theme in their work, the constant reduction of everything to "ultimate questions"—about God and Christ, about the Church, and about the world as an object of religious apprehension. Surely too much has already been said about Russian "God-seeking," much of it either incorrect or exaggerated. And yet it is hardly possible simply to ignore the constant presence of religious questioning and search in the most varied expressions of Russian culture. One cannot achieve a full understanding of the complicated and tragic path of Russia without considering it. The study of Russia will be incomplete and one-sided if, wholly concentrated on the contemporary Soviet period, it bypasses those themes and questions which, in various ways, have always disturbed the Russian conscience. The task of

3

this anthology is to indicate and provide some real awareness of these questions.

The texts collected here require a few introductory remarks. First of all, it would be a mistake to see in them an expression of the official teaching of the Orthodox Church. The authors represented here are independent thinkers whose views still give rise to disputes among theologians and philosophers. They still have their defenders and disciples, as well as their accusers and enemies. Thus for George Florovsky, author of the remarkable *Puti russkovo bogosloviye* ("The Ways of Russian Theology"), almost the whole development of Russian religious philosophy is a complete deviation from true Orthodoxy; it is the wandering and seeking of the Russian mind as it has torn itself away from the Church, and its return to her out of every possible type of spiritual and moral bondage. But according to Professor Zenkovsky, author of another study of the first rank, *History of Russian Philosophy*, all these searchings are, on the contrary, united precisely by one Orthodox theme, "total unity." The Church censorship at first prohibited the publication of Khomyakov's works in Russia, but now many see in him one of the most remarkable interpreters of Orthodoxy. Tolstoy was separated from the Church, but his very opposition to the Church is a significant fact in the history of Orthodoxy. The doctrine of Fyodorov is for some a blatant heresy, for others one of the best fruits of the Church's own world view. Berdyaev, Bulgakov, and Florensky have evoked bitter disputes up to the present day. Thus we are dealing here with a situation which is not yet finally settled and evaluated. The study of Russian religious thought is only just beginning, and whatever the results of this study will be, it is hardly possible to reject such thought as a phenomenon within Orthodoxy or closely related to it. The thinkers presented here have had a great influence on both theology and philosophy, and in my opinion they deserve study and attention.

This is not the place for a complete history of the religious development of Russia. However, for an understanding of the "specific gravity" of the texts gathered together in this book, a brief survey of certain basic features is in order.

The religious history of Russia begins with its adoption of Byzantine Orthodoxy, an event which determined its subsequent course once and for all. We know that the Slavs who united with Kiev in the first Russian state accepted Byzantine Christianity without much difficulty, and rapidly assimilated its content and general style. This was furthered, at first, by the fact that Byzantine Orthodoxy was sent to Russia in its Slavic "recension," which was begun in the ninth century by the Byzantine brothers St. Cyril and St. Methodius, and which later spread and took root in Bulgaria. Very soon after the so-called "Baptism of Russia" under the Kievan Prince Vladimir, the tradition of Russian sanctity, ecclesiastical architecture, and monasticism appeared. The depth and significance of this Kievan period was brilliantly analyzed by the late George P. Fedotov in *The Russian Religious Mind*. Indeed, Orthodoxy very quickly became "the faith of Russia," organically connected with the whole life and culture of the Russian people. It is important to emphasize, however, that this faith was received first of all in its aesthetic-moral content and in its liturgical form rather than in its intellectual or dogmatic aspect. This is explained not only by the cultural unpreparedness of Russia, her lack of a cultural tradition and schools, but also by the condition of Byzantium itself in the period of the Baptism of Russia.

About the time of the entrance of Russia into the Byzantine tradition of Orthodoxy, the golden age of intellectual and spiritual creativity of Byzantium was already past. The iconoclastic crisis of the eighth and ninth centuries was the last great "creative" crisis in the Eastern Church. It ended the often tragic but also infinitely rich history of the "establishment" of Byzantine Orthodoxy, of the development of its "canon." Toward the end of the ninth century, this "canon" may be con-

sidered complete. Whatever the area of the Church's life—
doctrine, divine worship, ascetic life—they all received their final
form precisely in the decades following the "Triumph of Orthodoxy" which officially celebrated the victory over the iconoclasts
(842). This triumph itself places a line between the earlier creative Byzantium and the later "conservative" Byzantium.

All the achievements of early Byzantium—the theological
writings of the Fathers, the Ecumenical Councils, the methods
of asceticism—were "canonized" not only in the sense of being
true but also as the *final* expression of Orthodoxy, which was to
be *preserved* for the most part by succeeding generations.

And so this completed, already "official" Orthodoxy was accepted by the Russians. In other words, they were only required
to receive and preserve but in no way to participate creatively in
that "adaptation" of the faith which was such a distinctive feature of the earlier Byzantine period. In the Russian form of
Orthodoxy therefore, from the very beginning, there was no
theological or intellectual "tempering process." This certainly
does not mean that there was a lack of depth to Russian religious
experience. "Prior to the silent pre-Petrine era," writes Florovsky,
"a great deal was tried and tested. The Russian school, with its
rather well-known receptivity, witnesses to the complexity and
depth, to the real brilliance of the old Russian spiritual experience, to the creative power of the Russian spirit" (*Puti*, p. 1). It
only means that throughout a very long period, in fact right up to
the revolutionary encounter with the West brought about in the
eighteenth century by Peter the Great, there was no tradition of
independent thought as a reflection of religious experience and
as its expression in words. Also, there were no theological schools
as the means for creating such thought. It is necessary to remember this in order to understand both the origins and the general
tone of the development of Russian religious thought.

A second essential feature of Russian religious development
must be discerned in its agelong isolation from the Christian

West. Russia received Orthodoxy when the latter had already in fact become "Eastern," had been formulated in its antagonism toward the West. The two ancient and primitive halves of the Christian world were gradually separated and transformed from "halves" into two independent, self-sufficient "wholes," tragically losing the consciousness of belonging to one another. The period in which Russia received Christianity was the "epoch of the division of the Church," the epoch not of dispute, not of dialogue, not even of polemic communication, but of a separation that had already become radical and irreparable. Contemporary historians often stress the fact that Kievan Russia before the Tatar devastation was open to the West. This is true, but the depth and significance of these Western ties should not be exaggerated. For in the very structure of Orthodoxy as received by Kievan Russia from Byzantium, there was already this antagonism toward the West, the limitation of the religious horizon to the Byzantine East. The further development of Russian history only strengthened and deepened this isolation of Russia from the West. The Tatar yoke, the expenditure of forces in the struggle against it, and, on the religious level, the Union of Florence (1439) and the fall of Constantinople (1453), increased and fixed the Russian "fear" of the West, or, at any rate, certainly did not encourage the development of intellectual ties with it. "The West" entered into Russian history as something dangerous and hostile—dangerous politically, hostile from the standpoint of religion. At the same time, the inner universalism of Byzantine Orthodoxy (retained in spite of its historical restriction to the "East") made Russia's "anti-Westernism" abnormal, artificial; it fettered the normal development of Russian thought. Hence the enthusiastic reception of the West in Russia after the reform of Peter the Great, the experiencing of it as a "return" to something closely related if not its very own. Just as Russian literature only discovered its national character as a result of the Petrine grafting on of the West, thereby also acquiring stature as world literature, Russian philosophy, too, found its own Rus-

sian and Orthodox themes in the school of the West, as a result
of the meeting of the Russian mind with Western intellectual
and philosophical traditions. The significance of Russian religious thought—not so much the significance of its individual
successes as of its whole development—lies most of all in the fact
that in it the historical identification of Orthodoxy with the
"East" is overcome from within and its universal perspective is
re-established. Before this, Orthodox theology had been subjected to Western influence and to the engrafting of Western
methods—in the Kievan school of the sixteenth and seventeenth
centuries, and through it, in the Russian theological schools
opened by Peter. But this led simply to "Western captivity," to
the internal latinization of Orthodox theology, from which it has
not freed itself completely even now. In Russian religious
thought, however, the "West" has been not only a method but
also the object of spiritual appraisal. As a result of this appraisal,
of this constant reflection or consideration of the West, communication with it was restored on a free basis as a dialogue
and exchange and not as a one-sided "subjugation." Vladimir
Weidlé's introductory essay, which follows, is devoted to this
theme of Russia and the West. It establishes that perspective in
which the real significance of Russian thought as a whole is made
plain.

Several first-class studies have already been devoted to the history of Russian thought and culture and there is no need for us
to enter into this subject here—a brief survey would in any case
scarcely further its understanding. In the General Bibliography
the reader will find the titles of the major and most useful works
in this area. The authors presented here do not, of course, exhaust all the representatives of Russian religious thought, nor is
each author's work by any means exhausted by the texts included. References are therefore given for further study in the
brief biographical sketches preceding each selection. We have
conceived this anthology as a kind of invitation—a searching

look into that area of Russian culture whose significance both for the understanding of the culture itself and for the history of the religious searching of our time has not yet, it seems to us, been properly defined. To this we may add that, according to reliable sources, Russian religious thought provokes great interest among young Soviet intellectuals. Quite recently an American student found a library including books by Berdyaev, Bulgakov, and others in the apartment of a worker in Stalingrad and this is one example among very many. The study of ultimate questions which these authors represent is therefore not only a study of the past. It may be related to the present and to the future in more than one way.

In preparing this anthology I was greatly helped by the Rev. Asheleigh E. Moorhouse. He not only translated many of the essays but also made valuable suggestions for the selection of the texts themselves.

Vladimir Weidlé

Russia and the West[1]

1

THE UNCONDITIONAL and irreconcilable contrasting of Russia with the West and of the West with Russia is at the heart of a complex of ideas that is curious above all in that it was created, and has been amicably developed, by minds having nothing else in common with one another: by the exclusive adherents of everything Russian in Russia and by the fanatical defenders of the West in the West. The former have this advantage over the latter, that even in the most extreme form, their views have furthered understanding of Russia's national peculiarities, while the European West represents a complex merger of national cultures whose positive development along such lines has long ago been completed. In spite of the unequal value of their theories, however, the fundamental error of both groups of theoreticians is the same: there is insufficient breadth and flexibility in their concept of Europe. Both are striving to exalt "themselves" by debasing "others," without realizing how relative is the difference between themselves and others; and this striving brings a deserved punishment, inevitably leading them as it does to a contraction of what is "theirs" in the face of new threats on all sides from the ever growing and extending "others." Fanatical

1 Translated from V. Weidlé, *Zadacha Rossii* (New York: Chekhov Publishing House, 1956), pp. 47–70.

11

Europeans are entrenching themselves behind the Rhine and the Danube, and our own isolationists are withdrawing from the Neva to the Moscow River, and even here Moscow does not seem to them sufficiently Eastern.

As applied to Russia (or to Slavic or Orthodox Europe in general), the concept of "the East" reveals its polemical origins by its very vagueness and changeability. What the "West" is, i.e., Western Europe, is more or less clear to everyone, but it is much less clear what the East is; this concept is construed in any way that is convenient, so long as it is opposed as sharply as possible, either positively or negatively, to the West which is under appraisal.

In any more or less consistent system of historico-cultural concepts, the European West must be contrasted with the European East, and then both of them, as Europe, must be contrasted with the Asiatic East, Near or Far. One may call Orthodoxy Eastern Christianity, but it is impossible to call Christianity Asiatic. One may call Russian culture Eastern European, but it was born and developed in Europe, not in Asia. The concept of Eurasia in relation to Russia is, from the standpoint of geography, as justifiable as the concept of Afro-Europe in relation to Spain, but it is impossible to speak either about a Eurasian or about an Afro-European culture. One may speak only about the national cultures of Russia and Spain, in which features brought in from the East have played a greater role than in the national cultures of other European countries. All these simple truths would be forgotten less easily if the comparatively precise concepts, "Asia," "the Near East," and "the Moslem world," were not constantly replaced by the meaningless word "East," which can, without difficulty, be used to support any sort of ideology. One only has to pronounce this word and everything that is European (but not related to Western Europe) is instantly turned into something not European at all, but alien, hostile, "Eastern." This magic operation has been performed countless times in the past century, and even now it has not lost

its power to darken Western as well as Russian minds. We have
it to thank for that erroneous interpretation of pre-Petrine Russia—stemming in equal measure from Chaadayev and the first
Slavophiles—which contrasts pre-Petrine Russia with Europe on
the grounds that it grew out of the Byzantine tradition.

Byzantium is not Asia; like the Western world, it too grew out
of the ancient and Christian foundations of European culture.
It is perfectly legitimate to contrast it with the West, but only
in its character as a *European* East. The East and West of
Europe are not two unrelated (although intercommunicating)
worlds but two halves of one and the same culture, a culture
based on Christianity and antiquity. It is fruitful to compare
them with one another, to contrast them with one another,
because they are inwardly united by a great spiritual heritage,
developed in different ways but not having thereby lost its
unity. This is why the Byzantine influence on the West, or later
the Western impact on the world nurtured by Byzantium, cannot be compared with such things as the Hellenization of northern India, Chinese Christianity, or the Arab's acceptance of
Aristotle. If the Byzantine Empire was geographically to a large
degree an Asiatic empire, is it not also true that ancient Greek
culture bloomed in the cities of Asia Minor, that Christianity
was born neither in Athens nor in Rome, and that while the
historian will regard St. Augustine, the greatest of the Western
fathers of the Church, as a European, the geographer will leave
him in Africa? The historical concept of Europe does not coincide with the geographical. Historically, Europe was born three
thousand years ago at the extreme eastern end of the Mediter-
ranean basin, while the northern part of the mainland of Europe
has in general been living a historical life for not much more (if
not less) than a thousand years. Undoubtedly there are more
genuinely Eastern or Asiatic elements in Byzantine culture than
in the culture of the Western Middle Ages. Even in Byzantium,
however, these elements are found not at the center but at the
periphery; more of these elements are found in the outlying

provinces than in the capital, more in secondary than in vital
and essential spheres of life. This can be seen very clearly in
the example of literary creativity, where the tradition of
Constantinople preserves the greatest fidelity to its Greco-Christian foundation, and where later Eastern (especially Persian)
influences, penetrating freely into the ornamental and decorative
realm, stopped short at the threshold of great architecture and
the pictorial art of the Church. It is true that, in the formation
of the Byzantine artistic style itself, Eastern elements played a
significant role, but the creative work leading to its development
consisted precisely in placing these elements in new relationships
and formulating them in new ways under the impulse of the
Hellenistic sense of rhythm and the Christian desire to spiritualize the corporeal.

Byzantine culture was primarily a Greco-Christian culture,
and only as such was it able to stand as the educator of the
nations of Eastern Europe which still lacked a higher culture.
There could also be some specifically Eastern features (largely
modified, however, by Hellenism and Christianity and in any
case not defining its ultimate value and historical significance)
in the composition of the tremendous gift received or inherited
from Byzantium. Educated by Byzantium, however, Old Russia
could not by this education have been torn away from Europe,
since above all, the education consisted in the transmittal to it
of the Greco-Christian tradition. Old Russia could only be torn
away from Europe to the extent that Byzantine Christianity differed from Western Christianity and to the extent that the
antiquity received via Byzantium differed from that received by
the West via Rome. It is true that even before the Tatar invasion, Russia was open to influences coming directly from the
eastern parts of the Byzantine Empire, from the Caucasus, and
from Transcaucasia through Trabzon. This, however, led only
to episodic borrowings, and there were as many of these as one
could want in Western Europe too. For it is becoming more and
more clear that certain ornamental and architectural motifs

wandered, partly by sea and probably also partly by land, through Russia to the far West. There is nothing which so presages Romanesque art as the art of Armenia in the early Middle Ages, and it is possible to explain the presence of similar decorative principles in the sculptural decoration of churches in the Suzdal area and of certain memorials in the Caucasus, southern Germany, and northern Italy by the same sort of migration from East to West. This movement of forms has nothing in common with Byzantine tradition as a whole. This tradition, in the realm of art as well as in other areas, did set Russia and the rest of the Orthodox world in contrast to the West, but it did not turn it into an Eastern or Asiatic nation. On the contrary, it determined it forever as a European nation.

Church Slavonic, which was a tutor for the Russian language and in the end combined with it in the new Russian literary language, is an exact copy of the Greek language in its cultural lexicon, word formation, syntax, and stylistic possibilities, and is much closer to Greek (not genetically, but in its internal form) than the Romance languages are to Latin. The sermons of Cyril of Turov stand closer to their Greek models in their musical quality, their subtle, rhythmical, syntactical formation, than do the Latin writings of his Western contemporaries to the great models of Latin prose. Rublyov's icon is closer to the Greek understanding of the fullness of form in the melodic quality of its lines and the luxuriance of its rhythm than the art of Masaccio or Fra Beato, his own contemporaries in Italy. Piety [*blagochestiye*], elegance [*blagolepiye*], veneration [*blagogoveniye*], beauty [*blagoobraziye*], purity of heart [*chistoserdechiye*], compassion [*miloserdiye*], wisdom [*tselomudriye*], emotion [*umileniye*]—all these words are constructed not only on Greek word forms but also according to Greek forms of life and thought, and were first used ecclesiastically, later also entering popular usage, as the starets in A *Raw Youth* reminds us, when we learn that he knew only a single denunciation: "They have no beauty [*blagoobraziye*] in them," and urged his followers to lead a "glorified"

[*blazhenny*] and "elegant" [*blagolepny*] life. "Orthodoxy,"
Rozanov has said, "answers to the spirit of harmony in the
highest degree, and in the highest degree does not answer to the
spirit of disorder." And if ever there was a culture of the spirit of
harmony, it is Greek culture. If we call this Greek Christianity
(which penetrated the whole spiritual life of ancient Russia)
either "Eastern" or "Asiatic," then what can we call European?

One may stress the peculiarity of Russian culture in relation to
the West by citing the fact of its Byzantine inheritance, but one
will also be confirming the fact that it belongs to the common
Christian culture of Europe, which in turn was the heir of classi-
cal antiquity. Thus the modern followers, and in part perverters,
of the Slavophile tradition base themselves not on this fact, not
on Russia's ties with Byzantium or a vague "East," but on facts
which bear witness in their eyes to the direct ties between Old
Russia and Turkish, Tatar, or Mongol Asia. These facts fall into
two categories. Some precede the formation of the Old Russian
culture as distinct from the culture of Byzantium (and therefore
can only touch the geographical, ethnic, and folk characteristics
of Russian cultural development). The others are connected
with the centuries when the Byzantine-Russian culture was already in existence and living a historical life (so that one must
see whether these facts do not simply form a combination of all
the imported, external, and borrowed features of this culture). It
can be said about both categories that the speculations about
Eurasia which cite them are true, but the conclusions drawn
from these speculations are incorrect. Eurasia, as a "natural
milieu" [*mestorazvitiye*], is a fruitful formula capable of explaining much in Russian history—as long as one does not consider
this natural milieu as a form of predestination and thus create a
new species of geographical determinism. In the same way,
speculations about the ethnic composition of the Russian people
or of certain features of the Russian language, of popular music
and popular ornamentation, suggesting a connection with analogous features among Asiatic peoples, are valuable in themselves,

but must be explained as referring to the material out of which the culture was formed or to the soil on which it grew and not to the culture itself. As an ethnic phenomenon the Russian language reveals certain points of similarity with the Turkish or Tatar language, but as a manifestation of a national culture, in other words as the Russian literary language, it was formed not under Tatar but under Greek influence, augmented later by the influences of Western European languages. In the great memorials of art, literature, and the religious life of Old Russia there is just as little of the Asiatic as there is in the culture of post-Petrine Russia. As for the individual elements adopted from the Tatars after the Tatar invasion or borrowed by Moscow from Persia, India, or China, they too, of course, have played their part, just as Arab influence played a far greater role in Spanish culture. But just as the Moors did not succeed in turning Spain into a non-European country, neither did these adopted elements eliminate Greek Christianity, Byzantium, and therefore Europe from Russia.

The positivistic or naturalistic premises of the concept of Eurasia are reflected in the endeavor to derive a culture wholly from the data of geography and ethnology, while forgetting that a spiritual evolution can in the end be stronger than both. Such premises are also reflected in the concept of national culture as a kind of direct secretion of the people, when in fact it may contain not only features that are extranational in origin but also features that are antinational. To stand on such a theory means not accepting the Hungarians as a European nation, not seeing that the Hellenistic nature of Goethe or Hölderlin is just as genuine as their German nationality, or that the Westernness and Russianness of Pushkin are one; in the last analysis it means that only Hebrews can be Christians or that it was an exclusively French (not at all a Christian or European) culture which flourished in mediaeval France. What is true in these theories is simply the fact that spiritual evolution does not occur within the kingdom of the spirit but within the conditions of historical existence, and as a result, Christianity, antiquity, Byzantium, and in general everything that is disseminated and transmitted inevitably changes its facial contours under the influence of local conditions, is colored in a new way in new ethnic surroundings. There is only one pathway open to anyone wishing to define the degree of "Easternness" in Old Russia and the degree to which it belonged to Europe: he must check the exact tones in which it tinted the Byzantine culture, in what way it made it Russian and thus modified it and reinterpreted it along new lines. If historians would agree to put the question properly and ask themselves whether Old Russia was, so to speak, more Western or more Eastern than Byzantium, then they would long ago have found the correct answer and would have been delivered from unnecessary disputes and perplexities.

Pre-Petrine Russian culture was Western Byzantine, and therefore Peter's work was but the legitimate conclusion of that circular historical journey which began with the transfer of the Roman capital to Constantinople and ended with the transfer of the Russian capital to St. Petersburg. For all its differences with the West, the religious, political, and legal life of Old Russia differed less from the West than the corresponding areas of Byzantine culture, and in some respects was closer to it than to its Byzantine tutor. St. Sergius of Radonyozh is, in the end, more like the Western saint of the Middle Ages—in part like Francis and in part like Bernard—than any Byzantine ascetic. In spite of all the features which so profoundly distinguish it from the Western Reformation, the Russian schism is nevertheless, in its social and spiritual consequences, closer to the Reformation than to any religious movement in the Byzantine world. In any case, the political and legal life of the period was less like that of Byzantium than that of the West, and the Byzantine ideology of Moscow was in sharp contrast to the reality of Moscow. While the great educational task of Byzantium was completed in a full assimilation of its gift and in independent creativity, above all in the realm of art, we see that the Russian masters departed from their Byzantine models precisely in a westerly rather than in an easterly direction. Nor are we referring here to more or less accidental and rare borrowings. The ornamentation of Novgorod is related to Scandinavian ornamentation, not by way of imitation, but by an internal relatedness; and Scandinavian stylistic principles also penetrated Novgorod iconography. Again, the village architecture of the Russian North is related to the Scandinavian and is inclined to verticalism, which, in the sixteenth century, found expression in the pyramid style of church building [v shatrovykh khramakh], breaking finally with the Byzantine tradition and tending rather to the creation of a kind of Russian Gothic, wholly independent of Western Gothic and in sharp contrast to it—indeed, knowing nothing about it, but closer to its basic aspirations than to the ancient religio-aesthetic canons of Byzantine architecture. From time immemorial the subconscious but deep needs, hopes, and aspirations of the spiritual life have been expressed most clearly in art. Pre-Petrine Russian art, primarily its ornament and architecture (less bound by ecclesiastical obedience than iconography), is an incontestable witness not only to Russia's European nature (its Byzantine inheritance has already made this clear) but also to its unpremeditated and intuitive turning to the West, that turning which was so furiously, convulsively, and also irrevocably completed by Peter.

2

Old Russia was already European by virtue of its Byzantine upbringing, i.e., it possessed the basic preliminary conditions of European cultural development. Its marked aloofness, however, especially in the Muscovite period, could have led in the end to a complete separation of Eastern from Western Europe; Russia could have fallen away from Europe. In the more than five centuries from the Tatar invasion to the time of Peter, this did

not happen, not only because Russia's weak though still preserved ties with the Western world prevented it, but still more
because of the Western (as opposed to Byzantine) features
which appeared in the spiritual life and cultural activity of
Muscovite Russia. The danger was finally eliminated by Peter;
Constantine sundered and Peter restored European unity. The
success—at least on the cultural level—of the far-reaching historical task which Peter accomplished is attested by everything
created by Russia in the more than two centuries of its Petersburg period. A nation should be judged as a person is judged, not
only by its roots, but also by its fruit. Too often we judge Russia
not on the basis of what it has become but on the basis of what it
seemed to be promising to become. Even if Old Russian culture
were not partly European, even if it were to correspond to all the
Slavophile or Eurasian concepts, there would be quite enough in
modern Russian culture to demonstrate the inevitability of a
European path for Russia. If Peter had been a Japanese Mikado
or an Aztec Emperor, airports and steel factories would have
multiplied on his land with time, but it would not have given
birth to Pushkin.

Reunion with the West was certainly not an easy task or one
without danger. The Slavophiles understood this, and there
would be nothing to reproach them for if their interpretation of
the danger had not been based on the same mistake that was
being made constantly by the Westernizers and which, more
than anything, impeded the fruitful development of their remarkable ideological conflict. The mistake consisted in contrasting the West with Russia, as that which is alien is contrasted
with that which is one's own, as two magnitudes in no way
organically bound together. The Westernizers prefer what is
alien and want to put it in the place of what is their own; the
Slavophiles prefer their own and want to purify it and mark it
off as separate from what is alien. For the Westernizer, his beloved West is nothing less than the bearer of a kind of abstract
civilization which must be transplanted into a half-wild Russia—

just as it must be transplanted even to the moon, once interplanetary communication has been discovered. For the Slavophile, better prepared to accept organically related cultural unities, Russia (or Orthodoxy, or the Slavic world) is conceived as such a unity, while in the West he sees only a cultural unity hostile to his own or more often, like the Westernizer, an abstract total of all the "fruits of the Enlightenment," which, however, he is inclined not to bless but to curse. Neither one sees that common rootedness of Russia and the West within the unity of Europe, which alone makes close intercourse between them fruitful and desirable. Both opponents argue on insufficiently historical grounds, too abstractly, as if the reunification of thé West and Russia—a Christian country educated by Byzantium (and therefore a country that is European not only in the geographical but also in the cultural sense) —could be, and in fact was, something like the Europeanization of Peru or China: a clash of two alien cultures which can be resolved only by the complete destruction of one or the other, or by the transformation of both into a mechanical mixture which cannot even be called a culture.

In reality, of course, something quite different took place. For Russia, becoming reunified with the West meant finding its place within Europe and in this way also finding itself. Russian culture was not on the point of losing its individuality, but of fully acquiring it for the first time—as part of another individuality. Europe is a multinational unity that is incomplete without Russia; Russia is a European nation which is incapable of attaining the fullness of its national life outside of Europe. The Europeanization of non-European cultural worlds is in a sense an unobstructed task, and also an unfruitful one; the rapprochement of Russia with the West was a difficult task, but also a fruitful one. The difficulty is explained by their prolonged estrangement and arises out of the constant possibility of exaggeration and one-sidedness, such as the Gallomania of the end of the eighteenth century, the Hegelianism of the forties, or the idle snobbishness and Westernizing conceitedness which has never disappeared from the Russian scene. The danger of a de-nationalization of Russia was real, and those who struggled against it were right to the extent that, deprived of its national individuality, the country would by this token also have been deprived of its place in European culture. This danger appeared from the very beginning, thanks to the excessively harsh and violent character of the Petrine reform; but the rise in creativity which it then evoked was also expressed very quickly. The Russian language in Peter's reign was cluttered and lacked vitality, and yet very soon there developed out of itsthat common literary language which was so unattainable in pre-Petrine Russia. Russian verse before Peter's reign had (under Western influence) adopted an inappropriate structure, but the efforts of Tredyakov-sky and Lomonosov, far from turning it back along the old path, *for the first time* placed it on firm ground and guaranteed its future development. The fate of Russian culture was revealed very clearly in the fate of Russian versification. The old path was narrow and could not lead to the creation of a great national (and not just folk) poetry. In putting an end to the old way the first impact of the West was chaotic and haphazard, as was much else in the Petrine reform and the borrowings which preceded it. But a more serious acquaintance, not just with the West close at hand, but with the sum total of Western European national cultures, led simultaneously to a perception of the national peculiarity of Russian versification and to its occupying a definite place among the national versifications of Europe. Russian verse was recognized as being close not to Polish or French but to German and English verse, even though it did not coincide with them in everything. Anyone who looks at Russian history in the light of this example will agree neither with the Slavophile, who is ready to be satisfied in a way with popular tonic verse, nor with the Westernizer, to whom the verse of Kantemir has to seem more radically "European" and therefore "progressive" than the verse of Pushkin.

In consolidating itself within Europe, Russia also became internally consolidated. This was so clear to Catherine's contemporaries that the conflicts connected with it seemed to be only a particular and not an essential feature of the task; it was almost as clear to the contemporaries of Alexander I. Slavophilism and the Westernizing party appeared in their characteristic form only after certain changes occurring within Western culture itself were perceived or at least sensed; and only by considering these changes is it possible to understand the real significance of both doctrines, to understand what separated them internally even though it was frequently glossed over in the official formulae of their polemic. The end result of the changes referred to was the slow transformation (already signaling its coming on the threshold of the new century) of the old family of organically matured and vitally interrelated national cultures into an international scientific and technical civilization. The Westernizers are followers of that stream of European thought which helped to bring about this transformation and received its fruits with enthusiasm; the Slavophiles are the pupils of its opponents who were attempting to fight against it even in the West. The Western European origin of both ideologies is apparent and also quite legitimate: their struggle is only part of that great struggle which has been carried on in the whole of Europe and has opposed the Enlightenment of the eighteenth century to the romantic defense of suprarational values. The existence of this struggle in Russia is proof of the fact that it belongs to Europe, not now to the old Europe, but to the new, problematical Europe of the nineteenth century. In this respect Chaadayev and the early Slavophiles occupy ideological positions that are not yet altogether precise (in particular Chaadayev's West was Catholic and not "enlightened" Europe); nevertheless it was from just this time—the thirties—that Russia took part not simply in the spiritual life of Europe but in that new, especially disturbed and critical phase of this spiritual life which the West had entered half a century earlier. Pushkin was

almost wholly beyond this rupture. His genius was related to
Raphael, Vermeer, Racine, Ariosto, Mozart and to the last two
old Europeans—Goethe and Stendhal. He was entirely turned
in the direction of old, prerevolutionary, and preromantic Europe; all of its heritage, its memory, all its love was innate in
him; his basic mission was to make it the spiritual homeland
of a future Russia. He fulfilled this mission to the full extent
of his talents, but the merging of Russia with the West into a
single Europe was accomplished in a new situation alien to
Pushkin and from which Pushkin seems directed not toward the
future but the past. Russia was finally developed, was finally
created in the roaring workshop of the nineteenth century.

The nineteenth century is to Russia what the age of the Renaissance was for Italy, what the end of the sixteenth and the
seventeenth century were for Spain, England, and France; it
is to Russia what the period roughly marked by the years of
Goethe's birth and death were for Germany. But if it holds a
special place in the history of Russia, this certainly does not
mean that Russia's nineteenth century is something set apart
from the nineteenth century of Europe and alien to it. The point
is that Russia attained its final individuality in the complex unity
of Europe in the century when Europe itself was more and
more ceasing to be what it had been in the past. Developing
now within Europe, Russia was also entering into Europe's
decline, into its tragic disintegration and homelessness. Hence
the extraordinarily complex structure of our "great age," not
only in comparison with the "great ages" of other nations, but
also in comparison with the same century in the West. The
contact with Europe's past led to the renaissance of Russia's
national culture, but the contact with the Europe of the present
tinted this renaissance with disturbing colors such as were not
present in the cultural renaissances of other European nations.
There were more elemental, vital forces (for example, those reflected in the protoplastic, earthy, corporeal genius of Tolstoy)
in the Russia of the past century than in the West, and what

they generated did not remain simply the property of Russia but merged into that nineteenth century Europe which was common to both Russia and the West. The art of Tolstoy or Dostoevsky is Russian art; Dostoevsky was a Russian just as Shakespeare was an Englishman or Pascal a Frenchman, but like them, the deeper he was rooted in his own country the deeper he grew into the life of Europe. The conditions which made possible the emergence of Shakespeare and Pascal appeared earlier in England and France than similar conditions in Russia, where Dostoevsky was as much a contemporary of Shakespeare as of Dickens, of Pascal as of Baudelaire, and where Tolstoy was a late-born epic poet, a visionary Homer, seduced by the stratagems of negative and demonstrative reason. The whole of Europe belongs to Russia and the whole of Russia to Europe as a result of the work of the generations from Peter to Pushkin. Everything that has been created in Russia after Pushkin belongs to the nineteenth century of Europe.

All Russian literature from Lermontov and Gogol down to our own time is a result of the upheaval produced by European romanticism; Russia has participated in this upheaval, continued it, and rejected no part of it. Russian music has taken more from Western music than from folk music; and above all it is connected with Western music after Beethoven. Russian painting, even that which (in Ivanov and Vrubel) remained faithful to its religious principle, was unable to return to iconography and still by-pass European art; it immediately found a form simultaneously European and independent of the West. Russian philosophy begins with Schelling and Hegel, Russian science with Western science. Even Russian theological thought derives as much from its own Eastern Christian tradition as from the tradition of Western philosophical and theological thought. The point here is not our imitativeness, nor Western superiority, but the fact that both in the West and in Russia the nineteenth century is one. Let us not cite the incomprehensibility of Russian culture to Germàns, Frenchmen, or Englishmen; in former

times it was far more difficult for them to explain themselves to
each other. Even now the Elizabethan drama is accessible only
to a select group in France, and the French tragedy is boring
to Englishmen; Milton is rarely read on the continent; and it
is not without difficulty that Frenchmen come to terms with
Dante and Goethe. On the other hand, if Russian writers of
the nineteenth century have not been assimilated by Europe,
then it is only out of laziness, out of a lack of knowledge of
the language, or as the result of the carelessness of translators.
These writers are all flesh of its flesh, they are all its blood rela-
tives, and there are no more European names in Europe's
literature over the past fifty years than the names of Tolstoy,
the pupil of Rousseau, and Dostoevsky, the disciple of Corneille
and Racine, George Sand, Dickens, and Balzac. The West is
now not only giving its culture to us, but also receiving ours in
return. The mutual interpenetration of Russia and the West,
their compatibility, the conditional and relative nature of every
contrast between them, are such that in many cases it is difficult
to decide whether Russia is returning its own forgotten gift to
the West, or offering something new and hitherto unknown.
And it is really impossible and unnecessary to decide this
question. The point is that Ivanov and Mussorgsky, Dostoevsky,
Tolstoy, or Solovyov are all profoundly Russian people, but to
the same extent they are also people of Europe. They would not
have existed without Europe; without them there would be
no Russia, and nineteenth century Europe would not have been
what it was. Russian culture stems from European culture, and
having become united with the West, having formed itself, it
returns into European culture. Russia is only one of the European countries, but already it is essential to Europe; it is only
one voice, but already it has full rights within the choir of
European voices.

"Europe is our mother, as is Russia; it is our second mother.
We have taken much from her, and will take from her again,
and we do not wish to be ungrateful to her." It was not a

Westernizer who said this; this is beyond the Westernizing
ideology as well as that of the Slavophiles; it was Dostoevsky
writing at the peak of his wisdom, on the threshold of death, in
The Diary of a Writer. His last hope was a messianism, but an
essentially European messianism, stemming from a sense of
Russia as being somehow better than Europe, as called to save
and restore Europe. Even if this hope was unjustified, still those
who held this faith were not "turning their face to the East";
they were turning to Europe, believing that an "Eastern" or Russian, fundamentally European light would begin to shine again
in Europe. The only thing they did not realize was that their
prophecy, to the extent that it was fulfilled, was being fulfilled
by themselves. Russian-European unity was never so powerfully
asserted as in the remarkable words of Ivan Karamazov. The
European cemetery of which he speaks was the cradle of modern Russia, the pledge of its cultural existence. "The dear departed" were so dear because, beside belonging to Europe, they
belonged equally to us. And it is not difficult for us to sense
now what Ivan Karamazov did not yet mention, and what
Dostoevsky did not yet feel. It is not hard for us to understand
that he himself, and in varying degrees all his contemporaries,
all the Russian people of his time, had not only inherited the
tombs of Europe but were also participating in the future of
Europe, were the creatures and creators of European culture,
were themselves speaking in the name of Europe without realizing that the task of their time and the destiny of the nineteenth
century were to merge Russia and Europe into one.

Translated by Asheleigh E. Moorhouse
August, 1963

Aleksei Stepanovich Khomyakov

1804 - 1860

Born in Moscow of an old aristocratic family, Khomyakov was a typical representative of the Muscovite intellectual elite. He received an excellent education, first at home, then at the University of Moscow. After a short military career and a tour of Europe, he settled at home, dividing his time between his estates and the famous intellectual salons of Moscow. Externally his life was almost eventless. In 1836 he married Yekaterina Yazykov and was very happy in his family life (she died in 1852). He counted among his closest friends some of the most brilliant men of his time: Nikolai Gogol, the brothers Piotr and Ivan Kireyevsky, the poet Zhukovsky, the brothers Aksakov, and Yuri Samarin. He was a successful and liberal landlord. On a deeper level, however, he shared in the tragedy of his generation and suffered from it. This tragedy was, on the one hand, the tragedy of that schism between the best minds of Russia—the Westernizers and the Slavophiles—which was never to heal and which constitutes the major drama of Russian intellectual and spiritual development. On the other hand, it was the tragedy of the suspicion and even the open enmity of the government. The Slavophiles, although they defended and confessed the traditional Russian values—Orthodoxy, monarchy, cultural independence from the West— were almost more suspicious to Nikolai I and his bureaucracy than their "Westernizing" rivals. For many years Khomyakov and his friends were condemned to silence. Even Khomyakov's theological essays had to be printed in France and Switzerland. He died of cholera in 1860.

The Slavophile movement, of which Khomyakov was the unquestioned and unchallenged leader, had a complex ideology. It included a philosophy of history centered on the defense of tradition, "organic" development, and a certain Russian "messianism"; a theory of state in its relation to the people; a social doctrine with the Russian *obshina* (the collective life of a Russian rural community) at its center; and, last but not least, a theology. Although Khomyakov was active in the elaboration of these aspects of Slavophilism (and was also a poet), his chief contribution to the history of Russian thought is undoubtedly in the field of theology. In the words of Fr. George Florovsky, "he was, in the years to come, to exercise an enormous influence on the ways of Russian theology. . . . He wanted to restate the Orthodox tradition in a new idiom which would be at the same time modern and traditional, i.e., in conformity with the teaching of the Fathers and with the continuous experience of the living Church. He wanted to liberate Russian theology, first of all, from the bondage of Western scholasticism, which had been cultivated for a long time in the schools" ("Orthodox Ecumenism in the Nineteenth Century," *St. Vladimir's Seminary Quarterly*, Vol. IV, 1956, p. 20).

Khomyakov's best known and most important theological essay, "The Church Is One," has been published in English several times. We give here another essay, essential to an understanding of Khomyakov's religious thought. It was first published in French (*Quelques mots à un chrétien Orthodoxe sur les Confessions Occidentales*, Paris, 1853) and appeared in Russian only after the death of the author. Khomyakov was very critical of Western spiritual and theological development, yet his best biographer, A. Gratieux, a Roman Catholic, agrees with Khomyakov's son Dmitri in evaluating this criticism as "supremely irenical." "For the best way of preparing union is to posit the problems in their depth and thus to dissipate all misunderstandings" (Gratieux, Vol. I, p. 147).

Bibliography

The collected works are available only in Russian: *Polnoe sobranie sochinenii* (Complete Collected Works), 8 vols. Moscow, 1900–14.

In English, see "The Church Is One," in W. J. Birkbeck, *Russia and the English Church*, Ch. 23, pp. 192 ff. New edition, London: SPCK, 1948 (reprinted in New York, 1953).

Books about Khomyakov:

Christoff, P. K., *An Introduction to Nineteenth Century Russian Slavophilism: A Study in Ideas*, Vol. I: A. S. Xomjakov. The Hague, 1961.

Zernov, N. M., *Three Russian Prophets: Khomyakov, Dostoyevsky, Solovyov*. London, 1944.

Gratieux, A., *A. S. Khomyakov et le Mouvement Slavophile*, 2 vols. Paris, 1939.

On the Western Confessions of Faith[1]

EVERY CHRISTIAN, when faced with an attack on the faith he confesses, is obliged to defend it to the extent of his intellectual ability, not waiting for any special authorization, since the Church has no official advocates. In the light of this observation I am taking up my pen to answer certain unjust accusations brought against the Ecumenical and Orthodox Church, writing in a language which is not my own, for the benefit of foreign readers.[2]

In an article printed in *La Revue des Deux Mondes* and apparently written by the Russian diplomat Mr. Tyuchev, mention was made of the supremacy of Rome, and in particular of the confusion of spiritual and worldly interests in the figure of a bishop-sovereign as being the chief reason for the delay in the solution of the religious question in the West. In 1852 this article was answered by Mr. Laurency, and it is this response which calls for a refutation.

I leave aside the question whether Mr. Tyuchev succeeded in expressing his thought in all its breadth (the merits of his article,

[1] Translated and abridged from the text printed in Yu. F. Samarin, ed., *Polnoe sobranie sochinenii Alekseya Stepanovicha Khomyakova* (Moscow, 1900), Vol. II.

[2] Khomyakov's article was first written and printed in French, and was later (1864) translated and published in Russian.

incidentally, are not even questioned by his opponent), and whether he did not to some extent confuse the reasons for the sickness with its external symptoms.

I shall begin neither by defending my countryman nor by criticizing him. My one purpose is to clear the Church of the strange charges brought against her by Mr. Laurency, and so I shall not go beyond the limits of the religious question. I would also wish to avoid countercharges, but am not able to do so. My travels in foreign lands and conversations with cultured and learned people of all the religious confessions of Europe have convinced me that Russia is still alien and virtually unknown to the Western world; and even more of a mystery to Christians following the Roman banner or the flag of the Reform is the religious thought of the Church's sons. Therefore, in order to give my readers an opportunity to understand our faith and the logic of its inner life, it will be necessary for me to show them, at least in part, how we regard those questions which Rome and the various German confessions are disputing. I am not even able to promise that I shall avoid unfriendliness in the expression of my thoughts. But I shall try to be just and to refrain from making any charges that are either slanderous or ill-founded. In any case, I am by no means seeking the honor of being known as one who is indifferent to what he regards as falsehood.

Mr. Laurency brings two basic charges against the Church. The first is this: that she supposedly acknowledges the supremacy of temporal power. On these grounds a comparison is drawn between the Roman confession and the Orthodox Church, which naturally does not turn out to our advantage. "The Pope," says the author, "is indeed a temporal sovereign, but not because he is a high priest; while the ruler of your Church is a high priest because he is a temporal sovereign. On whose side is the truth?" I shall not quote the actual and rather verbose language of the author, but I am sure I am giving its sense. First of all let me mention in passing that the word "high priest" (pontifex) is a most remarkable word, which the Latinists would be wise to stop using. It points all too clearly to a whole family of concepts whose Christian origins are more than doubtful. Even Tertullian noted this and used the expression "Pontifex Maximus" in an ironical sense. However, to the first charge leveled by Mr. Laurency I reply in few words: it is a downright lie; we acknowledge no head of the Church, either clerical or temporal. Christ is her head and she knows no other. I hasten to add that I certainly do not accuse Mr. Laurency of a deliberate slander. In all probability he has fallen into error unwittingly, and I am all the more ready to believe this in view of the fact that many times in my presence foreigners have made the same error; and yet it would seem that only the slightest reflection would be required to clear it up.

Head of the Church! But allow me to ask, if only in the name of common sense, head of precisely what church? Can it be of the Orthodox Church, of which we constitute only a part? In that case, the Russian Emperor would be the head of the churches which are governed by the patriarchs, of the church governed by the Greek Synod, and of the Orthodox churches in the regions of Austria. Even the most extreme ignorance, of course, does not permit such an absurd conclusion. Or perhaps he is the head of the Russian Church alone? But the Russian Church does not represent a distinct Church: she is no more than one of the eparchies of the Ecumenical Church. From this it would be necessary to conclude that what is being assigned to the Emperor is the title of head of his own eparchy, subject to the jurisdiction of general Church councils. There is no middle position here. Whoever insists on fixing upon us a head of the Church in the person of a visible sovereign must make a choice between two absurdities.

Temporal head of the Church! But does this head have the rights of the priesthood? Does he lay claim—I say nothing yet of infallibility (although it is precisely this that constitutes the distinctive mark of supremacy in the Church)—to some

kind of authority in questions of faith? Does he at least have
the right, by virtue of his office, to decide questions of general church order (discipline)? If it is impossible to give an
affirmative answer to these questions, then one can only be
amazed at the complete absence of good judgment which alone
could persuade a writer to hurl such an ill-founded accusation
against us, and at the complete ignorance which let this accusation stand and did not expose it to the ridicule it deserves. Of
course there is not a merchant, tradesman, or peasant in the
whole Russian Empire who would not, if he heard such an opinion about our Church, take it as a malicious taunt.

It is true that the expression "head of the territorial Church"[3]
is used in the laws of the Empire; but not at all in the sense in
which it is used in other lands; and in this case the difference
is so essential that one must not turn this expression into a
weapon against us without first attempting to understand its
meaning. Justice and scrupulousness require this.

When, after many afflictions and setbacks, the Russian people
in a general assembly elected Mikhail Romanov as their hereditary sovereign (such is the high origin of imperial power in Russia today), the people entrusted to their chosen one all the power
with which they themselves had been invested, in all its forms.
By right of this election the sovereign became the head of the
people in ecclesiastical matters as well as in matters of civic
government, I repeat—became head of the people in ecclesiastical matters, and only in this sense head of the territorial Church.
The people did not and were not able to transfer to the sovereign
a right which they did not possess, and hardly anyone will suggest that the Russian people once considered themselves called
to govern the Church. They had, from the beginning, as was the

[3] The Russian adjective here is *mestny*, which has the sense of "belonging
to or occupying a certain definite region or locality." I have used the word
"territorial" to render this idea rather than the word "local," which is often
used in modern English in a very restricted sense which would distort the
meaning of *mestny* as it occurs in this essay. (Trans.)

case with all the peoples which make up the Orthodox Church,
a voice in the election of their bishops, and this voice they could
transfer to their representative. They had the right, or rather
the obligation, to see that the decisions of their pastors and
councils were carried out in full; this right they could entrust to
their chosen one and his successors. They had the right to defend their faith against any hostile or violent attack; this right
also they could transfer to their sovereign. But the people had
no power whatever in questions of conscience, of general church
order, of dogma, of church government, and therefore could not
transfer such power to their Tsar. This is fully substantiated by
all subsequent events. The patriarchate was abolished;[4] this was
accomplished not by the will of the sovereign but by the decree
of the Eastern patriarchs and the native bishops. Later the synod
was established in place of the patriarchate; and this change was
brought about not by the sovereign's power but by those same
Eastern bishops who had, in an agreement with temporal power,
established the patriarchate in Russia in the first place. These
facts are sufficient to show that the title "head of the Church"
signifies "head of the people in ecclesiastical matters"; in fact it
neither has nor could have any other meaning. And once this
meaning is admitted, all the accusations based on confusion
come to nothing.

But does not Byzantine history provide our accusers with supporting evidence not given to them by the history of Russia? Do
they not imagine that they see in Byzantium, with its state seal
and the imperial title, a belief in a temporal head of the Church?
May it not be supposed that this belief is attested by reference
to the Paleologue who was precipitated into apostasy by despair
and the desire to purchase help from the West?[5] Or by reference

---

[4] The Russian patriarchate was abolished, or, rather, allowed to lapse
toward the end of the reign of Peter I, and was not re-established until 1917.
(Trans.)

[5] At the time of the capture of Constantinople by the Turks in 1453.
(Trans.)

to the Isaurians,[6] who by their exploits restored the military glory
of the Empire but were drawn into heresy by their misguided
zeal and blind self-assurance (for which the Protestant historians
of our time have not ceased to praise them)? Or to Iraclius, who
saved the state but openly embraced Monothelitism? Or finally to
Constantine's own son, Constantius, who crushed Pope Liberius
and was himself troubled by the holy fearlessness of the Bishop
of Alexandria? But the history of the Eastern Empire refutes the
charge directed against the Church—concerning a supposed subordination to the Emperor—even more clearly than the history
of Russia, so that we have no reason to deny the inheritance of
Byzantine thought. Even now we think, as do the Greeks, that
the sovereign, as head of the people in many matters touching
the Church, has the right (along with all his subjects) of freedom of conscience in faith and of the freedom of human reason;
but we do not consider him an oracle moved by some unseen
power, as the Roman bishop represents himself to the Latinists.
We think that the sovereign, being free and a man like any
other man, can fall into error and that if, God forbid, such a
misfortune should happen in spite of the constant prayers of
the Church, then the Emperor does not lose his right to the
obedience of his subjects in temporal matters; nor does the
Church sustain any injury whatever to her glory and fullness,
since her Head never changes. In a case like this the only thing
that would happen is that there would be one less Christian in
her bosom.

The Church permits no other interpretation. But is the slander
silenced? I am afraid not. Ill will may countercharge by referring
to the imperial signature attached to the synod's pronounce-
ments, as if the right of publication of laws and putting them
into effect was identical with the legislative power itself. Again,
it may refer to the influence of the sovereign in the appointment
of bishops and members of the synod which has replaced the
patriarchate, as if, in ancient times, the election of bishops and

[6] A dynasty of Byzantine emperors in the eighth century. (Trans.)

members of the synod (not even excluding those of Rome) did not depend on temporal power (either of the people or of the sovereign), and as if, finally, even today, in many countries of the Roman confession, such a dependency were not quite common.[7] It is difficult to imagine what other false conclusions might be drawn by malevolence and ill will; but after what I have said conscientious people (and I am sure Mr. Laurency is such a man) will not allow themselves to repeat accusations which lack foundation and are ridiculous in the eyes of any dispassionate and enlightened person.

It is not so easy to refute the second charge brought against the Church by Mr. Laurency, since it is based not on fact but on a supposed tendency. We are accused of Protestant leanings. I leave to one side the question whether this second accusation does not contradict the first. Since the insolvency of the first has now been proved, its contradiction of the second cannot serve as an argument on our behalf. I will attack the question directly. But first I must raise a question which is apparently new, or at least, so far as I know, not yet fully examined. For what reason has Protestantism, which has carried away almost half the followers of papism, stopped short at the borders of the Orthodox world? It is impossible to explain this fact by ethnic characteristics, since Calvinism has gained remarkable strength in Czechoslovakia, Poland, Lithuania, and Hungary, and has stopped suddenly, not before another ethnic group but before another faith. Thinkers ought to consider this question carefully.

The alleged tendency toward Protestantism can be examined only in the area of principles; but before I begin the survey of the inner logic of the Orthodox faith, and before I show its complete incompatibility with the charge made by Mr. Laurency (and by a great number of other Roman Catholic writers before him), I consider it desirable to review a historical fact.

---

[7] I am speaking only about the principle, from the Church's standpoint, and not about its application, which, like everything in the world, is often unsatisfactory and subject to abuse.

The Western Schism (my readers will permit me to use this term, since my conscience permits no other) has been in existence now for more than a thousand years.[8] How is it that during this time the Church governed by the patriarchs has not given birth to its own brand of Protestantism? How is it that it has not revealed, at least by now, a definite impulse toward reform of some kind? In the West things developed very rapidly. Scarcely three centuries passed before Luther and Calvin came forward with uplifted heads, strong words, definite principles, and fixed doctrines. A serious polemic will not begin to object by pointing to the heresies and schisms arising in Russia in the seventeenth century and later. Of course we bitterly mourn these spiritual sores; but it would be utterly ridiculous to compare some pitiful children of ignorance, or still more, the unreasonable zeal for the preservation of old ceremonies, with the Protestantism of the learned precursors of the Reform; since I am not speaking here of the Catharists or the Waldensians who appeared in the south, but about people who, like Ockham or Wycliffe or the immortal Hus, stood in the front rank of contemporary learning and could courageously enter into controversy with the whole theological armament of Rome, fearing no blows other than those which might be inflicted upon them by the arm of temporal power. I am speaking of people who, dying no less gloriously than the Christians of the first centuries, from the height of their victorious funeral pyres, turned to their executioners with words saturated with holy and tender love: "*Sancta simplicitas,*" and by these words proclaimed that they had not chosen their weapons from ignorance, nor was it upon ignorance that they had erected the building of their faith. How could it have happened that the East, with its alleged tendency toward Protestantism, did not produce similar people or similar religious movements? Do they ascribe this to the unfortunate

[8] Although the rupture between the Eastern and Western Church was formalized in 1054, controversy and strained relations had existed between Rome and Constantinople since the ninth century. (Trans.)

destiny of the Eastern Empire? If I am not mistaken, such an explanation has already been proposed by Comte de Maistre, but of course it satisfies nobody, with the exception of the most superficial minds.

However that may be, in the sphere of religious ideas the absence of this or that phenomenon, even if extended over a period of several centuries, only supports the more or less plausible argument that the tendency toward such a phenomenon does not yet exist. By no means does it prove the impossibility of the phenomenon appearing in the future. To be finally convinced of this impossibility, to raise a historical probability to the level of logical certainty, we must deduce this impossibility from the religious principle itself.

What is Protestantism? Does its distinctiveness lie, as some say, in the very act of protest made on behalf of faith? But if this were so then the apostles and martyrs who protested against the errors of Judaism and against the falsehood of idolatry would be Protestants; all the fathers of the Church would be Protestants, since they too protested against heresy; the whole Church would be constantly Protestant, since she has constantly and in all ages protested against the errors of the times. Clearly the word "Protestant" defines nothing if used in this way. Where then are we to seek a definition? Does the essence of Protestantism consist in "freedom of investigation"? But the apostles permitted free investigation, even made it an obligation; and the holy fathers defended the truth of the faith by their free investigations (cf. the great Athanasius in his heroic struggle against Arianism); and free investigation, understood in one way or another, constitutes the sole basis of true faith. Certainly the Roman confession seems to condemn free investigation; but here is a man who, having freely investigated all the authorities of Scripture and reason, has come to an acceptance of the whole teaching of the Latinists. Will they regard him as a Protestant? Another man, using the same freedom of investigation, has become convinced that the pope's dogmatic definitions are infallible, and that the only thing for him to do is to submit. Will they condemn him as a Protestant? Yet in the meantime, was it not by way of free investigation that he came to this conviction which compelled him to accept the whole doctrine? Finally, every belief, every discerning faith, is an act of freedom and must stem from previous free investigation, to which a man has submitted the phenomena of the external world or the inner phenomena of his soul, the events of transitory time or the testimonies of his contemporaries. I dare to go further. Even in those cases when the voice of God Himself has spoken immediately and raised a fallen or misguided soul, that soul has bowed down and worshiped only after having recognized the Divine voice. The act of free investigation is the beginning of conversion. In this connection, the Christian confessions differ from one another only in that some permit the investigation of all data, while others limit the number of subjects open to investigation. To ascribe the right of investigation to Protestantism alone would be to raise it to the level of the only discerning faith; but of course this would not be to the taste of its opponents; and all thinkers—even those who are not very serious—will reject such a proposition. One may ask, finally, if it is not in "reform," if it is not in the act of reformation itself that one must seek the essence of Protestantism? Certainly, in the first period of its development, Protestantism hoped to claim this meaning. But then the Church too has constantly been reforming her rites and regulations, and no one has thought to call her Protestant for this reason. Protestantism and reform in general are therefore not one and the same thing.

Protestantism means the expression of doubt in essential dogma. In other words, the denial of dogma as a living tradition; in short, a denial of the Church.

Now I ask every scrupulous person: Is this the Church which is being accused of Protestant tendencies, the Church which has always remained faithful to her tradition, never allowing herself to add anything to this tradition or subtract anything from it, the

Church which indeed looks upon the Roman confession as a schism due to innovations? Is it not absolute nonsense to bring such a charge against such a Church?

The Protestant world is by no means the world of free investigation. Freedom of investigation belongs to all people. Protestantism is one world simply negating another. Take away this other world which it is negating and Protestantism will die, since its whole life consists in negation. The body of doctrines it still holds, the work undertaken by the enterprise of a few scholars and later received by the apathetic credulity of several million uneducated people, is surviving only because the need is felt to oppose the Roman confession. As soon as this feeling disappears, Protestantism at once breaks down into private opinion with no common bonds whatever. Could this be the goal of that Church whose whole concern for other confessions, throughout eighteen centuries, has been inspired by the desire to witness the return of all people to the truth? To put the question is to answer it.

But this is not all. I hope to prove that if, in the future, the spirit of falsehood should ever give rise to some new heresy or schism in the bosom of the Church, her subsequent revival could not appear with the character of Protestantism at first; it could acquire such a character only later on, and then only after having passed through a whole series of transformations, precisely as it has happened in the West.

To begin with we must note that the Protestant world falls into two parts, far from equal in the number of their adherents and in their significance. These parts must not be confused. One has its own logical tradition, even though it denies a more ancient tradition. The other is satisfied with an illogical tradition. The first is composed of the Quakers, the Anabaptists, and other sects of that sort. The second includes all other so-called Reformation sects.

Both halves of Protestantism have one thing in common: their point of departure. Both acknowledge an interruption in the ecclesiastical tradition lasting for several centuries. From this point on they move apart in their principles. The first half, having broken almost all ties with Christianity, admits a new revelation, an immediate descent of the Holy Spirit, and on this foundation seeks to build one Church or many Churches, claiming for themselves an unquestionable tradition and constant inspiration. The basic datum may be false, but its application and development are completely reasonable: a tradition which is acknowledged as a fact receives also a logical justification. It is quite different with the other half of the Protestant world. There they accept a tradition, and at the same time deny the principle by which tradition is justified.

This contradiction may be clarified by an example. In 1847, traveling down the Rhine by steamer, I entered into conversation with a worthy pastor, a serious and educated man. Little by little our conversation shifted round to matters of faith, and in particular to the question of dogmatic tradition, the legitimacy of which the pastor did not accept. I asked him what confession he belonged to. It turned out that he was a Lutheran. On what grounds, I asked, did he give preference to Luther over Calvin? He presented me with exceedingly learned arguments. At this point his servant, who was accompanying him, offered him a glass of lemonade. I asked the pastor to tell me what confession his servant belonged to. He, too, was a Lutheran. "On what grounds," I asked, "does *he* give preference to Luther over Calvin?" The pastor remained silent and his face expressed displeasure. I hastened to assure him that I certainly had not intended to offend him, but had only wished to show him that even in Protestantism there is a tradition. Somewhat disconcerted, but good-natured as always, the pastor, in answer to my words, expressed the hope that with time the lack of education on which traditions depend would melt away before the light of knowledge. "But the people with limited abilities?" I asked. "And the majority of women; and the unskilled laborers who scarcely succeed in earning their daily bread; and children; and, finally, young people hardly more able than children to judge the learned questions

over which the followers of the Reform have become separated?"
The pastor was silent and, after a few moments of reflection,
said: "Yes. Yes, of course, the question still stands. . . . I am
thinking about it." We parted. I do not know if he is still thinking, but I do know that tradition as a fact undoubtedly exists
among the Reformers, although they deny its principle and
legitimacy with all their strength; I know, too, that they cannot
behave otherwise, nor can they extricate themselves from this
contradiction. Indeed, there is nothing contrary to logic in the
fact that those religious societies which acknowledge all their
scholars to be divinely inspired, and ascribe divine inspiration
to the founders with whom they are connected by ties of unbroken succession, at the same time also acknowledge tradition
—either secretly or openly. But by what right can those who base
their beliefs on the learned propositions of their forefathers begin
to use tradition as a means of support? There are people who
believe that the papacy receives inspiration from heaven; that
Fawkes or Johann of Leyden[9] were true organs of the Divine
Spirit. Perhaps these people are in error; nonetheless one can
understand that everything defined by these persons chosen from
above is obligatory for those who believe in them. But to believe
in the infallibility of learning, moreover of a learning which
works out its propositions dialectically, is against common sense.
Thus, while denying tradition as an uninterrupted revelation,
all the scholars of the Reformation are inevitably obliged to
regard all their less learned brothers as people utterly deprived
of true belief. If they were to be consistent they would say to
them: "Friends and brothers, you do not have right faith and you
will never have it until you become theologians like us. In the
meantime, you'll just have to get along somehow without it!"

[9] Guy Fawkes (1570–1606), Roman Catholic zealot and leading figure in
the so-called Gunpowder Plot, an attempt to blow up the English Houses
of Parliament in 1605. Johann Leyden (1508–1536) was a Dutch Anabaptist
fanatic, leader of a theocratic sect in Münster which revolted against the city's
prince-bishop in 1535. (Trans.)

Such a speech is unheard-of, naturally, but it certainly would be an act of sincerity. It is evident that the larger half of the Protestant world is quite satisfied with tradition, as understood in its own illegitimate way; the other, more consistent half has departed so far from Christianity that under the circumstances it is pointless to remain within it. Thus the distinctive characteristic of the Reform consists in the absence of legitimate tradition. What follows from this? It follows that Protestantism has by no means extended the rights of free investigation, but has only reduced the number of reliable data subject to the free investigation of its believers (by leaving them only the Scriptures), as Rome has reduced this number for most of its laity, too (by depriving them of the Scriptures).

Clearly Protestantism, as a Church, does not have the power to check itself, and having rejected legitimate tradition, it has deprived itself of every right to condemn a man who, while acknowledging the divinity of the Holy Scriptures, might not find in them the refutation of the error of Arius or Nestorius—since such a man would be wrong in the eyes of learning, but not in the eyes of faith. However, I am not attacking the Reformers here; what is important is to make clear the necessity which compels them to stand on the ground they now occupy, to trace the logical process which has forced them to this, and to show that within the Church such a necessity and process are impossible.

Since the time of her foundation by the apostles, the Church has been one. Embracing the whole world as it was then known, connecting the British Isles and Spain with Egypt and Syria, this unity was never violated. When a heresy arose the whole Christian world dispatched its representatives and highest dignitaries to solemn assemblies known as councils. By their world-wide character, because of the importance of the questions submitted for their decision, and in spite of the disorder and even violence which sometimes marred their purity, these councils stand out in the history of mankind as the noblest of all its

undertakings. The whole Church accepted or rejected the decisions of the councils depending on whether she found them
compatible or incompatible with her faith and tradition, and she
gave the name of Ecumenical to those councils whose determinations she acknowledged as the expression of her inner thought.
To their temporary authority in questions of discipline, this
further significance was added: they became certain and unalterable witnesses in questions of faith. The Ecumenical Council
became the voice of the Church. Even heresies did not violate
this divine unity; they bore the character of private errors and
not of schisms of whole regions or eparchies. Such was the structure of that ecclesiastical life the inner meaning of which has
long been completely incomprehensible to the whole West.

Let us shift now to the last years of the eighth, or the beginning
of the ninth century, and let us imagine a traveler, who has come
from the East to one of the cities of Italy or France. Filled with
the consciousness of this ancient unity, fully assured that he will
find himself among brothers, he enters a church to sanctify the
first day of the week. Moved by reverent motives and full of love,
he follows the service and listens carefully to the wonderful
prayers which have been dear to his heart from early childhood.
The words reach him: "Let us love one another, and with one
mind confess the Father, and the Son, and the Holy Spirit." He
listens. Now, in the church the Symbol of the Catholic and
Christian faith is pronounced, that Creed which every Christian
must serve all his life and for which he is obliged to sacrifice his
life if the occasion should arise. He listens carefully. But it is a
corrupted Creed he hears; this is some new and unknown Creed!
Has he really heard it, or is he perhaps the victim of some nightmare? He does not believe his ears; he begins to doubt his senses.
He makes inquiries, begs for explanations. He thinks that perhaps he has entered the gathering of some schismatics who are
denying the territorial Church. But alas no! He is hearing the
voice of that territorial Church herself. The entire patriarchate,
the whole vast world itself has lost its unity. The afflicted traveler

laments; they console him. "But we have only added a trifle," they say to him, just as the Latinists say to us now. "If it's a trifle, then why was it added?" "But it is a purely abstract matter." "How then can you be sure that you have understood it?" "Well, it's just our local tradition." "But how could it have found a place in the Ecumenical Creed, contrary to the written decree of an Ecumenical Council forbidding any such change?" "Well, this is a Church-wide tradition, the meaning of which we have put into words, guided by local opinion." "But we do not know such a tradition; and in any case, how can a local opinion find a place in an Ecumenical Creed? Is not the explanation of divine truths given to the whole Church together? Or have we somehow deserved excommunication from the Church? Not only have you not thought of turning to us for counsel, you have not even taken the trouble of notifying us of the change. Or have we already fallen so low? And yet not more than one century ago the East produced the greatest of Christian poets and perhaps the most glorious of her theologians: John of Damascus. And even now there are reckoned among us, confessors, martyrs for the faith, learned philosophers full of Christian understanding, ascetics whose whole lives are an uninterrupted prayer. Why, then, have you renounced us?" But no matter what the poor traveler may say, the deed is done, the breach confirmed. *By this very act* (i.e., the arbitrary changing of the Creed) *the Roman world clearly declared that in its eyes the East was nothing more than a world of helots in questions of faith and doctrine. For one entire half of the Church, ecclesiastical life was at an end.*

I am not touching the heart of the question, but let the believers in the sacredness of dogma and in the divine spirit of brotherhood which was bestowed by the Saviour on the apostles and on all Christians, let *them* ask if clarity of understanding and the divine grace which reveals the meaning of sanctity are to be obtained by neglect of one's brothers and by disowning the innocent. My task is simply to indicate the origin of the Protestant principle.

It is impossible to ascribe this modification to papism alone. This would be to render it too high an honor, or, from another viewpoint, too great an insult. Although the See of Rome apparently became wedded to its unique opinions, along with the territorial Churches under its care, still it firmly clung to the memory of unity. It persisted for some time; but then it was threatened by schisms, and temporal power began to press upon it with insistent demands. And so finally it yielded, perhaps rejoicing inwardly that it was now delivered from future obstructionism on the part of the independent Churches of the East. However that may be, the change was the deed not of one pope but of the whole Roman world, and this deed was justified not at all by belief in the infallibility of the Roman Bishop, but by the feeling of territorial pride. The belief in infallibility came later on; at the time when the rupture was accomplished, Pope Nicholas I was still writing to Photius that in questions of faith the least of Christians had the same voice as the first among bishops.[10] But the consequences of this change were not long in revealing themselves, and the Western world was carried away on a new path.

Having appropriated the right of independently deciding a dogmatic question within the area of the Ecumenical Church, private opinion carried within itself the seed of the growth and legitimation of Protestantism, that is, of free investigation torn

10 Let those who are unacquainted with the documents of this great litigation consult a biography of Photius, if only the one prepared by the Jesuit Jaeger. This work is not notable for its scrupulousness, but it contains important documents. Let me add: The legality of a case in no way depends on the scrupulousness of its advocates; moreover, in the present situation, the conscience of the Pope—as a fabricator of false documents—was hardly clearer than the conscience of the Patriarch—a usurper of the episcopal throne. (Photius became Patriarch of Constantinople in 858, following the illegal deposition of Ignatius. Nicholas supported Ignatius, and the dispute led to an exchange of mutual excommunications and the subsequent reinstatement of Ignatius in 867. After Ignatius' death in 878, Photius became Patriarch legally and held office until 886. Through all this he was regarded as the champion of the Eastern Church against the claims of papal supremacy. [Trans.])

from the living tradition of unity based on mutual love. Thus at
the moment of its origin, Romanism manifested itself as Protestantism. I hope that conscientious people will be convinced of
this, and that the following conclusions will make it even more
clear.

It was as if the right of deciding dogmatic questions were
suddenly altered. Previously this right had belonged to the whole
Ecumenical Church; now it was assigned to a regional Church.
For a regional Church, the right could be affirmed on two
grounds: by virtue of a freedom of inquiry which had abandoned
the living tradition; or by virtue of the claim of an exclusive inspiration by the Holy Spirit for a certain geographically defined
territory. Actually, the first of these principles was accepted, but
it was too soon to proclaim it as a right. The former order of
ecclesiastical life was still too well remembered, and the first principle was too indefinite and therefore too contrary to common
sense to permit an open affirmation.

So the thought naturally arose of associating the monopoly of
divine inspiration with one See, and Western Protestantism was
hidden beneath external authority. Such things are not uncommon in the political world. It could not be otherwise, since a
kingdom of purely rationalistic logic had been set up in place of
the Divine Spirit, who had withdrawn. The newly created despotism restrained the chaos which had been introduced into the
Church by the original novelty, that is, by the independence of
regional or local opinion.

The pope's authority was substituted for ecumenical infallibility, and his authority was external. Once a member of the
Church, once a responsible participant in her decisions, the
Christian man had now become a subject of the Church. She and
he had ceased to be one, he was outside her, although he remained in her bosom. The gift of infallibility assigned to the
pope was placed beyond the influence of ethical conditions, so
that neither the corruption of the whole Christian world nor
even the personal corruption of the pope himself could have any

effect on this infallibility. The pope became a kind of oracle deprived of all freedom, a kind of statue made of flesh and bones, put into motion by hidden springs. For the Christian this oracle fell into the category of things of a material nature, of things whose laws can and must be subjected to the investigation of reason alone. A purely external and consequently rational law had replaced the living, ethical law which alone does not fear rationalism, since it embraces not only man's reason but also the whole of his being.[11]

A this-worldly State took the place of the Christian Church. The single living law of unity in God was displaced by private laws, bearing in themselves the imprint of utilitarianism and juridical concerns. Rationalism grew up in the form of arbitrary definitions: it invented purgatory in order to explain prayers for the dead; it placed between God and man a balance of obligations and merits, weighing sins against prayers, crimes against meritorious exploits; it set up transferences from one man to another, legitimized the barter of illusory merits; in short, it brought the whole machinery of the banking house into the treasury of faith. At the same time, the Church-State introduced a state language: Latin. Then it appropriated to itself the judgment of worldly affairs; then it took up arm; and began to equip, first, informal bands of crusaders, and later, organized armies (the orders of knights-religious); and, finally, when the sword was torn from its hand, it moved into position the highly trained corps of the Jesuits. It is not now a matter of criticism. Seeking the sources of Protestant rationalism, I find it disguised in the form of Roman rationalism and I cannot avoid tracing its development.

[11] Some people assert that papal infallibility is given to the Church as a kind of reward for her moral unity. In what way, then, could she be rewarded for the insult borne by the whole Eastern Church? Others say that infallibility lies in the agreement between the pope's decision and that of the whole Church convoked in council, or even if not actually gathered in council. How then was it possible to accept a dogma not subjected to prior examination and not even communicated to one entire half of the Christian world? None of these shifts stands up under serious investigation.

Without dwelling on abuses, I am concentrating on the principle. The Church inspired by God became, for the Western Christian, something external, a kind of negative authority, a kind of material authority. It turned man into its slave, and as a result acquired, in him, a judge.

"The Church is an *authority*," said Guizot in one of his remarkable works, while one of his adversaries, attacking him, simply repeated these words. Speaking in this way neither one suspected how much untruth and blasphemy lay in the statement. Poor Romanist! Poor Protestant! No—the Church is not an authority, just as God is not an authority and Christ is not an authority, since authority is something external to us. The Church is not an authority, I say, but the truth—and at the same time the inner life of the Christian, since God, Christ, the Church, live in him with a life more real than the heart which is beating in his breast or the blood flowing in his veins. But they are alive in him only insofar as he himself is living by the ecumenical life of love and unity, i.e., by the life of the Church. Such is the blindness of the Western sects that, up to now, not one of them has understood how radically the ground on which they stand differs from that on which the original Church has been standing from earliest times, and on which she will stand eternally.

In this the Latinists are completely wrong. They themselves are rationalists, and yet they accuse others of rationalism; they themselves were Protestants from the first moment of their falling away, and yet they condemn the spontaneous rebellion of their rebellious brothers. On the other hand, while they have every right to return the accusation, the Protestants are unable to do so because they themselves are no more than developers of the Roman teaching. The only difference is that they have adapted it to suit themselves. No sooner did authority become external power, and no sooner was knowledge of religious truths cut off from religious life, than the relationship among people was altered too. Within the Church the people constituted a single whole; one spirit was alive in all. Now this bond disappeared,

another replaced it: the common, subject-like dependence of all
the people on the supreme power of Rome. No sooner did the
first doubt of the legitimacy of this power arise than unity was
destroyed, since the doctrine of papal infallibility was not
founded on the holiness of the Ecumenical Church; nor did the
Western world lay claim to a relatively higher level of moral
purity at the moment when it arrogated to itself the right to
change (or, as the Romanists say, to expound) the Creed and
disregard the opinion of its Eastern brothers. No, it simply cited
the accidental circumstance of episcopal succession, as if the
other bishops established by the apostle Peter, regardless of their
location, were not just as much his successors as the Bishop of
Rome! Rome never said to the people: "Only the perfectly holy
man can judge me, but such a man will always think as I do." On
the contrary, Rome destroyed every bond between knowledge
and inner perfection of soul; it gave free reign to reason while at
the same time obviously trampling it under foot.

It would not be difficult to show in the doctrine of the Reformers the indelible mark of Rome and the same spirit of utilitarian rationalism which characterizes papism. Their conclusions
are not the same; but the premises and the definitions assumed
and contained in these conclusions are always identical. The Papacy says: "The Church has always prayed for the dead, but this
prayer would be useless if there were not an intermediate state
between heaven and hell; *therefore* there is a purgatory." The
Reform answers: "There is not a trace of purgatory either in Holy
Scripture or in the early Church; *therefore* it is useless to pray
for the dead and I will not pray for them." The Papacy says:
"The Church appeals to the intercession of the saints, *therefore*
this is useful, *therefore* this completes the merits of prayer and
works of satisfaction." The Reform answers: "The satisfaction
for sins made by the blood of Christ and appropriated by faith
in baptism and in prayer is sufficient for the redemption not only
of man but also of all creation, *therefore* the saints' intercession
for us is useless, and there is no reason to appeal to them in

prayer." Clearly the sacred Communion of Saints is equally in-comprehensible to both sides. The Papacy says: "According to the witness of the apostle James faith is insufficient,[12] *therefore* we cannot be saved by faith, and *therefore* works are useful and constitute merit." Protestantism answers: "Faith alone saves, ac-cording to the witness of the apostle Paul, and works do not constitute merit, *therefore* they are useless." And so on, and so on.

In this way the warring parties have gone back and forth at each other with syllogisms through the centuries, and are still going back and forth at each other, but always over the same ground, the ground of rationalism; and neither side can choose any other. Even Rome's division of the Church into the teaching and the learning Church has been transmitted to the Reform; the only difference is that in the Roman confession it exists by right, by virtue of acknowledged law, while in Protestantism it exists only as a fact; and a scholar has taken the place of the priest.

I have tried to prove that Protestantism is impossible for us and that we can have nothing in common with the Reform, since we stand on completely different soil. But in order to make this conclusion quite plain I will present one more explanation of a more positive nature. Speaking through Holy Scripture, teaching and sanctifying through the sacred tradition of the Ecumenical Church, the Divine Spirit cannot be apprehended by reason alone. He is accessible only to the whole human spirit under the influence of grace. The attempt to penetrate into the realm of faith and its mystery by the light of reason alone is a presumption in the eyes of the Christian, a criminal and stupid presumption. Only the light which comes down from heaven and which pene-trates the whole spirit of man can show him the way; only the

[12] It is hardly necessary to prove that the apostle James is misinterpreted in this citation. He is obviously ascribing the name "faith" to knowledge, but this certainly does not mean that he is identifying the one with the other; he wishes to show in this way the complete illegitimacy of any claim knowledge might have to the name "faith" when it does not in fact have faith's dis-tinctive marks.

power given by the Divine Spirit can raise him to those unapproachable heights where Divinity is revealed. "Only he can
understand a prophet who is a prophet himself," says St. Gregory
the Wonder-worker. Only Divinity can comprehend God and
His everlasting wisdom. Only he who bears within himself the
living Christ can approach His throne without being annihilated
by that glory before which the purest spiritual powers prostrate
themselves in joyful trembling. The right and the power to contemplate the grandeur of heaven and penetrate its mystery are
given only to the Church, holy and eternal; to the living ark of
the Divine Spirit which bears Christ, her Lord and Saviour; to
her alone, bound to Him by a close and inner unity which neither
human thought can grasp nor human words express. I speak of
the Church in her wholeness, of which the Church on earth is an
inseparable part; since what we call the visible Church and the
invisible Church are not two Churches, but one, under two
different aspects. The Church in her fullness, as a spiritual organism, is neither a collective nor an abstract entity; she is the
Divine Spirit, who knows Himself and is unable not to know.
The whole Church wrote the Holy Scriptures and then gave life
to them in Tradition. To put it more accurately, Scripture and
Tradition, as two manifestations of one and the same Spirit, are a
single manifestation. Scripture is nothing but written Tradition,
and Tradition is nothing but living Scripture. Such is the mystery
of this harmonious unity; it is formed by the fusion of the purest
holiness with the highest reason, and only by way of this fusion
does reason acquire the ability to comprehend things in that
realm where reason alone, separated from holiness, is as blind as
matter itself.

Will Protestantism rise on this soil? Will a man stand on this
ground who thinks of himself as a judge of the Church and thus
makes the claim to perfect holiness and perfection of reason? I
doubt if such a man would be received as a welcome guest by
that Church which has as its first principle the doctrine that
ignorance and sin are the inevitable result of isolation, while

fullness of understanding and incorruptible holiness belong only
to the unity of all the members of the Church together.

Such is the teaching of the Ecumenical Orthodox Church, and
I say boldly that no one will find in it the seeds of rationalism.

But, we are asked, whence comes the power to preserve a teaching so pure and exalted? Whence the weapons for its defense?
The power is found in mutual love, the weapons in the communion of prayer; and divine help does not betray love and
prayer, since God Himself inspires both.

Where, then, will we find a guarantee against error in the
future? There is only one answer to this question: Whoever
seeks beyond hope and faith for any guarantee of the spirit of
love is already a rationalist. For him the Church, too, is unthinkable, since he is already, in his whole spirit, plunged in
doubt.

I do not know if I have succeeded in making my thought clear,
so that my readers will really see the difference between the basic
principles of the Church and those of the Western confessions.
The difference is so great that it is hardly possible to find one
point on which they might agree. It even happens that, the more
similar in appearance are the expressions or external forms, the
more essential is the difference in their significance.

So many of the questions which have been argued for so many
centuries in the religious polemic of Europe find a simple resolution within the Church; or, to speak more accurately, for her
they do not even exist as questions. Thus, taking it as a first
principle that the life of the spiritual world is nothing but love
and communion in prayer, she prays for the dead, even though
she rejects the fable of purgatory invented by rationalism; she
asks for the intercession of the saints, not ascribing to them,
however, the merits contrived by the utilitarian school, and not
acknowledging the necessity for any intercession other than that
of our Divine Mediator. Thus, aware of her living unity, she cannot even understand the question whether salvation lies in faith
alone or in faith and works together. In her eyes life and truth

are one, and works are nothing but the manifestation of a faith which, without this manifestation, would not be faith but logical knowledge. Thus also, feeling her inner union with the Holy Spirit, she offers thanks to the One Who is Good for every good thing, ascribing nothing to herself and to man except the evil which, in him, resists the work of God. Man must be helpless if the power of God is to be perfected in his soul.

Here I must fix the reader's attention on a phenomenon which is especially significant. The bifurcation of the Church into the Teaching Church and the Church of Pupils (this name really ought to be given to the lower division), while acknowledged as a basic principle in Romanism (conditioned as it is by the structural properties of a Church-State with its division into clergy and laity), has passed into the Reform and is preserved in it as a result of the abrogation of legitimate tradition or the encroachment of knowledge on faith. Here then is the common feature of both Western confessions. Its absence in the Orthodox Church defines her character in the most decisive way.

In saying this I am not proposing a hypothesis, not even a logical conclusion from a combination of other principles in Orthodoxy (I drew such a conclusion and put it into writing many years ago).[13] I am saying much more. The feature which I have pointed out is an indisputable dogmatic fact. The Eastern patriarchs, having assembled in council with their bishops, solemnly pronounced in their reply to the Encyclical Letter of Pius IX that "infallibility resides solely in the *ecumenicity* of the Church bound together by mutual love, and that the unchangeableness of dogma as well as the purity of rite are entrusted to the care not of one heirarchy but of all the people of the Church, who are the Body of Christ."[14] This formal declaration of all the Eastern clergy, which was received by the territorial Russian Church

13 Khomyakov is probably referring here to his article, "The Church Is One," first published in 1864 but written much earlier, perhaps in the forties. (Trans.)

14 Encyclical dated May 6, 1848.

with respectful and brotherly gratitude, has acquired the moral authority of an ecumenical sanction. This is unquestionably the most significant event in Church history over many centuries.

In the True Church there is no Teaching Church.

Does this mean that there is no edification in the Church? There is not only edification, but more edification there than anywhere else. Every word inspired by the feeling of truly Christian love, and living faith, and hope, is edification. Every deed carrying the imprint of the Spirit of God is a lesson. Every Christian life is a pattern and example. The martyr who dies for the truth, the judge who judges righteously (not as pleasing men, but God), the farmer in his humble labor continually being lifted in thought to his Creator—all such men live and die for the edification of their brothers; and not without reason, for the Spirit of God puts words of wisdom on their lips such as the scholar and theologian will never find. "The bishop is at the same time both the teacher and disciple of his flock," said the modern apostle to the Aleutian Islands, Bishop Innokenti. Every man, no matter how high he is placed in the hierarchy, or conversely, no matter how hidden from view he may be in the shadow of humble circumstance, both edifies and is edified, for God clothes whom He wills with the gifts of His infinite wisdom, without regard to person or calling. It is not just the word that edifies, but a man's whole life.

The question of edification brings us again to the question of investigation, since the one presupposes the other. Faith is always the consequence of revelation recognized as revelation; it is the perceiving of an invisible fact manifested in some visible fact; faith is not *belief* or logical conviction based on conclusions, but much more. It is not the act of one perceptive faculty separated from others, but the act of all the powers of reason grasped and captivated in all its depth by the living truth of the revealed fact. Faith is not known only or sensed only, but is known and sensed together, so to speak; in a word, it is not knowledge alone but knowledge and life. So, then, the process of investigation in matters of faith borrows from faith the essential nature of faith, and differs completely from investigation in the usual meaning of the word. First, in the area of faith, the world which is under investigation is not a world external to man, since man himself, and the whole man, with all his fullness of reason and will, belongs to this world and is an essential part of it. Second, investigation in the area of faith presupposes certain basic data, moral or rational, which, for the soul, stand above all doubt. Actually, investigation in the area of faith is nothing but the process of the reasonable unveiling of these data; since full doubt, knowing no limits (if such a thing could really exist), would not only exclude all possibility of faith but also any thought of serious investigation. Once admitted by an absolutely pure soul, the least of these data would give it all the other data by virtue of an unbreakable although perhaps unrecognized sequence of deductions. For the Orthodox Christian the sum of these data includes the whole universe, with all the phenomena of human life and the whole word of God, both written and expressed in the dogmatic ecumenical tradition.

Thus investigation itself in the area of faith, both by the variety of data subject to study and by the fact that its goal lies in living and not merely in abstract truth, demands the use of all intellectual powers in the will and reason, and beyond that also the inner investigation of these powers themselves. It is necessary to take into account not only the world that is seen, as object, but also the power and purity of the organ of sight.

The initial principle of such investigation is the humble acknowledgment of one's own frailty. It cannot be otherwise; since the shadow of sin already contains the possibility of error, and the possibility turns into inevitability when a man unconditionally relies on his own powers or the gifts of grace bestowed on him as an individual. One would have to claim perfection of the perceptive faculty as well as moral perfection in order to be in a position to make a truly independent investigation of the subjects of faith. It would take more than just satanic pride to make such a claim; one would have to be quite mad. The truth exists only where there is pure holiness, that is, in the wholeness of the Ecumenical Church, which is the manifestation of the Spirit of God in mankind.

Edification, then, is accomplished, not by Scripture alone, as the Protestants think (nevertheless we thank them with all our heart for increasing the number of copies of the Bible); nor by verbal interpretation; nor by the Creed (the necessity of which, however, we by no means deny); nor by preaching; nor by the study of theology; nor by works of love; but by all these things together.

Of course Christianity is expressed in logical form in the Creed; but this expression is not separated from its other manifestations. Christianity is taught as a learned discipline under the title of theology; but this is no more than a branch of the teaching as a whole. Whoever truncates the teaching, that is, whoever separates teaching in the narrow sense of lecturing and interpreting from its other forms, errs grievously; whoever turns teaching into an exclusive privilege descends into foolishness; whoever makes of teaching a kind of official function, supposing that the divine gift of teaching is inseparably connected with this official function, falls into heresy, since in this very way a new, unheard-of sacrament is created: the sacrament of rationalism or logical knowledge. The *whole* Church teaches—the Church in all her fullness. The Church does not acknowledge a Teaching Church in any other sense.

I hope that I have said enough to prove that the second charge brought against us by Mr. Laurency, the Comte de Maistre, and by many others, is just as ill-founded as the first, and that Protestantism could arise in the Church only by way of the Roman schism, out of which it inevitably flows.

However, an objection may perhaps be raised on the strength of my own words. It could be said that in tracing the genealogy of Protestantism through Romanism I have proved that the rationalistic soil of the Reform was created first by the Roman schism; but since this schism (at the moment of its appearance) was an act of Protestantism, surely it must follow that Protestantism can arise directly within the Church. I hope, however, that my answer will justify me. Certainly, by its falling away from the Church, Rome performed an act of Protestantism; but in those times the ecclesiological spirit, even in the West, was still so strong and so opposed to the spirit of the later Reform that Romanism was compelled to hide its character from the sight of Christians and from itself too, masking the principle of rationalistic anarchy it had brought into the midst of the Church by a despotism in matters of faith. Even if it could be demonstrated, however, that *in former times* Protestantism or the Protestant principle could be generated in the bosom of the Church, it is nevertheless clear now that this possibility *no longer exists.*

From the very beginning of the Christian world, no small number of heresies have arisen to disturb its harmony. Even before the apostles had finished their earthly task, many of their pupils were seduced by falsehood. Later on, with each succeeding century, heresies multiplied. Many of the faithful were torn away from the Church by Nestorianism and Eutychianism, with all their ramifications, and especially by Arianism, which provided, incidentally, the occasion for the Roman schism. The question is raised: Can these heresies be revived? No! At the time when they arose, the dogmas which they opposed were not yet clothed in the form of clear definitions, even though they were included implicitly in the Church's tradition. Thus it was possible for a frail, personal faith to fall into error. Later, by Divine Providence, by the grace of His eternal Word and the inspiration of the Spirit of truth and life, dogma received a precise definition at the councils—and from then on error (in its old form) became impossible even as a result of personal frailty. Unbelief is still possible, but not Arianism. The same is true with the other heresies; they too are no longer possible. They involved misconceptions concerning the revealed dogma of the inner being of God, or of God's relationship to human nature; distorting the dogmatic tradition, they claimed to be the true tradition. These were more or less culpable errors, but they did not infringe upon the dogma of ecclesiastical ecumenicity; on the contrary, all the above-mentioned heresies tried to prove the truth of their teachings by referring to their supposed acceptance by all Christians. Romanism began at the moment it placed the independence of individual or regional opinion above the ecumenical unity of faith; it was the first to create a heresy of a new type, a heresy against the dogma of the nature of the Church, against her own faith in herself. The Reform was only the continuation of this same heresy under another name.

All the Western sects may be defined in this way; but an error once defined is no longer possible for members of the Church. Does this mean that members of the Church are immune to error? By no means. Just as it would be unreasonable to assert that they are immune to sin. Such perfection belongs only to the Church in her living wholeness, and cannot be ascribed to anyone individually.

Only the person able to call himself a living organ of the Spirit of God would have the right to claim infallibility. But does it follow from this that the faith of an Orthodox Christian is open to error? No. Since the Christian, by the very fact that he believes in the Ecumenical Church, lowers his belief (in questions that have not yet been clearly defined) to the level of a personal opinion, or to that of a regional opinion if the doctrine has been accepted by a whole eparchy. However, although an error in opinion holds no danger for the Church, it cannot be considered harmless for the individual Christian. It is always a sign and consequence of moral error or weakness, making a man to some extent unworthy of heavenly light, and, like every sin, it can be wiped out only by divine mercy. A Christian's faith must overflow with joy and gratitude, but also with fear. Let him pray! Let him beg for the light he lacks! If only he will not lull his conscience to sleep, like the Reformer who says: "Of course I may be mistaken, but my intentions are pure and God will take them into account, as He does my weakness." Or like the Romanist, who says: "Let us suppose then that I'm mistaken—so what? The pope knows the truth for me, and I submit in advance to his decision!"

I have clarified as well as I could the difference in character between the Church and the Western confessions. I have stated plainly the heresy against the dogma concerning the ecumenicity and holiness of the Church contained in both Latinist and Protestant rationalism. Now I must say a few words about our relations with these two confessions, their relations with each other, and their contemporary position.

Since the Reform is nothing but a continuation and development of Romanism, I must first speak about our relations with the latter. Is a rapprochement possible? One can only answer this question with a decisive "No." Truth does not permit compromises. It is understandable why the papacy has devised the Greek Uniat Church. The Church-State can, if it sees fit, bestow certain rights of citizenship upon its former Eastern brothers, as helots in the realm of faith. It can give these rights to them as a reward for their humble submission to the authority of the pope, without demanding from them the oneness of faith expressed in the Creed. Of course, for the true Latinist such half-citizens can only arouse pity and contempt. They are far from being real Roman citizens, and not one theologian, not one teacher would undertake to prove the logic of their religion. It is an absurdity which is being tolerated—and nothing more. In the eyes of the Church such a union is unthinkable, but it is in complete harmony with the principles of Romanism. The Church admits no compromises in dogma or faith. She requires full unity, nothing less; on the other hand, she gives full equality, since she recognizes the spirit of brotherliness and not subjection. Thus a rapprochement is impossible without the full renunciation by the Romanists of an error which is now more than a thousand years old.

But would not a council bridge the chasm separating the Roman schism from the Church? No—since a council can be called only after the chasm has been bridged. It is true that people intoxicated by false opinions participated in the Ecumenical Councils; some of them returned to the truth, others were stubborn in their errors and as a result were finally separated from the Church. But the point is that these people, in spite of their errors, did not deny the divine principle of ecumenicity in the most fundamental dogmas of the faith. They held, or at least declared the hope of defining in clear terms, the dogma confessed by the Church, and also hoped to be worthy of the grace of testifying to the faith of their brothers. Such was the aim of the councils, such was their significance, such was the concept implied in the usual introductory formula to all their decisions: "It has pleased the Holy Spirit. . . ." These words do not express a haughty claim, but a humble hope, justified or repudiated later by the acceptance or nonacceptance of the decisions by the whole people of the Church or, as the Eastern patriarchs put it, by the whole Body of Christ. There were, from time to time, heretical councils. Why were these councils rejected, when outwardly they did not differ from the Ecumenical Councils? Solely because their decisions were not acknowledged as the voice of the Church *by the whole people of the Church,* by that people and within that world where, in questions of faith, there is no difference between a scholar and an untutored person, between cleric and layman, between man and woman, king and subject, slaveowner and slave, and where, if in God's judgment it is needed, a youth receives the gift of knowledge, a word of infinite wisdom is given to a child, and the heresy of a learned bishop is confuted by an illiterate cowherd, so that all might be joined in that free unity of living faith which is the manifestation of the Spirit of God. Such is the dogma lying beneath the idea of the council. Now then, why have a council if the Western world has been deemed worthy of such a clear revelation of divine truth that it has considered itself empowered to insert its revelation into the Symbol of Faith without waiting for confirmation from the East? What might a wretched Greek or Russian helot do

at a council seated alongside these chosen vessels, these representatives of people who have anointed themselves with the
chrism of infallibility? A council is impossible until the Western
world returns to the idea of the council and condemns its own
infringement of the council principle and all the consequences
stemming from this infringement. Or, to put it another way,
until it returns to the original Creed and submits its opinion, by
which the Creed was impaired, to the judgment of the Ecumenical Faith. In a word, when rationalism is clearly understood and
condemned, then and only then will a council be possible. So it
is not a council which will bridge the chasm; the chasm must first
be bridged before the council can assemble.[15]

It was noted above that Romanism had been forced to renounce its own nature, so to speak, as long as it bore anarchy
within itself as a principle and feared its manifestation in practice. It was compelled to masquerade in its own eyes and transform itself into despotism. This transformation has not failed
to bring important consequences. The unity of the Church was
free; more precisely, the unity was freedom itself, the harmonious
expression of inner agreement. When this living unity was rejected, ecclesiastical freedom was sacrificed for the maintenance
of a contrived and arbitrary unity. The spiritual intuition of
truth was replaced by an external token or sign.

The Reform followed another path. Remaining steadfast to
the principle of rationalistic self-determination which had generated the Roman schism, it demanded its freedom (with every
right), and was forced to sacrifice all semblance of unity. As
with papism, so also with the Reform: everything leads to ex-

15 This was the conviction of the great Mark of Ephesus who, at the
Florentine Council, demanded that the Creed be restored to its original purity
and the insertion be declared an opinion standing outside its formula. Excluded from the list of dogmas, the error would become harmless. This was
what Mark wanted, leaving the actual correction of the error to God's providence. Thus the heresy would have been removed and the possibility of communion restored. But the pride of rationalism has not yet permitted Rome to
go this far.

ternality. Such is the nature of all the children of rationalism. The unity of papism is an external unity, deprived of living content; the freedom of the Protestant mind is also an external freedom, without real content.

The papists, like the Judaizers, base their position on a sign (or token); Protestants, like the Hellenizers, base their position on logic. A true understanding of the Church, as freedom in unity and life in reason, is equally inaccessible to both.

On the other hand, conflict is possible, even inevitable, since they occupy the same ground and have the same rights. Both Romanism and Protestantism have been plunged wholly (without suspecting it) into that logical antinomy into which every living thing falls as long as it sees things only from the logical point of view. But what are the results of the conflict? In all truthfulness, there is nothing comforting here for either side. Both are strong in attack and weak in defense, since both are equally wrong, and equally condemned by reason and the witness of history. At every moment each of the warring parties can pride itself on a spectacular victory; but in the meantime both are constantly defeated, and the field of battle is left to unbelief. If the need for faith had not compelled many people to close their eyes to the inconsistency of a religion accepted only because it was impossible to get along without it, and if the same need had not compelled even those who do not seriously believe in religion to continue to hold on to what they once accepted, unbelief would long ago have conquered the field.

Since the conflict between the Western confessions has been conducted on the soil of rationalism, one cannot even say that *faith* has been its real subject. Beliefs and convictions, no matter how sincere or passionate, have yet to deserve the name of faith. Nevertheless, as a subject of study this conflict is extraordinarily interesting and profoundly instructive. The characteristics of the parties are defined in it clearly.

A criticism that is serious but dry and imperfect; a learning that is broad but unsubstantial because of its lack of inner unity;

an upright and sober morality worthy of the first centuries of the Church, combined with a narrowness of vision set within the limits of individualism; ardent outbursts of feeling in which we seem to hear a confession of their shortcomings and their lack of hope in ever attaining atonement; a constant lack of depth scarcely masked by a fog of arbitrary mysticism; a love of the truth combined with an inability to understand it in its living reality; in a word—*rationalism within idealism:* such is the fate of the Protestants. A breadth of view that is large enough, yet quite insufficient for true Christianity; an eloquence that is brilliant but too often marred by passion; a bearing that is majestic but always theatrical; a criticism that is almost always superficial, catching at words and not probing far into meaning; an illusory display of unity with an absence of real unity; a certain peculiar poverty of religious need, which never dares to raise its sights to higher levels and is always ready to settle for a cheap satisfaction; a certain uneven depth, hiding its shoals in clouds of sophisms; a hearty and sincere love for external order combined with a disregard for internal order, i.e., truth; in a word—*rationalism within materialism:* such is the fate of the Latinists. Nor do I mean to accuse all the writers of this party of deliberate falsehood, or to say that none of their opponents deserves the same reproach; but the inclination of the papist party to sophisms, its systematic side-stepping in the face of real objections, its feigned ignorance—which has finally become a regular habit of textual distortions, omissions, and inaccuracies in quotation—all this is so well known that it is beyond dispute. Not wishing, however, in such an important accusation, to limit myself to simple assertions, and having made it a rule for myself never to cite facts which are in any way doubtful, I will remind my readers of the long-drawn-out affair of the False Decretals, upon which the theory of papal supremacy rested until the belief became so entrenched that it was possible to remove the false props; I mention also the false Deeds of Donation which formed the basis for the temporal power of the Roman primate; and the endless series of deliberately mutilated editions of the holy fathers. Close to our own time, I mention the fact that the work of Adam Zernikavius, in which it is demonstrated that all the testimony drawn from the works of the holy fathers in support of the addition to the Creed was intentionally altered or misquoted, still stands unrefuted. Finally, moving into our own time, I point to the writings of the eloquent proto-sophist Comte de Maistre,[16] and to the remarkable work of Newman ("On the Development of Christian Doctrine").[17] It should be noted that this last writer was scrupulous indeed as long as he confessed Anglicanism, but after converting to Romanism out of scrupulousness (so I assume), there was a sudden loss of scruple. However, in pointing out the falsity which always marks the Roman polemic, I by no

[16] Cf. the argument in defense of Romanism drawn by de Maistre from the works of St. Athanasius: "The whole world," says St. Athanasius to the heretics, "calls the true Church the Catholic Church. This alone is enough to prove that you are heretics." "But which Church is it," de Maistre asks, "that all Europe calls Catholic? The Church of Rome. Consequently all other Churches are in schism." But surely St. Athanasius was talking to Greeks, who clearly understood the meaning of the word "catholic" (as "world-wide," "ecumenical"), so that his argument had full force. But, I ask, what does this prove in the case of modern Europe, where the word has lost all meaning? Let them ask about the world-wide or ecumenical Church in England, or Germany, or especially in Russia, and listen carefully to the answers!

[17] In this work Newman supplements Moeller's theory about the gradual perfecting and development of the Church. "All her doctrine," he says, "was contained implicitly in her primitive teaching, and was gradually developed out of it, or more accurately, gradually acquired a clarity of logical expression. Thus it was with the basic dogma of the Trinity, thus also with the doctrine of papal supremacy in matters of faith, and so on." And so Newman pretends that he has never heard about the apostasy of Pope Liberius, or about the condemnation of Pope Honorius by an Ecumenical Council and the acceptance of this condemnation by the whole West. What is important here is not the fact that Honorius erred, nor does it matter whether this was proved or not; what is important is that an Ecumenical Council acknowledged the possibility of papal fallibility, something Newman could not help but know. Thus the new doctrine of infallibility was not a development of ecumenical doctrine, but its direct contradiction. The author's silence and pretended ignorance on this point is nothing more than a barefaced lie.

means wish to condemn too harshly the writers who have taken part in it, and I will not dwell on the question of the extent of their moral responsibility.

Neither Orthodox writers nor the defenders of Protestantism are above reproach in this matter, although occasions for just complaint are encountered much less frequently with them than with the Latinists; and the degree of personal guilt is far from being the same. A falsehood coming from the pen of an Orthodox writer is an absurd infamy, definitely harming the cause which he is undertaking to defend; in the case of a Protestant, a falsehood is a culpable absurdity and at the same time completely unprofitable; but with the Romanist, falsehood is a necessity, and to a certain extent forgivable. The reason for this difference is clear. Falsehood is essentially opposed to Orthodoxy, as it is to truth. In Protestantism, the realm of searching for truth, falsehood is simply out of place. In Romanism, however, the teaching which denies its own root principle, falsehood is inevitable. Here is the real source of that moral corruption which, in the Roman confession, perverts the brightest minds and discredits the loftiest intellects (we need only recall the remarkable Bossuet).

The moral exhaustion of the two parties becomes more and more apparent every day. A horror in the face of common danger is overwhelming the rationalistic sects of the West: Papism and the Reform. They still go on struggling with one another (they are unable to stop) but they have lost all hope of victory, having more or less clearly recognized their own inner weaknesses. Unbelief rapidly grows up before them, not that unbelief of the powerful, the rich, and the learned which marked the eighteenth century, but the unbelief of the masses, the scepticism of ignorance. Such are the legitimate offspring of the open or hidden rationalism which has passed for faith in the European world for hundreds of years.

I have fulfilled my duty. I have defended the Church against false accusations which I do not consider, however, to be deliber-

ate slanders. In order to make my refutation intelligible I have
had to develop the distinctive features both of Orthodoxy and of
the Western schism, which is nothing but patched up rationalism, and to present the contemporary religious question in
the light in which it appears to us. As I said at the beginning, I
have not tried to gloss over my hostility of thought by an affected
moderation of terms. I have boldly put forward the Church's
teaching and her attitude toward the different forms of the
schism. I have openly expressed my opinion about the conflict
between the sects. I dare to hope, however, that no one will accuse me of malice or conscious injustice.

I repeat: I have fulfilled my duty in answering the charges
brought against the Church—not only my duty in relation to
the Church, but still more in relation to you, my readers and
brothers, who have unfortunately been separated from us by an
error which arose in ages long passed out of view. No fear of any
kind, or any sort of calculation, has constrained my pen, nor have
I written out of any hope of profit.

Readers and brothers! A ruinous legacy has come down to you
from the ignorance and sinfulness of past ages—the embryo of
death; and you are suffering punishment for it without being
directly responsible, since you have had no definite understanding of the error involved. You have done much for mankind in
science and art, in constitutional law and in the civilization of
peoples, in the practical realization of the meaning of truth and
in the practical application of love. More than that, you have
done all you could for man in his relation to God, preaching
Christ to people who had never before heard His Divine Name.
All honor and thanks to you for your immeasurable labors, the
fruits of which mankind is gathering now and will continue to
gather in the future. But as long as it still inspires you, this
ruinous legacy will kill your spiritual life.

The cure is within your power. Of course, as long as the
disease is alive in popular prejudices and in the ignorance of the
means to stop its spread (and this will last a long time), it is

impossible to expect the healing of the masses; but the cure is accessible now to private individuals. If any one of my readers is convinced of the truth of my words, of the validity of my definition of the origins of the schism and its rationalistic character, then I beg him to consider. If he will make but one acknowledgment of the truth, then he must accept all the practical consequences flowing from it; if he will make but one confession of error, he must then repair it, to the extent that this is possible.

I beg him to undertake a moral exploit—to tear himself away from rationalism, to condemn the excommunication which was once pronounced upon his Eastern brothers, to reject all the later decrees flowing from this falsehood, to accept us once more in his communion with the rights of brotherly equality, and to restore in his soul the unity of the Church, so that by this fact he might have the right to repeat with her: "Let us love one another, and with one mind confess the Father, and the Son, and the Holy Spirit."

The disease carries death within itself, but the cure is not difficult; it only requires an act of justice. Will people want to undertake this exploit, or will they prefer to perpetuate the reign of falsehood, deluding their own consciences and the minds of their brothers?

My readers, judge for yourselves!

Translated by Asheleigh E. Moorhouse
April, 1964

Vladimir Sergeyevich Solovyov

1853 - 1900

To admirers and enemies alike, Solovyov is the most important Russian philosopher; his influence on the "renaissance" of the twentieth century was enormous. He died at the age of only forty-seven, but what an intense, rich, and even mysterious life was his! Son of the famous Russian historian, Sergei Solovyov, Vladimir received a traditional and religious education. But already at the age of fifteen he proclaimed himself a total materialist and socialist, endorsed enthusiastically the radical creed of the sixties, and enrolled in the Faculty of Science. The return to faith, however, followed almost immediately, and Solovyov remained thereafter not only a Christian but a militant defender of the Christian faith. This need to *defend* Christianity, to expose it as the supreme wisdom, is probably the mainspring of his whole philosophy. Upon graduation from the university in 1873, Solovyov spent a year studying at the Moscow Theological Academy. His master's dissertation, *Krisis Zapadnoy Filosofii* ("The Crisis of Western Philosophy: Against the Positivists"), which he presented and defended at the age of twenty-one, made him famous overnight. But Solovyov was not only an academic philosopher. From his very first years he had

"peculiar dreams" and visions, and all his life he remained oriented toward the mysterious and the esoteric. And here, the theme is Sophia, the mysterious personification of Eternal Womanhood. Not only was Solovyov interested in "Sophiology," he had personal contacts with Sophia—they are related in his poem, *Three Meetings*. When, in 1875, he left Russia for what seemed to be an academic leave, he in fact went to "meet" Sophia, first in the British Museum (!) and then in Cairo. "Basically," writes S. L. Frank, "the idea of Sophia is, with Solovyov, a mystical intuition and not a metaphysical conception. Solovyov's mysticism is of the gnostically-theosophical type. . . . What is essential in this doctrine of Sophia is not its abstract logical justification . . . but its 'spirit,' its concrete religious significance—and that consists in religious love for the world and mankind in its sacred, potentially divine, and beautiful primary nature" (A *Solovyov Anthology*, p. 13). From 1876 to 1881 Solovyov lectured, first in Moscow, then in St. Petersburg. In 1878 his famous *Lectures on God-Manhood* appeared, and in 1880 his doctoral dissertation, *Kritika Otvlechennykh Nachal*, "The Critique of Abstract Principles." But his academic career came to an abrupt end in 1881, when, after the assassination of Alexander II by terrorists, Solovyov, in a public lecture, begged the Tsar to forgive his father's assassins. He was forced to resign his teaching post and from then on remained all his life a wandering free lance. From systematic philosophy, he first went to history. This was his "utopian" period: in his *Istoria i Budushee Teokratii*, "History and Future of Theocracy" (only one of the three volumes appeared in 1886), he described the fulfillment of Christianity as embracing all aspects of life. It was also his "Romanizing" period, for the Roman Catholic Church had, in his theocratic dream, to unite all churches. In his French book, *La Russie et l'Eglise Universelle* (1889), Solovyov gave one of the most intelligent, although often exaggerated, criticisms of Orthodoxy. He even received communion from a Catholic priest, which led some biographers to speak of his "conversion" to Catholicism. It is clear, however, that Solovyov understood this act as an anticipation of that Christian unity without which the fulfillment of his theocratic dream was impossible.

In the nineties, Solovyov almost completely dropped his theocratic optimism, and his thought acquired an apocalyptic and pessimistic orientation. His *Three Conversations* (1900) finds its climax in the eschatological "Tale of the Antichrist." In July 1900, Solovyov died, and his last prayer was for the Jews.

Bibliography

Collected works in Russian: *Sobranie Sochinenii Vi Solovyova*, 2nd ed., 10 vols. St. Petersburg: Prosveshchenie, 1911–1914.

Available in English:

War and Christianity, From the Russian Point of View: Three Conversations, Introd. by Stephen Graham. London: Constable's Russian Library, 1915.
The Justification of the Good: An Essay in Moral Philosophy, trans. by Natalie A. Duddington. New York: Macmillan, 1918.
Plato, trans. by R. Gree. London: Stanley Nott, 1935.

God, Man, and the Church: The Spiritual Foundations of Life, trans. by Donald Attwater. London: L. Clarke, 1938.
The Meaning of Love, trans. by Jane Marshall. New York: International Universities Press, 1947.
Lectures on God-Manhood, Introd. by P. P. Zonboff. London & Dublin: Dennis Dobson, 1948.
Russia and the Universal Church. London: Centenary Press, 1948.
A Solovyov Anthology, arranged by S. L. Frank. New York: Charles Scribner's Sons, 1950.

Beauty, Sexuality, and Love

1 Beauty in Nature

It SHOULD BE remembered that every philosophical theory of art and beauty, while explaining its subject in its present state, must open out for it wide future horizons. A theory which merely registers and generalizes in abstract terms the actual connection between events is sterile: it is merely empirical and scarcely rises above the wisdom of popular sayings and beliefs. A truly philosophical theory, in explaining the meaning of a fact, i.e., its relationship to all that is akin to it, connects it thereby with an endlessly ascending series of new facts. However bold such a theory may appear, it will be neither arbitrary nor fantastic, provided that its broad generalizations are based upon the true essence of the object, discovered by the intellect in that object's particular condition or appearance. For the essence of a thing is necessarily greater and deeper than a particular appearance of it, and therefore necessarily is the source of new appearances which express or realize it more and more fully.

But in any case the essence of beauty must be grasped first of all in its actual concrete appearances. Of the two kinds of beautiful appearances—nature and art—we will take first that which is wider in extent, simpler in content, and prior to the other in the order of time. The aesthetics of nature will give us the necessary basis for a philosophy of art.

A diamond, i.e., crystallized carbon, is, in its chemical composition, the same as ordinary coal. Similarly, there is no doubt that the song of a nightingale and the frantic caterwauling of a lovesick cat are the same in their psycho-physiological nature—namely, both are vocal expressions of an intensified sexual instinct. But the diamond is beautiful and highly valued for its beauty, whereas even the humblest savage is not likely to use a piece of coal as an ornament. And while the nightingale's song has always and everywhere been regarded as one of the manifestations of beauty in nature, cat's music, no less vividly expressive of the same psycho-physical motive, has never given aesthetic pleasure to anyone.

These elementary instances are enough to show that beauty is something formally distinct and specific, not directly determined by its material basis of fact and not reducible to it. Being independent of the physical substratum of things and events, beauty is not conditioned, either, by the subjective valuation of practical utility or sensuous pleasure which those objects or events may have for us. It requires no proof that beautiful things are often completely useless for the satisfaction of our practical needs and that, on the contrary, the most useful things are often by no means beautiful.

Whatever its material elements may be, formal beauty as such is always completely useless. But this pure uselessness is highly valued by man, and, as we shall see later, not by man alone. And since beauty cannot be valued as a means of satisfying practical or physiological needs, it follows that it is valued as an end in itself. In beauty—even in the case of its simplest and most elementary manifestations—we come across something that is *unconditionally valuable*, that exists for its own sake and not for the sake of anything else, something that by its very presence gives joy and satisfaction to the human heart which, in beauty, finds peace and freedom from the struggles and labors of life.

Let us turn once more to the actual instances of beauty in nature. The beauty of the diamond is in no way inherent in its substance (for that substance is the same as that of a plain lump of coal) and evidently depends upon the play of light upon its crystals. This does not imply, however, that the property of beauty belongs not to the diamond itself but to the ray of light refracted in it. For the same ray reflected by some plain object produces no aesthetic impression, and if it is not reflected by, or refracted in anything, produces no impression at all. Accordingly, beauty which belongs neither to the diamond's material body nor to the ray of light refracted by it is the result of interaction between the two. The play of light, retained and transformed by that body, completely conceals its crudely material appearance, and although the dark substance of carbon is present here as in coal, it is merely the bearer of the principle of light which reveals its own content in the play of colors. A ray of light falling upon a lump of coal is absorbed by its substance, and the blackness of coal is the natural symbol of the fact that in this case the power of light has not conquered the dark forces of nature.

In the union of substance and light, without division or confusion, both retain their nature but neither is visible in its separateness; all that is visible is light-bearing matter and embodied light—illuminated coal and petrified rainbow.

. . . Seeing that the beauty of the diamond wholly depends upon the transfiguration of its substance, which retains and breaks up or unfolds rays of light, we must define beauty as the *transfiguration of matter through the incarnation in it of another, a supermaterial principle.*

. . . This conception of beauty based upon an elementary instance of beautiful visual appearances in nature is entirely confirmed by the equally elementary instance of beautiful sounds. Just as in the diamond the heavy and dark substance of carbon is clothed with radiant light, so in the song of the nightingale the physical sexual instinct is clothed in harmonious sounds. In this case the objective auditory expression of sexual passion completely hides its material basis, acquires an independent significance, and may be abstracted from its direct physiological cause:

one may listen to the bird's song and receive an aesthetic impression from it, completely forgetting what it is that urges the bird to sing, just as in admiring the diamond's brilliance we have no occasion to think of its chemical substance. But, in fact, just as it is necessary for the diamond to be crystallized carbon, so it is necessary for the nightingale's song to be an expression of sexual attraction partly transmuted into an objective auditory form. That song is the transfiguration of the sexual instinct, its liberation from crude physiological fact—it is the animal sex instinct embodying in itself *the idea of love*.

. . . Thus in the case of sound, too, beauty proves to be the result of the interaction and mutual interpenetration of two factors: here, too, as in the visual instance, the ideal principle takes possession of the material fact and becomes embodied in it, while the material element receiving the ideal content into itself is illumined and transfigured thereby.

Beauty is an actual fact, the product of real natural processes taking place in the world. We have beauty in nature when ponderable matter is transformed into a luminous body, or when a fierce striving for a tangible physiological act is transformed into a series of harmonious and rhythmical sounds. Beauty is absent when the material elements of the world appear as more or less *bare*—whether as crude, formless bulk in the inorganic world or as unbridled animal instinct in the world of living organisms. . . . Beauty in nature is not the expression of *any* content but only of an ideal content; in other words it is the *embodiment of an idea*.

The word "idea" in the definition of beauty as "an embodied idea" dispenses with the view that beauty may express *any* content; and the word "embodied" corrects the still more prevalent view that although beauty must have an ideal content it is not an actual realization of it, but is merely an appearance or semblance (*Schein*) of the idea. On the second view, the beautiful as a subjective psychological fact, i.e., as the sensation of beauty or its appearance in our mind, takes the place of beauty itself as an objective form in nature. In truth, however, beauty is an idea that is actually realized and embodied in the world prior to the human mind, and its incarnation is no less real and far more significant (in the cosmogonic sense) than the material elements in which it finds embodiment. The play of light in a crystalline body is in any case no less real than that body's chemical substance, and the modulations of a bird's song are as much a natural reality as is the instinct of reproduction.

Beauty, or the embodied idea, is the best portion of our real world; it is that portion of it which not merely exists but deserves to exist. We give the name of ideal in general to that which is in itself worthy of being.

It is essential to distinguish the general ideal essence of beauty from the specifically aesthetic form. Only the latter differentiates beauty from goodness and truth, for their ideal essence is the same—being that has value, absolute "all-unity," freedom of particular existence in the universal unity. It is *this* that we desire as the highest good, it is *this* that we think of as truth, and *this*, too, that we sense as beauty; but in order that we may sense an idea, it must be embodied in material reality. Beauty as such, in its specific quality, depends upon the completeness of such embodiment.

The criterion of worthy or ideal being in general is the greatest possible independence of parts combined with the greatest possible unity of the whole. The criterion of aesthetic worth is the most complete and many-sided embodiment of this ideal in the given material. It is obvious that in their application to particular cases these two criteria may not coincide and must be carefully distinguished. A very small degree of worthy or ideal being may be embodied with the highest degree of perfection in the given material, and the loftiest ideal motives may be expressed very poorly and imperfectly indeed. In the domain of art the distinction is obvious and only quite uncultured minds can confuse the two criteria—the generally ideal and the specifically aesthetic. The distinction is less obvious in the domain of nature, but it is undoubtedly present there too, and it is very important not to lose sight of it. Let us take two instances again—a tapeworm and a diamond. The first, as an animal organism, expresses, to a certain extent, the idea of life; the second, in its ideal content, stands for a certain degree of transfiguration of inorganic matter. The idea of organic life, even if it be on the level of a worm, is higher than the idea of a crystallized body, even though it be a diamond. In the diamond, matter is illumined from outside only, while in the worm it is inwardly vitalized. In the simplest organism we find a greater number of separate parts and a greater unity among them than in the most perfect stone; every organism is more complex, and at the same time more individual, than a stone. Thus, according to the first criterion, a tapeworm is higher than a diamond because it is richer in content. But in applying the purely aesthetic criterion we come to a different conclusion. In the diamond the elementary idea of a mineral transfused with light (a precious stone) is expressed more completely and perfectly than the higher and more complex idea of organic or, more specifically, of animal life is expressed in the tapeworm. A diamond is an object perfect of its kind, for nowhere else is such a power of resistance or impenetrability united with such luminosity, nowhere else do we find such vivid and subtle play of light upon so hard a body. The worm, on the contrary, is one of the most imperfect embryonic expressions of the idea of organic life. . . . Thus, from the purely aesthetic point of view, the worm, as an extremely imperfect embodiment of a comparatively high idea (of an animal organism), must be placed incomparably lower than a diamond, which is a complete and perfect expression of the poorer idea of a luminous stone.

Matter is inert and impenetrable being—the direct opposite of the Idea as positive all-penetrability or all-unity. Only in *light* is matter liberated from its inertia and impenetrability, and through it, the visible world is for the first time divided into two polarities. Light is the primary reality of the Idea in contradistinction to ponderable matter, and in that sense it is the first principle of beauty in nature. Further manifestations of beauty are conditioned by combinations of light with matter. Such combinations are of two kinds: mechanical or external, and organic or inward. The first result in the natural phenomena of light as such, and the second in the phenomena of life.

... In the inorganic world, beauty belongs either to events and objects in which matter directly becomes a bearer of light or to those in which lifeless nature becomes, as it were, animated and manifests in its movements the character of life.

... Let us first say a few words about the beauty of inorganic nature *at rest*, of beauty dependent solely upon light.

The order in which the Idea becomes incarnate, or beauty is manifested in the world, corresponds to the general cosmogonic order: at the beginning God created *heaven*. . . . Our ancestors regarded heaven as the father of gods; we, though not worshiping Svarog or Varuna, nor detecting any signs of a personal, living being in the arch of heaven, admire its beauty no less than the pagans did; consequently, that beauty does not depend upon our subjective ideas, but is connected with actual properties inherent in the interstellar space visible to us. The aesthetic qualities of the sky are conditioned by light: it is beautiful only when it is illuminated. On a grey, rainy day or a dark, starless night the sky has no beauty whatever. In speaking of its beauty we really mean only the phenomena of light taking place in the cosmic space visible to us.

The all-embracing sky is beautiful as the image of universal unity, as the expression of serene triumph, of the eternal victory of the principle of light over chaotic confusion, of the eternal incarnation of the Idea in the whole of material existence.

We now pass from the appearances of calm, triumphant light to those of moving and seemingly free life in inorganic nature. Life in its most general sense is the free play or movement of particular forces and positions united in an individual whole. Insofar as that play expresses one of the essential characteristics of worthy or ideal being, its embodiment in material phenomena

—the real or the apparent life of nature—has an aesthetic significance. This beauty of visible life in the inorganic world is
noticeable, first of all, in flowing water in its various forms—
streams, mountain rivers, waterfalls. The aesthetic significance
of this living movement is enhanced by its boundlessness, which
seems, as it were, to express the insatiable longing of finite beings
separated from the absolute all-inclusive unity.

And the boundless sea itself acquires a new beauty in its stormy
motion as the symbol of rebellious life, of the gigantic struggle
of elementary forces which cannot break the universal intercon-
nectedness of the cosmos or destroy its unity, but can only fill it
with movement, brilliance, and thunder.

. . . Chaos, i.e., utter formlessness, is the necessary background
of all earthly beauty, and the aesthetic value of such things as
the stormy sea depends precisely on the fact that chaos is stirring
beneath them.

Outbursts of elemental forces or strivings of elemental impotence, having no beauty in themselves, become willy-nilly the
material for the more or less clear and complete expression in
nature of the universal Idea or the positive all-embracing unity.

The architectonic principle of the universe, the Logos, reflected by matter from without as light and kindling the flame of
life in matter from within, builds up in animal and plant
organisms definite and stable forms of life which, gradually
ascending to greater and greater perfection, may at last serve as
the material and the soil for the true embodiment of the all-
embracing and indivisible Idea.

The actual substratum of the organic forms, the material of
the biological process, is *entirely* taken from the inorganic world:
that is the booty won by the creative mind from chaotic matter.
In other words, organic bodies are merely transformations of
inorganic substance—in the same sense in which St. Isaac's
Cathedral is a transformation of granite, or Venus of Milo is a
transformation of marble.

. . . On the formal side we have, in the structure of living organisms, a new and comparatively higher degree of the expression of the same architectonic principle which has been at work in the inorganic world—a new and comparatively more perfect way of embodying the same Idea which was already finding expression in inanimate nature, though more superficially and less definitely. The same image of the all-embracing unity which the cosmic artist has sketched in bold and simple strokes in the starry heaven or in the many-colored rainbow is painted by him in subtle detail in plant and animal organisms.

. . . The general picture of the organic world presents two fundamental characteristics, both of which must be recognized if we are to understand cosmic life and have a philosophy and an aesthetic theory of nature. In the first place, there is no doubt that the organic world is not the product of so-called direct creation, nor can it be *directly deduced* from one absolute creative principle, for if it were, it would have to be unconditionally perfect, serene, and harmonious, not only as a whole but also in every one of its parts. But reality by no means corresponds to such an optimistic conception. In this respect certain facts and discoveries of positive science are of decisive significance. In considering organic life on earth, especially in the paleontological age, sufficiently well known in our day, we find a clear picture of a complex and difficult process, determined by the struggle between different principles, which only after long periods of great effort reaches a certain stable equilibrium. This is utterly unlike absolutely perfect creation proceeding directly from the creative will of the divine artist alone. Our biological history is a slow and painful process of birth. We see in it clear signs of inner opposition, blind groping, jerks and spasmodic shocks, unfinished sketches of failures—and what a number of monstrous creatures and abortions! All those paleozoa, those antediluvian monsters: megatheria plesiosauri, ichthyosauri, pterodactyls—can they be direct and perfect creations of God? If they fulfilled their end and deserved the Creator's approbation, how could it have happened that they finally disappeared from our earth, making room for more balanced and harmonious forms?

The second fundamental characteristic of organic nature is that, although the life-giving agent of the cosmic process throws over his unsuccessful attempts without regret, he values not only the final result of the process but also each of its innumerable stages, provided they embody the idea of life as well and as fully as they can. Winning, step by step, from chaotic elements the material for its organic creations, the cosmic mind treasures every one of its gains, abandoning only those which prove to be apparent only and on which boundless chaos has set its indelible mark.

At every new stage of cosmic development, with every new increase in the depth and complexity of natural existence there opens out a possibility of new and more perfect embodiments of the all-inclusive Idea in beautiful forms—but only a possibility.

We know that increase in the power of natural life is not, as such, a guarantee of beauty; that the cosmogonic criterion does not coincide with the aesthetic, and indeed is, in part, directly opposed to it. That is understandable. The elemental basis of the world, blind natural will, when raised to a higher level of being and thus inwardly intensified, is enabled thereby to submit more fully to the ideal principle of the cosmos—which then embodies in it a new and more perfect form of beauty. But at the same time its power of resistance to the ideal principle is also intensified, and at this higher stage it is able to carry out such resistance by more complex and significant means. The beauty of living, organic beings is higher, but at the same time rarer, than the beauty of inorganic nature; we know, too, that positive hideousness begins only where life begins. Passive plant life offers but little resistance to the ideal principle which embodies in it the beauty of pure and clear forms having little content. The chaotic element, petrified in the mineral, and slumbering in the vegetable kingdom, first awakes to active self-assertion in the

animal life and mind, opposing its inner insatiableness to
the objective idea of a perfect organism.

... The general paleontological history of the animal kingdom
as a whole and the individual embryological history of each
animal organism bear the clear stamp of the obstinate resistance
of vivified chaos to the higher organic forms designed, from all
eternity, in the mind of the cosmic artist. In order to win lasting
victories, he has to narrow the battlefield more and more. And
each new victory opens up possibilities of a new defeat: each
time a higher stage of beauty and organization is reached, there
appear greater deviations and greater ugliness as a more vivid
manifestation of the primary formlessness that lies at the bottom of life and of all cosmic being.

The cosmic artist had to work long and hard to embody ideal
beauty in the domain of animal life, the basic matter of which is
formless protoplasm and the typical representative—a worm.

The cosmic artist knows that the basis of the animal body is
ugly and tries in every way to cover it up and adorn it. His
purpose is not to destroy or thrust aside the ugliness, but to make
it, first, clothe itself in beauty and, finally, transform itself into
beauty. Therefore, by means of secret suggestions which we call
instinct, he incites creatures to make out of their own flesh
and blood all kinds of beautiful coverings; he causes the snail
to get into a fancifully colored shell of its own making, which, for
the purposes of utility (if it had any), did not in the least need
to be ornamental; he impels the disgusting caterpillar to put on
multicolored wings which it had itself grown; he induces fishes,
birds, and beasts to cover themselves completely with sparkling
scales, bright feathers, smooth and fluffy fur.

The higher animals—birds and, still more, certain mammals
(those of the feline family and also deer, gazelles, etc.)—in addition to their handsome outer covering are, in their whole appearance, a beautiful embodiment of the idea of life: of graceful
strength, harmonious co-ordination between the parts, and free
mobility of the whole. This ideal definition includes all the

multifarious types and varieties of animal beauty, the description and enumeration of which does not form part of my task. It is the business of descriptive zoology. We must also leave aside the question of how, in what ways, the constructive power of the cosmic artist leads nature to create beautiful animal forms. That question can only be dealt with by metaphysical cosmogony. The present argument concerning beauty in nature may be concluded by pointing out facts which, as mentioned above, empirically confirm the objective character of that beauty.

The facts of sexual selection observed by Darwin and other naturalists are quite insufficient for explaining the beauty of all animal forms: they refer almost exclusively to outer ornamental beauty of various animals. What matters in this connection, however, is not the actual importance of the facts, but the unquestionable proof they provide of the independent, objective significance of the aesthetic motive even in its most superficial expressions.

While many unbending minds were attempting, in the interests of scientific positivism, to reduce human aesthetics to a utilitarian basis, the greatest modern representative of that same school of thought showed that the aesthetic motive is independent of utilitarian purposes, even in the animal kingdom, and thus, for the first time, provided a positive basis for a truly idealistic aesthetic. This indisputable merit would alone be sufficient to immortalize Darwin's name, even if he had not created the theory of the origin of species through natural selection in the struggle for existence—a theory that clearly defined and carefully traced one of the most important material factors of the cosmic process.

An animal's life is determined by two main interests: supporting itself by means of nutrition and perpetuating its species by means of reproduction. The latter aim is not, of course, consciously present to the animal, but is achieved by nature indirectly through exciting sexual attraction in individual members of the opposite sex. The cosmic artist, however, makes use of sexual attraction in order not merely to perpetuate but also to adorn the particular animal forms. Creatures belonging to the active sex, the males, pursue the female and struggle with one another on her account; and it appears, says Darwin, that contrary to all expectations, the power *to please* the female is in certain cases of more importance than that of overcoming other males in open battle.

The meaning of these facts is both simple and significant. Man finds certain things in nature beautiful; they give him aesthetic pleasure. Most philosophers and scientists are convinced that this is merely a subjective peculiarity of the human mind and that in nature as such there is no beauty, any more than there is truth or goodness. But it appears that those very combinations of forms, colors, and sounds which in nature please man, also please the creatures of nature—the animals of all types and classes. They please them so much, have so great an importance for them, that the upkeep and development of these useless peculiarities, sometimes actually harmful from the utilitarian point of view, underlies their existence as a species. Accordingly, we cannot possibly say that the wings of a tropical butterfly or a peacock's tail are beautiful only on our subjective view, for their beauty is valued just as much by the female butterflies and peahens. But in that case we are bound to go further. Once it has been admitted that a peacock's tail is objectively beautiful, it would be the height of absurdity to insist that the beauty of the rainbow or of the diamond is merely a subjective appearance in the human mind. Of course, if in a particular case there is no sentient subject at all, there is no sensation of beauty. What matters, however, is not the sensation but the quality of the *object* capable of producing similar sensations in the most different subjects. But if, in general, beauty in nature is objective, it must have a certain general ontological basis—it must be, on different levels and in different ways, a sensuous embodiment of one absolutely objective, all-inclusive Idea.

The cosmic mind, in obvious opposition to the primeval chaos and in secret agreement with the world soul or nature, rent by that chaos and more and more amenable to the suggestions of the architectonic principle, creates in and through that principle the complex and magnificent body of our universe. This creation is a *process* having two closely interconnected purposes, the general and the particular. The general purpose is the embodiment of the real Idea, i.e., of light and life, in different forms of natural beauty; the particular purpose is the creation of man, i.e., of the form which, together with the greatest bodily beauty, presents the highest inner concentration of light and life, which is called self-consciousness. Even in the animal world, as has just been shown, the general cosmic purpose is attained with the help and co-operation of the creatures themselves through exciting in them certain inner feelings and strivings. Nature does not build up or adorn animals as some external material, but makes them build up and adorn themselves. Finally, man not merely participates in the activity of cosmic principles, but is capable of *knowing the purpose* of that activity and consequently of striving to achieve it freely and consciously. The same relation that obtains between human self-consciousness and animals' inner feeling holds between beauty in art and beauty in nature.

2   The Meaning of Art

A tree growing beautifully in the open and the same tree beautifully painted on canvas produce the same kind of aesthetic impression, are subject to the same aesthetic valuation; it is not for nothing that in both instances the same word is used to express it. But if it were merely a case of such visible, superficial similarity, the question might well be asked—and indeed it has been asked—why this reduplication of beauty? Is it not a childish amusement to repeat in a picture what already has a beautiful existence in nature? The usual answer to this is (given, for instance, by Taine in his *Philosophie de l'art*) that art does not reproduce the actual objects and events as such but only as seen by the artist—and a true artist sees in them merely their typical, characteristic features: that the aesthetic element of natural events, after passing through the artist's consciousness and imagination, is cleansed of all material accidents and thus intensified and seen more clearly; that beauty, disseminated in nature in forms and colors, appears concentrated, condensed, emphasized in a picture. This explanation is not completely satisfactory, if only because it is quite inapplicable to vast and important domains of art. What natural events are emphasized, for instance, in Beethoven's sonatas? The aesthetic connection between art and nature is obviously much deeper and more significant. In truth it consists not in the repetition but in the continuation of the artistic work begun by nature, in a further and more complete solution of the same aesthetic task.

The result of the natural process is man—to begin with, as the most beautiful,[1] and secondly, as the most conscious of natural beings. In this second capacity man is not simply the result of the cosmic process but an *agent* in it, thus answering more perfectly its ideal purpose: the complete mutual interpenetration and free solidarity of the spiritual and the material, the ideal and the real, the subjective and the objective elements of the universe. But why, then, do we consider the cosmic process begun by nature and continued by man from the aesthetic point of view, as the solution of some artistic problem? Would it not be better to regard its purpose as the realization of truth and goodness, the triumph of the supreme reason and will? If, in answer to this, we recall that beauty is simply an embodiment in sensuous forms of that very ideal content which, prior to such embodiment, is called truth and goodness, this will call forth a fresh objection. A strict moralist will say that goodness and truth need no aesthetic embodiment. To do good and to know truth is all that is needed.

[1] I am speaking in this connection of beauty in a general and objective sense, and mean that man's exterior is capable of expressing a more perfect (a more ideal) inner content than can be expressed by other animals.

In answer to this objection let us suppose that the good is realized not merely in someone's personal life but in the life of the whole society, that an ideal social order is established, that there is complete solidarity and universal brotherhood. The impenetrability of egoism is done away with: all find themselves in each, and each in all. But if this universal mutual interpenetrability, which is the essence of moral good, stops short of material nature, if the spiritual principle, having conquered the impenetrability of human psychological egoism, cannot overcome the impenetrability of matter—the physical egoism—this means that the power of goodness or love is not strong enough, that the moral principle cannot be finally realized and fully justified. The question then arises: if the dark force of material being triumphs in the end, if it is unconquerable by the principle of the good, is it not then the ultimate truth of all that is, and is not the good, as we call it, merely a subjective mirage? And, indeed, how can one speak of the triumph of the good when a society organized on the most ideal moral principles may perish at any moment because of some geological or astronomical cataclysm? Asbolute alienation of the moral principle from material being is fatal for the former, but certainly not for the latter. The very existence of the moral order in the world presupposes its connection with the material order, a certain co-ordination between the two. It might be imagined that this co-ordination should be looked for, apart from any aesthetics, in the direct power of human reason over the blind forces of nature and in the absolute mastery of the spirit over blind matter. Apparently several important steps have already been taken in this direction. When the end is reached, and when, owing to the achievements of applied science, we conquer, as some optimists believe, not only space and time but death itself, the existence of moral life in the world, on the basis of the material, will be finally safeguarded. This will have no relation to the aesthetic motive, so that even then the contention that the good does not need beauty will remain valid. And yet, will the good itself, in that case, be *complete*? It consists, not in the triumph of one over another, but in the solidarity of all. But can the beings and agents of the natural world be excluded from that *all?* They cannot be regarded as merely the means or instruments of human existence. They too must enter as a positive element into the ideal structure of life. To be *secure*, the moral order must rest upon material nature as the medium and the means of its existence, but to be *complete* and perfect it must include the material basis of existence as an independent part of moral activity, which at this point becomes aesthetic; for material being can enter into the moral order only through spiritualization and enlightenment, that is, only in the form of beauty. Beauty, then, is needed for the fulfillment of the good in the material world, for it is beauty alone that enlightens and subdues the evil darkness of this world.

But has not this work of bringing light to the universe been done already, apart from us? Natural beauty has already clothed the world with its radiant veil; formless chaos stirs uneasily under the harmonious form of the cosmos, but cannot throw it off either in the limitless expanse of the heavenly bodies or in the narrow range of earthly organisms. Should not art strive merely to clothe human relations in beauty and embody in sensible images the true meaning of human life? But in nature dark forces are merely subdued, and not won over by the universal reason; the victory is superficial and incomplete, and the beauty of nature is merely a veil thrown over the evil life and not the transfiguration of that life. That is why man, with his rational mind, must be not only the final end of the natural process but also, in his turn, a means to a more profound and complete action of the ideal principle upon nature. We know that in nature the realization of that principle differs in degree and that every increase in depth on the positive side is accompanied by a corresponding increase or inner intensification on the negative. In inorganic matter the evil principle acts merely as heaviness and inertia; in the organic world it manifests itself as death and dissolution (and here, too, hideousness is less obviously triumphant in the destruction of plants than in the death and decomposition of animals, and in the case of the higher animals this is more true than in that of the lower); in man, in addition to showing itself more completely and intensely on the physical side, it also expresses its deepest essence as moral evil. But on the other hand, it is possible for man to triumph over it finally, and to embody that triumph in eternal and incorruptible beauty. According to the old conception, now widely prevalent again, moral evil is identical with the dark, unconscious physical life, and moral goodness with the rational light of consciousness that develops in man. That the light of reason is in itself good is unquestionable; but physical light cannot be called evil. Both have the same significance in their respective spheres. In the case of physical light,[2] the universal idea (positive all-unity, the life of all for one another in the one) is realized in a reflected form only: ill events and objects are able to exist for one another, or are revealed to one another in their mutual reflections by means of a common imponderable medium. In a similar way all that exists is reflected in reason by means of general abstract notions which do not express the inner being of things but only their superficial logical schemata. Hence, in rational knowledge we find only a reflection of the universal idea and not its real presence in the knower and the known. For their true realization, goodness and truth must become a creative power in the subject, transforming reality and not merely reflecting it. In the physical world, light is transformed into life and becomes the organizing principle of plants and animals, so that it is not merely reflected by bodies but is incarnate in them; in the same way, the light of

[2] I am speaking here, of course, not of the visual sensations of light in man and in animals, but of light as the movement of an imponderable medium which interconnects material bodies and thus conditions their objective being for one another independently of our subjective sensations. "Light" alone is mentioned for shortness, but the same thing may be said of other dynamic phenomena: heat, electricity, etc. We are not concerned here with hypotheses of physical science, but only with the fact that there is an unquestionable difference between the nature of those phenomena and ponderable matter.

reason cannot be confined to knowledge alone, but must artistically embody the apprehended meaning of life in a new setting that is more in keeping with it. Of course, before creating in beauty or transforming the not-ideal reality into an ideal one, the difference between the two must be known—and known not merely in the abstract, but first of all through immediate feeling inherent in the artist.

The difference between ideal, that is, valuable or worthy being and unworthy or wrong being depends, generally speaking, upon the particular relation of the given elements to one another and to the whole. When, to begin with, particular elements do not exclude one another but, on the contrary, mutually posit themselves in one another and are at one; when, secondly, they do not exclude the whole but build up their particular being upon one universal basis; when, thirdly, that universal basis or absolute principle does not suppress or engulf the particular elements but, manifesting itself in them, gives them complete freedom within itself—such being is ideal or valuable, that which ought to be. Indeed, in itself it *is* already, though to us it appears, not as a given reality, but as an ideal only partly and gradually realized; in this sense it becomes the final end and absolute norm of our vital activities. The will strives toward it as the highest good, thought is determined by it as the absolute truth, and it is partly sensed and partly divined by our feelings and imagination as beauty. These positive ideal determinations of valuable being are essentially identical, just as are the corresponding negative principles. Every kind of evil consists, at bottom, in the violation of the mutual solidarity and balance between parts and whole; and all falsehood and ugliness can be reduced to that too. When a particular or single element asserts itself in its separateness, striving to exclude or to suppress other beings; when particular or single elements, together or separately, strive to put themselves in the place of the whole, to exclude or deny its independent unity and consequently the common bond between themselves; or when, on the contrary, the freedom of particular being is diminished or taken away in the name of unity; all this—exclusive self-assertion (egoism), anarchic separatism, and tyrannical uniformity—must be pronounced *evil*. The same thing transferred from the practical sphere to the theoretical is *falsehood*. An idea is false when it is solely concerned with some one particular aspect of reality to the exclusion of all the others; an intellectual outlook is false when it admits only an indefinite collocation of particular empirical events and denies the general meaning or the rational unity of the cosmos; equally false is abstract monism or pantheism that denies all particular existence in the name of absolute unity. The same essential characteristics that determine evil in the moral sphere and falsity in the intellectual determine ugliness in the aesthetic sphere. Everything in which one part grows out of all proportion and predominates over others, all that is lacking in wholeness and unity and, finally, all that is deficient in free multiplicity is ugly. Anarchic multiplicity is as much opposed to goodness, truth, and beauty as is dead, crushing unity. The attempt to realize such a unity in a sensuous form results in the idea of infinite emptiness, devoid of all special and definite forms of being, that is, in mere formlessness.

Worthy or ideal being requires equal freedom for the whole and for the parts. Consequently it does not mean freedom from particular determinations but only from their exclusiveness. The fullness of such freedom requires that all particular elements should find themselves in one another and in the whole, that each should posit itself in the other and the other in itself, that each should be aware of its own particularity in the unity of the whole, and of the unity of the whole in its own particularity— in short, that there should be absolute solidarity between all that is, and God should be all in all.

Complete sensuous realization of that universal solidarity or positive all-unity—perfect beauty not merely as an idea reflected from, but as actually present in matter—presupposes, in the first instance, the closest and deepest interaction between the inner or spiritual and the outer or material being. This is the fundamental aesthetic requirement, the specific difference between beauty and the two other aspects of the absolute idea. An equal content which remains merely an inner property of the spirit, of its will and thought, is devoid of beauty, and absence of beauty means that the idea is impotent. Indeed, so long as the spirit is incapable of giving direct external expression to its inner content and of incarnating itself in material phenomena, and, on the other hand, so long as matter is incapable of receiving the ideal action of the spirit and of being penetrated by or transmuted into spirit, there is no true unity between these two main realms of being. This means that the idea which is the perfect harmony of all that is has not as yet, in this particular manifestation, sufficient power fully to realize or fulfill itself. Neither abstract spirit, incapable of creative incarnation, nor soulless matter, incapable of spiritualization, corresponds to ideal or worthy being, and both bear a clear stamp of their unworthiness inasmuch as neither can be beautiful. The fullness of beauty requires, first, direct material embodiment of the spiritual essence and, secondly, complete spiritualization of the material appearance as the inherent and inseparable form of the ideal content. To this twofold condition there is necessarily added a third—or, rather, it follows from it of necessity. When the spiritual content is immediately and indissolubly united in beauty to its sensuous expression and there is complete mutual interpenetration between them, the material appearance that has really become beautiful, that has actually embodied the idea, must become as permanent and immortal as the idea itself. In Hegelian aesthetics, beauty is the incarnation of the eternal, universal idea in particular and transitory events, which still remain transient and disappear like separate waves in the stream of the material process, reflecting but for a moment the radiance of the eternal idea. But this can only be if the relation between the spiritual principle and the material event is one of impassive indifference. True and perfect beauty, however, expressing as it does complete oneness and mutual interpenetration between these two elements, must, of necessity, make the material actually participate in the other's eternity.

The beautiful appearances of the physical world are far from conforming to these demands or conditions of perfect beauty. To begin with, in natural beauty the ideal content is not sufficiently transparent; it does not reveal itself in all its mysterious depth, but only manifests its general outline, illustrating, so to speak, through concrete, particular facts the simplest characteristics of the absolute idea. Thus light, in its sensuous qualities, expresses the all-pervading and imponderable character of the ideal principle; plants show, in their visible form, the expansiveness of the idea of life and the general striving of the earthly soul toward the higher forms of being; beautiful animals express the intensity of vital motives united in a complex whole and sufficiently balanced to admit free play of the forces of life, and so on. The idea undoubtedly is embodied in all this, but only externally, in a general and superficial way. The superficial materialization of the ideal principle in natural beauty is in keeping with the equally superficial spiritualization of matter, which leads to the possibility of apparent contradictions between form and content (a typically ferocious beast may be very beautiful). The contradiction is only apparent because, being superficial, natural beauty expresses the idea of life, not in its inner moral quality, but merely in its external physical characteristics, such as swiftness, force, freedom of movement. The third essential imperfection of natural beauty is connected with the same fact: since it does not wholly and inwardly pervade the chaotic nature of material being, but merely throws an external covering over it, it remains eternal and unchangeable *in general* only—in the genera and species—while each particular beautiful appearance and entity remains in the power of the material process which first damages its beautiful form and subsequently destroys it altogether. From the naturalistic point of view, this instability of all individual appearances of beauty is a fatal and unalterable law. But in order to be even theoretically reconciled to this triumph of all-destroying material process, it is necessary to admit—as consistent adherents of naturalism do—that beauty and all other ideal contents of the world are a subjective illusion of human imagination. We know, however, that beauty has an objective significance, that it acts outside the human world, and that nature herself is not indifferent to beauty. And if nature has not succeeded in realizing perfect beauty in the domain of physical life, it is with good reason that through great labors and efforts, terrible catastrophes and monstrous creations—necessary, however, for the final end—she rises from that lower realm into the sphere of conscious human life. The task that cannot be fulfilled by means of physical life must be fulfilled through human creativeness.

Hence the threefold task of art in general is: (1) to give a direct, objective expression to the deepest inner qualities and determinations of the living Idea which nature is incapable of expressing, (2) to spiritualize natural beauty, and through this (3) to perpetuate its individual appearances. This means transforming physical life into spiritual life, that is, into a life which, in the first place, has its own word or revelation in itself and is capable of direct outward expression; which, in the second place, is capable of inwardly transforming and spiritualizing matter or of being truly incarnate in it; and which, thirdly, is free from the power of the material process and therefore abides forever. To embody this spiritual fullness completely in our actual world, to realize absolute beauty in it, or to create a universal spiritual organism is the highest task of art. Clearly the fulfillment of this task must coincide with the end of the cosmic process as a whole. While history still continues, there can be only partial and fragmentary anticipations of perfect beauty. In their highest achievements the arts that exist at present catch glimpses of eternal beauty in our transitory existence and, extending them further, anticipate and give us a foretaste of the reality beyond, which is to come. They are thus a transition stage or a connect-

ing link between the beauty of nature and the beauty of the life
to come. Interpreted in this way, art ceases to be empty play
and becomes important and instructive work, not, of course, in
the sense of a didactic sermon but of an inspired *prophecy*. The
indissoluble connection that once existed between art and religion proves that this exalted significance of art is not an arbitrary demand. The original inseparability between the religious
and the artistic work is certainly not to be regarded as an ideal.
True and complete beauty demands greater scope for the human
element and presupposes a higher and more complex development of social life than could be attained in primitive cultures.
The present alienation of art from religion is a transition from
the ancient fusion to a future free synthesis. The perfect life,
anticipations of which true art gives us, will also be based, not
upon the submergence of the human element by the divine, but
upon their free interaction.

We can now formulate a general definition of real art as such:
every sensuous expression of any object or event from the point
of view of its final state or in the light of the world to come is
a work of art.

The anticipations of perfect beauty in human art are of three
kinds: (1) direct or *magic*, when the deepest inner states connecting us with the true essence of things and the transcendental
world (or, if preferred, with the *an-sich-Sein* of all that is) break
through all conventions and material limitations, and find direct
and complete expression in beautiful sounds and words (music
and, partly, pure lyrics); (2) indirect, through the intensification
of the given beauty. The inner, essential, and eternal meaning
of life, concealed in the particular and accidental appearances of
the natural and the human world, is but vaguely and insufficiently expressed by their natural beauty; it is revealed and
clarified by the artist, who reproduces those appearances in a
concentrated, purified, and idealized form. Thus, architecture
reproduces, in an idealized form, certain regular shapes of natural bodies, expressing in this way the victory of those ideal

forms over the fundamental anti-ideal property of matter—gravity; classic sculpture, in idealizing the beauty of the human form and strictly observing the fine but definite line that distinguishes bodily beauty from the carnal, anticipates in its achievement the spiritual corporeality which shall one day be revealed to us in actual fact; landscape painting (and, partly, lyric poetry) reproduces, in a concentrated form, the ideal aspect of the complex phenomena of physical nature, cleansing them of all material accidents (and even of three-dimensional extendedness); religious painting and poetry are an idealized reproduction of such facts of human history as had revealed in advance the higher meaning of our existence. (3) The third kind of aesthetic anticipation of the perfect reality of the future is also indirect, and consists in reflecting the ideal from an environment alien to it and intensified by the artist to make the reflection more vivid.

The disharmony between the given reality and the ideal or higher meaning of life may be of different varieties. To begin with, a certain human reality, perfect and beautiful after its own kind (namely, after the kind of the *natural* man), falls short of the absolute ideal intended for the *spiritual* man and humanity. Achilles and Hector, Priam and Agamemnon, Krishna, Arjuna and Rama are unquestionably beautiful, but the more artistically they and their deeds are depicted, the clearer it is that they are not what true men should be and that true human achievement is different from their exploits. Homer probably—and the authors of the Indian poems certainly—had no such idea in mind, and we must regard heroic epic poetry as a vague and unconscious reflection of the absolute ideal from a beautiful but inadequate human reality.

. . . A more profound attitude toward the unrealized ideal is to be found in tragedy, where the characters themselves are imbued with the sense of an inner contradiction between their given reality and that which ought to be. Comedy, on the other hand, intensifies and deepens the feelings for the ideal, first by emphasizing that aspect of reality which cannot in any sense be called beautiful, and secondly by representing men who live in that reality as perfectly content with it, thus making them still more at variance with the ideal. It is this *complacency*, and not the outer setting of the plot, that constitutes the essential nature of the comic as distinct from the tragic element.

In order to see that even the greatest poetical works express the meaning of spiritual life merely by *reflecting* it from the nonideal human reality, let us take Goethe's *Faust*. The positive meaning of this lyric-epic tragedy is directly revealed only in the last scene of the second part and is abstractly summed up in the final chorus, *Alles Vergängliche ist nur ein Gleichnis*, and so on. But what is the direct organic bond between this apotheosis and the rest of the tragedy? The heavenly powers and *das ewig Weibliche* appear from above, and therefore, after all, from outside, and are not revealed from within the subject. The idea of the last scene is present in *Faust* throughout, but it is merely reflected from the partly real, partly fantastic plot of the tragedy itself. Just as a ray of light plays on a diamond to the delight of the spectator, but without producing any change in the material composition of the stone, so the spiritual light of the absolute ideal refracted in the artist's imagination illumines the dark human reality without in the least altering its essence. Let us suppose that a poet mightier than Goethe or Shakespeare did present, in a complex poetic work, an artistic, that is, a true and concrete picture of truly spiritual life—of the life which ought to be and which realizes the absolute ideal to perfection. Even that miracle of art, not achieved so far by any poet,[3] would, in our present world, be merely a magnificent mirage in an arid desert, heightening but not satisfying our spiritual thirst. The final task of perfect art is to realize the absolute ideal, not in imagination only but in very deed—to spiritualize and transfigure our actual life. If it be said that such a task transcends the

[3] In the third part of the *Divine Comedy*, Dante describes paradise in a way which may be true, but is certainly not sufficiently vivid and concrete— a fundamental defect which cannot be redeemed by the most musical verses.

limits of art, it may well be asked who has laid down those limits. We do not find them in history. We see there a changing art, art in the process of development. Separate branches attain their perfection and develop no more; to make up for this, other branches come into being. All are probably agreed that sculpture was brought to its final perfection by the ancient Greeks; nor is it likely that further progress will be made in heroic epic poetry and pure tragedy. I venture to go further and do not think it too bold to assert that just as the ancients had perfected those forms of art, so the modern European nations have exhausted all other species of art known to us. If art has a future, it lies in quite a new sphere of activity. Of course, this future development of aesthetic creativeness depends upon the general course of history, for art in general is the sphere of the embodiment of ideas and not of their original inception and growth.

3   The Meaning of Love

The meaning of sexual love is generally supposed to consist in subserving the propagation of the species. I consider this view to be mistaken—not on the ground of any ideal considerations as such, but first and foremost on grounds of natural history. That the reproduction of living creatures does not need sexual love is clear if only from the fact that it does not even need the division into sexes. A considerable number both of vegetable and of animal organisms multiply sexlessly; by division, budding, spores, grafting. True, the higher forms in both the organic kingdoms reproduce themselves sexually. But to begin with, the organisms that do so *may* also multiply sexlessly (grafting in the plant world, parthenogenesis among the higher insects), and secondly, admitting that, as a general rule, higher organisms multiply by means of sexual union, the conclusion to be drawn is that the sex factor is connected not with reproduction as such (which may take place without it) but with the reproduction of *higher* organisms. Hence, the meaning of sexual differentiation (and, consequently, of sexual love) must be sought, not in the idea of generic life and its reproduction, but only in the idea of a higher organism.

A striking confirmation of this is provided by the following important fact. Among animals that reproduce themselves solely in the sexual way (the vertebrates), the higher we go in the organic scale, the more limited is the power of reproduction and the greater the force of sexual attraction. In the lowest class of this section—the fishes—the rate of reproduction is enormous: the spawn produced yearly by every female are counted in millions; they are fertilized by the male outside the body of the female, and the way in which this is done does not suggest strong sexual attraction. Of all vertebrate creatures, this cold-blooded class undoubtedly multiplies most and shows least trace of love-passion.[4] At the next stage—among the amphibians and the reptiles—the rate of reproduction is much lower than among the fishes, though some of the species of this class justify the biblical description of them as "swarming"; but, with a lower rate of reproduction, we find in these animals closer sexual relations. In birds the power of reproduction is much smaller than, for instance, in frogs, to say nothing of fishes, while sexual attraction and mutual affection between the male and the female are developed to a degree unexampled in the two lower classes. Among mammals (or the viviparous), reproduction is much slower than among the birds, and sexual attraction is much more intense, though for the most part less constant. Finally, in man the rate of reproduction is lower than in the rest of the animal kingdom, but sexual love attains the greatest force and significance, uniting in the highest degree the permanence of

[4] Solovyov distinguishes three forms or levels of love, which correspond to the three Greek words for love—"love-passion" (*eros*), "love-feeling" (*philia*), and "love-union" (*agape*).

relations (as with birds) with the intensity of passion (as with the viviparous).

Thus sexual love and reproduction of the species are in *inverse proportion* to each other: the stronger the one, the weaker the other. In this respect, the animal kingdom as a whole develops in the following order: at the lowest level there is an enormous power of reproduction and a complete absence of anything like sexual love (since there is no division into sexes); in more perfect organisms there appear sexual differentiation and, corresponding to it, a certain sexual attraction, very weak at first; at further stages of organic development it increases, while the power of reproduction diminishes (i.e., it increases directly with the perfection of the organism and inversly with the power of reproduction); until at last, at the top of the scale, in man, there may be intense sexual love without any reproduction whatever. If, then, at the two opposite poles of animal life we find, on the one hand, reproduction without any sexual love, and on the other, sexual love without any reproduction, it is perfectly clear that these two facts cannot be indissolubly interconnected; it is clear that each of them has an independent significance of its own, and that the meaning of one cannot consist in serving as a means for the other. The same conclusion follows if we consider sexual love exclusively in the human world, where it acquires, incomparably more clearly than in the animal kingdom, an individual character, in virtue of which *precisely this* person of the opposite sex has an absolute significance for the lover as unique and irreplaceable, as an end in itself.

At this point we meet with a popular theory which, while admitting that sexual love as such serves the generic instinct and is a means of reproduction, attempts to explain the individualization of love in the case of man as a certain trick or deception practiced by nature or the cosmic will for its own ends. In the human world, where individual peculiarities have far more significance than in the animal or the vegetable kingdoms, nature aims not merely at preserving the species but also

at realizing within its limits a number of possible specific types
and individual characters. Apart from this general purpose of
manifesting the greatest possible variety of forms, the life of
mankind as a historical process has for its purpose raising and
improving human nature. This requires not merely as many different specimens of humanity as possible but also its *best* specimens, valuable both in themselves as individual types and for
their uplifting and improving influence upon others. Thus the
moving power of the cosmic and the historical process—whatever we may call it—is concerned not only with the continual
reproduction of human individuals after their own kind but also
in certain particular and, as far as possible, significant specimens
being born. For this purpose simple reproduction through pro-
miscuous and fortuitous union of the sexes is insufficient. To
produce individually determined offspring, the union of individually determined parents is required, and consequently the
general sexual attraction that serves the purposes of reproduction
among animals is not enough. With human beings, it is not
producing offspring as such that matters, but producing a particular kind of offspring, most suitable for world purposes; and
since this given individual can produce such offspring, not with
any individual of the opposite sex, but only with one particular
person, that person alone must have for him or her a special power of attraction and appear exceptional, irreplaceable,
unique, and capable of bestowing the highest bliss. It is this
individualization and exaltation of the sexual instinct that distinguishes human from animal love, but it, too, is aroused in us
by an alien, though perhaps a higher power, for its own ends,
foreign to our personal consciousness. It is aroused as an irrational, fatal passion that takes possession of us and disappears
like a mirage as soon as the need for it is over.

If this theory were correct, if the individual and exalted nature of the love-feeling had its whole meaning, reason, and purpose in something external to itself, namely, in the quality of
the offspring required for world purposes, it would logically fol-

low that the degree of the individualization and intensity of love was in direct proportion to the character and significance of the offspring to which it gave rise: the more valuable the offspring, the greater the love between the parents, and, *vice versa*, the stronger the love between two particular persons, the more remarkable their offspring should be. If, speaking generally, the love-feeling is aroused by the cosmic will for the sake of the required offspring and is merely *a means* for producing it, in each given case the strength of the means used by the cosmic mover must be proportionate to the importance of the end to be achieved. The more the cosmic will is interested in the offspring-to-be, the more strongly it must attract to each other and bind together the two necessary progenitors. Suppose a world genius of enormous importance for the historical process has to be born. In so far as a genius is more rare than ordinary mortals, the higher power controlling the historical process would obviously be proportionately more interested in his birth than in others; and consequently the sexual attraction, by means of which the cosmic will (according to this theory) secures the end so important to it, should be proportionately more intense than usual. The champions of the theory may, of course, deny the presence of an exact quantitative ratio between the importance of a given individual and the intensity of his parents' passion, since such things admit of no exact measurement; but it is absolutely indubitable (from the standpoint of the theory in question) that if the cosmic will is *extremely interested* in the birth of some person, it must take *extreme measures* to secure the desired result; it must arouse in the parents a passion of extreme intensity, capable of overcoming all obstacles to their union.

In reality, however, we find nothing of the kind. There is no correlation whatever between the intensity of the love-passion and the importance of the progeny. To begin with, there is the fact, utterly inexplicable for the theory we are considering, that the most intense love often remains unrequited and produces no offspring whatever, let alone valuable offspring. If, as a result of such love, people take monastic vows or commit suicide, why should the cosmic will concerned with posterity have troubled about them? But even if the ardent Werther[5] had not committed suicide, his unhappy passion would remain an inexplicable riddle for the theory of qualified offspring. From the point of view of that theory, Werther's intense and highly individualized love for Charlotte showed that it was only with Charlotte he could produce the offspring of special value and importance for humanity, for the sake of which the cosmic will aroused in him this extraordinary passion. But how was it, then, that this omniscient and omnipotent will proved incapable or did not think of similarly affecting Charlotte, without whose reciprocity Werther's passion was quite unnecessary and served no purpose? For a teleologically acting substance, *love's labor lost* is an utter absurdity.

Exceptionally intense love is generally unhappy. Unhappy love very often leads to suicide in one form or another, and each of these suicides through unhappy love disproves the theory that intense love is aroused solely for the purpose of producing descendants whose importance is indicated by the intensity of the love. But in all such cases it is the very intensity of love that rules out the possibility of any descendants at all.

As a general rule, from which there are hardly any exceptions, particular intensity of sexual love either altogether excludes reproduction or results in offspring, the importance of which in no way corresponds to the power of the love-feeling and to the exceptional character of the relations arising from it.

To find the meaning of sexual love in successful childbearing is the same as to find meaning where there is no love; where there is love, it is to deprive it of all meaning and justification. When put to the test of facts, this fictitious theory of love proves to be not an explanation but rather a refusal to explain anything.

---

[5] I illustrate my arguments by instances taken chiefly from great literary works. They are better than instances from real life, for they represent types and not particular cases.

Both with animals and with man, sexual love is the finest flowering of the individual life. But since in animals the life of the genus is of far more importance than that of the individual, the highest pitch of intensity achieved by them merely profits the generic process. Although sexual attraction is not simply a means for the propagation or the reproduction of organisms, it serves to produce *more perfect* organisms through sexual rivalry and selection. An attempt has been made to ascribe the same significance to love in the human world but, as we have seen, quite in vain. For in the human world, individuality has an independent significance and in its strongest expression cannot be merely a means for the ends of the historical process external to it. Or, to put it better, the true end of the historical process does not admit of the human personality being merely a passive and transitory means to it.

The conviction that man has absolute worth is based neither upon self-conceit nor upon the empirical fact that we know of no other more perfect being in the order of nature. Man's unconditional worth consists in the absolute form (or image) of *rational* consciousness undoubtedly inherent in him. Being aware —as animals are—of his experiences, detecting certain connections between them and, on the basis of these, anticipating future experiences, man also has the faculty of passing judgments of value on his own states and actions, and on facts in general, in their relation not only to other particular facts but to universal ideal norms. Man's consciousness is determined not only by empirical facts but by the *knowledge of truth.* Conforming his actions to this higher consciousness, man can infinitely perfect his life and nature *without transcending the human form.* This is why he is the highest being in the natural world and the true end of the process of world creation; for, next to the Being which is Itself the absolute and eternal truth, comes the being which is capable of knowing and realizing truth in itself; man is highest in the natural world, not relatively, but unconditionally. What rational ground can be adduced for creating new and essentially

more perfect forms when there already exists a form capable of
infinite self-perfectibility and of receiving the whole fullness of
the absolute content? Once such a form has appeared, further
progress can only consist in new degrees of its own development
and not in replacing it by some other creature, some hitherto
nonexistent form of being. This is the essential difference between the cosmogonic and the historical process. The first (before the appearance of man) creates a succession of new kinds
of beings: the old are partly destroyed as unsuccessful experi-
ments and partly coexist with the new in a purely external way,
accidentally coming together, but forming no *real* unity because
they have no common consciousness to connect them with one
another and with the cosmic past. Such common consciousness
appears in man. In the animal world the succession of the
higher forms upon the lower, however regular and purposive, is
a fact utterly external and foreign to the animals themselves and
indeed nonexistent for them. An elephant or a monkey can know
nothing about the complex process of geological and biological
transformation that conditioned his actual appearance upon the
earth; the comparatively high level of intelligence reached by
this or that animal or by a particular species does not mean
any progress in the *general* consciousness in which those intelligent animals are as completely lacking as a stupid oyster. The
complex brain of a higher mammal is as little use for throwing
light upon nature as a whole as the rudimentary nerve ganglia
of a worm. In humanity, on the contrary, general consciousness
progresses through the achievements of the individual consciousness in the realms of religion or science. The individual intelligence is, in the case of man, not only an organ of personal life
but also an organ of memory and anticipation for all mankind
and even for the whole of nature.

    ... *The whole truth*—the positive unity of all—is latent from
the first in man's living consciousness and is gradually realized
in the life of humanity, being consciously handed down. This
successive consciousness can be expanded indefinitely and is con-

tinuous, and therefore man can, while remaining himself, understand and realize all the infinite fullness of being, so that he
need not be, and cannot be replaced by any higher kinds of entities. Within the limits of his given reality, man is only a part
of nature; but he is constantly and consistently transcending
those limits. In his spiritual progeny—religion and science, morality and art—he manifests himself as the center of the universal consciousness of nature, as the soul of the world, as the
self-realizing potency of the absolute all-unity; consequently only
that absolute itself, in its perfect actuality or its eternal being,
that is, God, can be higher than man.

Man's privilege over other natural beings—his power of understanding and realizing the truth—is both generic and individual: *every* man is capable of knowing and realizing the
truth; everyone can become a living reflection of the absolute
whole, a conscious and independent organ of universal life. The
rest of nature also contains truth (or the image of God), but
only in its objective universality, unknown to particular beings.
This truth forms them and acts in and through them as the
power of fate, as the law of their being, unknown to them, to
which they involuntarily and unconsciously submit. In themselves, in their inner feeling and consciousness, they cannot rise
above their given, partial existence; they find themselves only
in their separateness, in solution from *all*—consequently outside
truth. Therefore truth, or the universal unity, can only triumph
in the animal kingdom through the change of generations, the
permanence of the species, and the destruction of the individual
life incapable of comprehending the truth. The human individuality, however, just because it is capable of comprehending the
truth, is not cancelled by it, but is preserved and strengthened
through its triumph.

But in order that an individual being should find in truth—in
the all-unity—its own affirmation and justification, it must not
only be conscious of truth but be *in* it. Primarily and immediately, however, an individual man is not in truth any more than

an animal is. He finds himself as an isolated particle of the cosmic whole and in his egoism affirms this partial existence as a whole for himself; he wants to be all in his separation from the whole, outside truth. Egoism, as the real, basic principle of individual life, penetrates it right through, directing and concretely determining everything in it, and therefore a merely theoretical consciousness of truth cannot possibly outweigh and abolish it. Until the living force of egoism meets, in man, with another living force opposed to it, consciousness of truth is only an external illumination, a reflection of another light. If man could accept the truth only in this sense, his connection with it would not be inward and indissoluble; his own being—remaining, like that of animals, outside truth—would be, like theirs, doomed to disappear in its subjectivity and would be preserved only as an idea in the absolute mind.

Truth as a living power taking possession of man's inner being and really saving him from false self-affirmation is called love. Love as the actual abolition of egoism is the real justification and salvation of individuality. Love is higher than rational consciousness, but without it, it could not act as an inner saving power which sublimates and does not destroy individuality. It is thanks to rational consciousness alone (or, what is the same thing, the consciousness of truth) that man can distinguish himself, that is, his true individuality, from his egoism. In sacrificing this egoism and surrendering himself to love, he finds both a living and a life-giving power; he does not lose his individual being, together with his egoism but, on the contrary, preserves it forever.

. . . The meaning of human love in general is *the justification and salvation of individuality through the sacrifice of egoism.* Starting with this general position, we can deal with our specific task and explain the meaning of sexual love. It is highly significant that sexual relations are not only called love, but are generally recognized as pre-eminently representative of love, being the type and the ideal of all other kinds of love (see The Song of Songs and the Revelation of St. John).

The evil and falsity of egoism certainly do not consist in the fact that man prizes himself too highly or ascribes absolute significance and infinite dignity to himself. In this he is right, for every human subject, as an independent center of living powers, as the potency of infinite perfection, as a being capable of embracing in his life and consciousness the absolute truth, has unconditional significance and dignity, is something absolutely irreplaceable and cannot prize himself too highly (in the words of the Gospel, what shall a man give in exchange for his soul?). Not to recognize one's absolute significance in this sense is tantamount to renouncing one's human dignity. The fundamental evil and falsity of egoism lie, not in the recognition of the subject's own absolute significance and value, but in the fact that while he justly ascribes such significance to himself, he unjustly denies it to others; in recognizing himself as a center of life, which he is in reality, he refers others to the circumference of his being, setting upon them only an external and relative value.

Of course, theoretically and in the abstract, every man who is in his right mind always admits that other people have exactly the same rights as he. But in his vital consciousness, in his inner feeling and in practice, he is aware of an infinite, incommensurable difference between himself and others: he, as such, is all; they, as such, are nothing. But it is precisely this exclusive self-affirmation that prevents man from being, in fact, what he claims to be. The unconditional significance and absoluteness which, speaking generally, he rightly recognizes in himself but wrongly denies to others is in itself merely potential—it is only a possibility demanding realization. God *is* all, i.e., possesses in one absolute act all the positive content, all the fullness of being. Man (in general, and every individual man in particular), being, in fact, not only *this* and not *another*, may become all only by abolishing in his consciousness and in his life the inner limits which separate him from others. "This" man may be "all" only *together with others*; only together with others can he realize his absolute significance and become an inseparable and irreplaceable part of the universal whole, an independent, unique, and living organ of the absolute life. True individuality is a certain form of universal unity, a certain definite way of apprehending and assimilating the whole. In affirming himself outside all else, man robs his own existence of its meaning, deprives himself of the true content of life, and reduces his individuality to an empty form. Thus egoism is certainly not the self-affirmation and self-consciousness of individuality, but, on the contrary, its self-negation and destruction.

The physical and metaphysical as well as the social and historical conditions of human existence modify and soften our egoism in many ways, putting various formidable obstacles before its undisguised manifestations with all their terrible consequences. But this complex system of correctives and obstacles, predetermined by Providence and realized by nature and history, does not affect the actual basis of egoism which constantly peeps out from under the cover of personal and public morality and at times manifests itself in its full force. There is only one power which may, and actually does undermine egoism at the root, from within, and that is love, and chiefly sexual love. The evil and falsity of egoism consist in ascribing absolute significance exclusively to oneself and denying it to others; reason shows that it is unwarranted and unjust, and love abolishes this unjust relation in fact, compelling us to recognize, not in abstract thought but in inner feeling and vital will, the absolute significance of another person for us. Through love we come to know the truth of another, not in abstraction but in reality, and actually transfer the center of our life beyond the confines of our empirical separateness. In doing so we manifest and realize our own truth, our own absolute significance, which consists precisely in the power of transcending our actual phenomenal existence and of living not in ourselves only but also in another.

All love is a manifestation of this power, but not every kind of love realizes it to the same extent or undermines egoism with the same thoroughness. Egoism is a real and fundamental force rooted in the deepest center of our being and spreading from there to the whole of our reality, a force that is continually active in every department and in every detail of our existence. If egoism is to be undermined, it must be counteracted by a love as concretely determined as it is itself, a love which penetrates and possesses the whole of our being. The "other" which is to liberate our individuality from the fetters of egoism must be correlated with the whole of that individuality. It must be as real, concrete, and objectivized as we are, and at the same time must differ from us in every way, so as to be really "other." In other words, while having the same essential content as we, it must have it in another way, in a different form, so that our every manifestation, our every vital act should meet in that "other" a corresponding but not an identical manifestation. The relation of the one to the other must thus be a complete and continual exchange, a complete and continual affirmation of oneself in another, a perfect interaction and communion. Only then will egoism be undermined and abolished, not only in principle, but in all its concrete actuality. Only this so to speak chemical fusion of two beings of the same kind and significance, but throughout different in form, can render possible (both in the natural and the spiritual order) the creation of a new man, the actual realization of the true human individuality. Such fusion, or at any rate the nearest approximation to it, is to be found in sexual love, and that is the reason why it has an exceptional significance as a necessary and irreplaceable basis of all further growth in perfection, as the inevitable and constant condition which alone makes it possible for man to be actually in truth.

Fully admitting the great importance and the high dignity of other kinds of love by which false spiritualism and impotent moralism would like to replace sexual love, we nevertheless find that only the latter satisfies the two fundamental conditions without which there can be no final abolition of selfhood through complete vital communion with another. In all other kinds of love, either the homogeneity, the equality and interaction between the lover and the beloved, or the all-inclusive difference of complementary qualities is absent.

Thus in mystical love the object of love is the absolute indifference that engulfs human individuality; egoism is here abolished only in the very insufficient sense in which it is abolished in deep sleep (with which the union of the individual soul with the universal spirit is compared and sometimes actually identified in the Upanishads, or Vedanta). A living man and the mystic "abyss" of absolute indifference are so heterogeneous and incommensurable that the two cannot coexist, to say nothing of being in any vital communion. If the object of love is there, there is no lover—he has disappeared, lost himself, sunk, as it were, into a deep, dreamless sleep; and when he returns to himself, the object of love disappears, and absolute indifference is replaced by the variegated multiplicity of actual life against the background of his own egoism adorned by spiritual pride. There have certainly been mystics in history—whole schools of mysticism, in fact—that interpreted the object of love not as absolute indifference, but as an object which was able to assume concrete forms allowing vital relations with it; very significantly, however, those relations acquired the perfectly clear and consistent character of sexual love.

Parental, and especially maternal love approximates to sexual love both in respect of the intensity of feeling and the concreteness of its object, but on other grounds it cannot have the same significance for the human personality. It is conditioned by the fact of reproduction and the law that successive generations replace one another—a law that dominates life in the animal world but has not, or at any rate ought not to have, the same significance in human life. With animals the succeeding generation directly and rapidly cancels its predecessors, shows their existence to be meaningless, and then, in its turn, is convicted of the same meaningless existence by its own progeny. Maternal love, which in human beings at times attains heights of self-sacrifice not to be found in a hen's love, is a relic, no doubt still necessary, of that order of things. In any case, it is unquestionable that in maternal love there can be no complete reciprocity and lifelong communion, if only because the lover and the beloved belong to different generations and that for the latter, life is in the future, with new and independent problems and interests among which representatives of the past appear only as pale shadows. It is sufficient to say that the parents cannot be the object of the children's life in the same sense in which the children can be the object of life for the parents.

A mother who puts her whole soul into her children certainly sacrifices her egoism, but she also loses her individuality, and though her love may strengthen the children's individuality, it preserves and even intensifies their egoism. Besides, in maternal love there is really no recognition of the beloved's absolute significance and true individuality, for although a child is precious to its mother above all, this is precisely because it is *her* child; as with animals, the apparent recognition of another's absolute significance is really conditioned by an external physiological bond.

Other varieties of sympathetic feeling have even less claim to replace sexual love. Friendship between persons of the same sex lacks the all-round formal distinction between the mutually complementary qualities, and when, in spite of this, such friendship attains particular intensity, it becomes an unnatural substitute for sexual love. As to patriotism and love for humanity, however important those feelings are, they cannot in themselves concretely and actually eradicate egoism, for the lover and the object of love are incommensurable: neither humanity nor the nation can be, for the individual man, as concrete an entity as he himself is. It is possible, of course, to sacrifice one's life for the nation or for humanity, but to make oneself into a new creature, to manifest and realize true human individuality on the basis of this extensive love is impossible. The old egoistic self still remains the real center, while the nation and humanity are relegated to the periphery of consciousness as ideal objects. The same thing must be said about love of science or art.

. . . The meaning and value of love as a feeling consists in the fact that it makes us actually, with our whole being, recognize in *another* the absolute, central significance which, owing to egoism, we feel only in ourselves. Love is important, not as one of our feelings, but as the transference of our whole vital interest from ourselves to another, as the transposition of the very center of our personal life. This is characteristic of every kind of love, but of sexual love[6] pre-eminently. It differs from other kinds of love in its greater intensity, its greater absorption, and the possibility of a more complete and comprehensive reciprocity. This love alone can lead to the actual and indissoluble union of two lives made one, and only of it does the word of God say that the two shall be one flesh, i.e., shall become one real being.

The love-feeling demands such fullness of inner and final union, but as a rule things go no further than this subjective striving, and that, too, proves to be transitory. Instead of the poetry of the eternal and central union we have a more or less continuous, but in any case temporal, a more or less intimate, but in any case external and superficial nearness between two limited beings within the narrow framework of everyday prose. The object of love does not preserve, in fact, the absolute significance ascribed to it by the dream of love. To an outsider, this is obvious from the first, and the involuntary tinge of irony that inevitably colors other people's attitudes to lovers proves to be merely an anticipation of their own disillusionment. Sooner or later the ecstatic element of love disappears.

. . . And so if we consider only that which generally happens and look only at love's actual outcome, love must be recognized as a dream possessing us for a time and then disappearing without

[6] For lack of a better term I give the name of "sexual love" to an exclusive attachment (both reciprocal and one-sided) between persons of the opposite sex capable of being in the relation of husband and wife, but I do not in the least prejudge the significance of the physiological side of the matter.

any practical result (since childbearing is not the work of love as such). But if evidence compels us to admit that the ideal meaning of love is not realized in fact, must we admit that it is *unrealizable?*

. . . It would be quite unjust to deny that love is realizable simply because it has never yet been realized: the same was true in the past of many other things—all arts and sciences, civic society, control of the forces of nature, and so on. Rational consciousness itself, before it became a fact in man, was only a vague and fruitless striving in the animal world. A number of geological and biological epochs passed in unsuccessful attempts to create a brain capable of becoming an organ for the embodiment of rational thought. So far, love is for man what reason was for the animal world: it exists in its rudiments or tokens, but not as yet in fact. And if stupendous cosmic periods—witnesses of unrealized reason—have not prevented that reason from manifesting itself at last, the fact that love has not been realized in the course of the comparatively few thousands of years lived by historical humanity gives us no right to conclude that it cannot be realized in the future. It must be remembered, however, that while the reality of rational consciousness appeared *in* man but not through man, the realization of love as the highest step in humanity's own life must take place both in him and *through* him.

The task of love is to *justify in fact* the meaning of love which is at first given only as a feeling—to create such a union of two given, limited beings as would make of them one absolute, ideal personality. Far from containing any inner contradiction or being at variance with the meaning of the world as a whole, this task arises directly out of our spiritual nature, the distinguishing characteristic of which is that man can, while remaining himself, comprehend the absolute content and become an absolute personality. But in order to be filled with absolute content (which in religious language is called eternal life or the Kingdom of God), the human form itself must be reinstated in its wholeness. In empirical reality there is no man *as such*—he exists only in a one-sided and limited form as a masculine or a feminine individual (all other differences develop upon this basis). The true human being, in the fullness of his ideal personality, obviously cannot be merely a man or merely a woman, but must be the higher unity of the two. To realize this unity or to create the true human being as the free unity of the masculine and the feminine elements, which preserve their formal separateness but overcome their essential disparity and disruption, is the direct *task* of love. If we consider the conditions required for carrying it out, we shall see that it is only because those conditions are not observed that love invariably comes to grief and has to be pronounced an illusion.

The first step toward successfully solving any problem is to state it consciously and correctly; but the problem of love has never been consciously formulated and therefore has never been properly solved. People have always regarded love solely as a given fact or as a state (normal for some and painful for others) experienced by man but not imposing any obligations upon him. True, two concerns are bound up with it—physiological possession of the object of love and permanent alliance with it—which do impose certain duties. But the matter is subject to the laws of animal nature on the one hand, and to the laws of civic community on the other, and love, left to itself from beginning to end, disappears like a mirage. Of course, love is, in the first place, a fact of nature (or a gift of God), a natural process arising independently of us. But this does not imply that we cannot and must not stand in a conscious relation to it and of our own will direct this natural process to higher ends.

Everyone knows that in love there is always a special *idealization* of the object of love—which appears to the lover in quite a different light from that in which it appears to other people. I am speaking of light not only in a metaphorical sense; I am speaking not only of a particular moral and intellectual valuation, but of special sensuous perception as well: the lover actually *sees,* visually apprehends, something different. True, for him, too, this light of love soon disappears. But does that imply that it was false, that it was merely a subjective illusion?

The true being of man in general, and of every man in particular, is not confined to his given empirical expressions; no rational grounds to the contrary can be adduced from any point of view.

. . . We know that in addition to his material, animal nature man has an ideal nature connecting him with the absolute truth or God. Beside the material or empirical content of his life every man contains the image of God—a special form of the absolute content. That image of God is known to us in the abstract and in theory through reason, and concretely and actually through love. In love, the revelation of the ideal being, generally concealed by the material appearance, is not confined to an inner feeling, but sometimes becomes apprehensible by the outer senses; and this imparts greater significance to love as the beginning of the visible reinstatement of the image of God in the material world, the incarnation of true ideal humanity. The power of love transforming itself into light, transfiguring and spiritualizing the form of external appearance, reveals to us its objective force, but it is for us to do the rest. We must understand this revelation and make use of it so that it should not remain an enigmatic and fleeting glimpse of some mystery.

The spiritual-physical process of the reinstatement of the image of God in material humanity cannot possibly happen of itself, apart from us. Like all that is best in this world, it begins in the dark realm of unconscious processes and relations; the germ and the roots of the tree of life are hidden there, but we must tend its growth by our own conscious action. Passive receptivity of feeling is enough to begin with, but it must be followed by active faith and moral endeavor in order to preserve, strengthen, and develop the gift of radiant and creative love and by means of it to embody in oneself and in the other the image of God, forming out of two limited and mortal beings one absolute and immortal personality. Idealization, inevitably and involuntarily present in love, shows us the far-off, ideal image of the loved one through the material appearance—not in order that we should merely admire it, but in order that, by the power of true faith, active imagination, and real creativeness, we should transform the reality that falls short of it in accordance with that true image, and embody the ideal in actual fact.

But who has ever thought anything of the kind apropos of love? Mediaeval minstrels and knights, strong in faith but weak in intellect, were content simply to identify the ideal of love with a given person, refusing to see the obvious discrepancy between them.

... In addition to the faith which merely made them piously contemplate and ecstatically sing the praises of the fictitiously embodied ideal, mediaeval love was, of course, connected with a longing for heroic deeds. But those military and destructive deeds, being in no way related to the ideal that inspired them, could not lead to its realization.

... The whole of mediaeval chivalry suffered from the severance between the celestial visions of Christianity and the "wild and furious" forces of actual life, until finally the last and most famous of knights, Don Quixote de la Mancha, having killed many sheep and broken down many windmills, but not having brought the Toboso dairymaid the least bit nearer to the ideal of Dulcinea, arrived at the just but purely negative conviction of his error.

... Don Quixote's disappointment was the legacy of chivalry to the new Europe. We are still feeling its effects. The idealization of love, having ceased to be the source of absurd heroic deeds, does not inspire any deeds at all. It proves to be merely a bait which causes us to desire physical and practical possession, and disappears as soon as this hardly ideal purpose is attained. The light of love serves no one as a guide to the lost paradise; it is regarded as a fantastic illumination of a short "love prologue in heaven," extinguished by nature at the proper time as utterly unnecessary for the subsequent earthly performance. But in truth the light is extinguished by the weak and unconscious character of our love, which distorts the true sequence.

External union, practical and especially physiological, has no definite relation to love. It may exist without love, and there may be love without it. It is necessary for love, not as its essential condition and independent goal, but only as its final realization. If this realization is made an end in itself, prior to the ideal work of love, it ruins love.

... The actual feeling of love is merely a stimulus suggesting to us that we can and must recreate the wholeness of the human being. Every time that this sacred spark is lit in the human heart, groaning and travailing creation waits for the first manifestation of the glory of the sons of God. But without the action of the conscious human spirit, the divine spark dies, and disappointed nature creates new generations of the sons of men for new hopes.

These hopes will not be fulfilled until we decide fully to recognize, and to realize to the end, all that true love demands, all that is contained in the idea of true love. Given a conscious attitude to love and real determination to accomplish the task it sets us, we are first of all hindered by two facts which apparently doom us to impotence and justify those who regard love as an illusion. In the feeling of love, in accordance with its essential meaning, we affirm the absolute significance of another personality and, through it, of our own. But an absolute personality cannot be *transitory* and it cannot be *empty*. The inevitability of death and the emptiness of our life are incompatible with the emphatic affirmation of one's own and another's personality contained in the feeling of love. That feeling, if it is strong and fully conscious, cannot resign itself to the certainty that decrepit old age and death are in store both for the beloved and for the lover. And yet, the indubitable fact that men have always died and go on dying is taken by everyone, or almost everyone, to be an absolutely unalterable law of nature. True, many believe in the immortality of the soul; but it is precisely the feeling of love that shows best the insufficiency of that abstract faith. A discarnate spirit is an angel and not a man; but if we love a human being, a complete human personality, and if love is the beginning of that being's spiritualization and enlightenment, it necessarily demands the preservation, the eternal youth and immortality, of this particular person, this living spirit incarnate in a bodily organism.

. . . But if the inevitability of death is incompatible with true love, immortality is utterly incompatible with the emptiness of our life. For the majority of mankind, life is merely an alternation of hard mechanical labor and crudely sensuous pleasures that deaden consciousness. And the minority that has a chance of actively concerning itself not only with the means but also with the ends of life uses its freedom from mechanical labor chiefly for following meaningless and immoral pursuits.

. . . It is obvious at first glance that such an existence is incompatible with immortality. But closer inspection will show that even apparently fuller lives are equally incompatible with it. If, instead of a society lady or a gambler, we take, at the opposite pole, great men, geniuses who have bestowed on mankind immortal works of art or have changed the destiny of nations, we shall see that the content and the historical fruits of their lives have significance only as given, once and for all, and would lose all meaning if those geniuses continued their earthly life forever. The immortality of works obviously does not require, and indeed excludes, the infinitely continued existence of the persons who produced them. It is impossible to imagine Shakespeare endlessly writing his plays, or Newton endlessly studying heavenly mechanics, to say nothing of the absurdity of continuing forever the kind of activity for which Alexander the Great or Napoleon are famed. Art, science, and politics, while providing the content of certain particular strivings of the human spirit and satisfying the temporary, historical needs of humanity, obviously do not impart an absolute, self-sufficient content to the human *personality* and therefore do not require that it should be immortal. Love alone needs this, and it alone can achieve it. True love not only affirms in subjective feeling the absolute significance of human personality in another and in oneself but also justifies this significance in reality, actually delivers us from the inevitability of death and fills our life with absolute content.

"Dionysos and Hades are one and the same," said the most profound thinker of the ancient world. Dionysos, the young and blooming god of material life in the full intensity of its seething forces, the god of turbulent and fruitful nature, is the same as Hades, the pale lord of the silent and tenebrous realm of departed shades; the god of life and the god of death are one and the same god. This is an indisputable truth for the natural organic world. The fullness of vital forces seething in an individual creature does not constitute the particular life of that creature but the alien life of the genus, indifferent and pitiless, which for the individual is death. On the lower levels of the animal world this is perfectly clear; there, individual entities exist solely in order to reproduce themselves, and then die. In many species they do not survive the act of reproduction, but die on the spot; in others they survive for a short time only. But although this connection between birth and death, between the preservation of the species and the destruction of the particular entity is a law of nature, nature herself, in her progressive development, limits and relaxes this law more and more. It still remains necessary for the particular entity to serve as a means for carrying on the life of the genus and then to die, but the necessity manifests itself less and less directly and exclusively as the organic forms increase in perfection and individual entities grow more conscious and independent. Thus the law of identity between Dionysos and Hades, generic life and individual death—or, what is the same thing, the law of conflict and opposition between the genus and the individual entity—is most pronounced at the lower levels of the organic world and becomes less and less stringent as the higher forms develop. If that be the case, does

not the appearance of what is unconditionally the highest organic form, embodying a self-conscious and self-active being
which separates itself from nature, regards nature as an object,
and is consequently capable of inwardly liberating itself from the
demands of the genus—does not the appearance of such a being
suggest an end to this tyranny of the genus over the individual?
If, in the course of the biological process, nature strives to limit
the law of death more and more, ought not man in the historical
process to abolish this law altogether?

It is self-evident that so long as man reproduces himself like
an animal, he also dies like an animal. But it is equally evident
that mere abstention from the act of procreation does not in any
way save one from death. Persons who have preserved their
virginity die, and so do eunuchs, and neither enjoy even particular longevity. This is quite understandable. Speaking generally,
death is the disintegration, the falling apart of a creature's con-
stituent elements. But the division between the masculine and
the feminine elements of the human being is in itself a state of
disintegration and the beginning of death. To remain in sexual
dividedness means to remain on the path of death, and those who
cannot or will not leave that path must, of natural necessity,
tread it to the end. He who supports the root of death must
necessarily taste its fruit. Only the whole man can be immortal,
and if physiological union cannot reinstate the wholeness of the
human being, it means that this false union must be replaced by
a true union and certainly not by abstention from all union, i.e.,
not by a striving to retain *in statu quo* the divided, disintegrated,
and consequently mortal human nature.

In what, then, does the true union of the sexes consist and how
is it realized? In this respect, our life is so far from the truth that
we regard as a norm what is in reality only the less extreme and
outrageous abnormality.

Numerous perversions of the sexual instinct studied by psy-
chiatry are merely curious varieties of the general and all-pervading perversion of sexual relations in mankind—the perversion

which supports and perpetuates the kingdom of sin and death. The three relations or bonds between the sexes which are normal for the human being in his wholeness do actually exist in the human world—the bond according to the lower nature, in the animal life; the moral-civic bond under the law; and the bond in the spiritual life, or union in God—but they are realized unnaturally, that is, separately from one another, in an order contrary to their true meaning and interdependence, and to an unequal degree.

The animal, physiological bond is given the first place in our reality, while in truth it ought to have the last. It is regarded as the basis of the whole, while it ought to be only its final culmination. For many, the basis in this case coincides with the culmination. They do not go beyond animal relations. Others build upon this broad foundation the social and moral superstructure of the legal family union. Then the level of everyday existence is taken for the culminating point, and that which ought to be a free and conscious expression, in the temporal process, of the eternal unity becomes an involuntary channel of meaningless material life. As a rare exception, pure spiritual love is left for the few elect. But it is robbed beforehand by the other, lower bonds of all actual content, so that it has to be satisfied with dreamy and sterile sentimentality which has no real task or vital purpose. This unfortunate spiritual love resembles the little angels in old paintings who have nothing but heads and wings. Such angels cannot move forward, for their wings are only strong enough to hold them up at a certain height. Spiritual love finds itself in the same exalted but extremely unsatisfactory position. Physical passion has a certain task before it, though a shameful one; legal family union also fullfils a function, necessary at present, though of middling value. But spiritual love, as it has so far appeared, has no task whatever to accomplish, and therefore it is not surprising that the majority of practical people *glaubt an keine Liebe, oder nimmt's für Poësie.*[7]

′ Does not believe in love, or takes it for poetry.

This exclusively spiritual love is obviously as much of an anomaly as exclusive physical passion or a loveless legal union. The absolute norm is the reinstatement of the wholeness of the human being, and in whatever direction that norm is violated, the result is always abnormal and unnatural. Pseudo-spiritual love is not merely abnormal but also utterly purposeless, for the separation of the spiritual from the sensuous for which it strives is, in any case, performed in the best possible way by death. True spiritual love, on the other hand, is not a feeble imitation and anticipation of death but triumph over death; it is not the separation of the immortal from the mortal, of the eternal from the temporal, but the transformation of the mortal into the immortal, the reception of the temporal into eternity. False spirituality is the negation of the flesh; true spirituality is its regeneration, salvation, and resurrection. . . .

"So God created man in His own image, in the image of God created He him; male and female created He them." "This is a great mystery, but I speak concerning Christ and the Church." The mysterious image of God in which man was created refers not to one separate part of the human being, but to the true unity of his two essential aspects, the male and the female. The relation that God has to His creation and that Christ has to His Church must be the relation of the husband to the wife. These words are generally known, but their meaning is little understood. As God creates the universe, as Christ builds the Church, so must man create and build his feminine complement. It is, of course, an elementary truth that man stands for the active and woman for the passive principle and that a man ought to have a formative influence upon a woman's mind and character. We are concerned, however, not with this superficial relation, but with the "great mystery" of which St. Paul speaks. That great mystery is essentially analogous to, though not identical with, the relation between the human and the divine.

. . . God's relation to the creature is that of everything to nothing, i.e., of the absolute fullness of being to the pure potency of being; Christ's relation to the Church is that of actual to potential perfection, which is being raised into actuality; but the relation between husband and wife is the relation between two differently acting but equally imperfect potencies which attain perfection only through a process of interaction. Or, to put it differently, God receives nothing, that is, He gains no increase from the creature, but gives everything to it; Christ receives no increase from the Church in perfection, and gives all perfection to it, but He does receive from the Church increase in the fullness of His collective body; finally, man and his feminine *alter ego* complete each other both really and ideally, attaining perfection through interaction only. Man can creatively reinstate God's image in the living object of his love only by reinstating that image in himself as well. But he has no power of his own to do it, for if he had, he would not need any reinstatement; and not having the power, he must receive it from God. Hence man (husband) is the creative and formative principle in relation to his feminine complement, not in himself, but as a mediator of divine power.

. . . The work of true love is based, first of all, upon *faith*. The basic meaning of love, as already shown, consists in recognizing the absolute significance of another personality. But in its actual, sensuously apprehended existence, that personality has no unconditional significance; it is imperfect and transitory. Consequently, we can only ascribe absolute significance to it through faith which is "the substance of things hoped for, the evidence of things not seen." But what is the object of faith in this case? What exactly does it mean to believe in the unconditional and therefore infinite significance of this individual person? To affirm that the individual as such, as separate and particular, has absolute significance would be both absurd and blasphemous.

. . . By faith in the object of our love we must mean the affirmation of that object as existing in God and in that sense possessing infinite significance.

. . . Since for the eternal and indivisible God everything is to-

gether and at once, to affirm an individual being in God means
to affirm it, not in its separateness but in all, or, more exactly, in
the unity of all. Since, however, this individual being, in its
given actuality, does not enter into the unity of all, but exists
separately, as a materially isolated fact, the object of our believing
love necessarily differs from the empirical object of our instinctive love, though it is indissolubly bound up with it. It is one
and the same person in two different aspects or two different
spheres of being—the ideal and the real. The first is so far only
an idea. But in true, believing, and clear-sighted love we know
that this idea is not our arbitrary invention; it expresses the *truth*
of the object, unrealized as yet in the sphere of outward existence.

Although this true idea of the beloved shines through its material embodiment at moments of love's ecstasy, it appears more
clearly at first as an object of imagination. Its concrete form, the
ideal image with which I clothe the beloved at the moment, is, of
course, created by myself; but it is not created out of nothing.
The subjectivity of that image as such, the fact, that is, that it
appears here and now before my mental vision, in no way proves
that the imagined object itself is subjective and exists for me
alone. If for me, standing on this side of the transcendental
world, a certain ideal object appears as a product of my imagination, this does not prevent it from being fully real in another,
higher realm of being. And although our actual life lies outside
that higher realm, our mind is not quite a stranger to it, and we
can have some speculative knowledge of its laws. And this is its
first and fundamental law: while in this world separate and isolated existence is an actual fact and unity is only a concept or
idea, there, on the contrary, it is the unity, or, more exactly, the
all-unity, that is real, and isolation and separateness have only
potential and subjective existence.

It follows that the being of *this* person in the transcendental
sphere is not individual in our sense of the term. There, i.e., in
truth, an individual person is only a ray—living and actual, but
an inseparable ray—of one ideal light, of the one universal sub-

stance. This ideal person or personified idea is merely an individualization of the all-unity which is indivisibly present in each one of its individual expressions. And so when we imagine the ideal form of the beloved, the all-embracing unity itself is given us in that form. How, then, is it to be conceived?

God as one, in distinguishing from Himself His 'other,' i.e., all that is not He, unites that other to Himself, positing it before Him, together and all at once, in an absolutely perfect form, and consequently as a unity. This *other* unity, distinct though inseparable from God's primary unity, is, in relation to God, a passive, feminine unity, for in it eternal emptiness (pure potency) receives the fullness of the divine life. But though pure nothing lies *at the bottom* of this eternal femininity, for God this nothing is eternally concealed by the image of absolute perfection which He bestows upon it. This perfection, which for us is still in the process of being realized, actually *is* already for God, i.e., in truth. The ideal unity toward which our world is striving and which is the goal of the cosmic and historical process cannot be merely a subjective idea (for whose idea could it be?), but is truly the eternal object of divine love, as God's eternal "other."

This living ideal of divine love is prior to our love and contains the secret of its idealization. The idealization of the lower being is the beginning of the realization of the higher, and herein lies the truth of love's exaltation. The complete realization, the transformation of an individual feminine being into a ray of the divine eternal feminine, inseparable from its radiant source, will be the real—both the subjective and the objective—reunion of the individual human being with the Deity, the reinstatement of the living and immortal image of God in man.

The object of true love is not simple but twofold. We love, first, the ideal entity (ideal not in an abstract sense, but in the sense of belonging to a higher realm of being) which we must bring into our real world, and second, the natural human entity which provides the real personal material for such realization; this natural human entity is idealized through love, not in our subjective imagination, but in the sense of being actually and objectively regenerated. Thus, true love is indivisibly both *ascending* and *descending* (*amor ascendens* and *amor descendens*, or the two Aphrodites whom Plato rightly distinguished but wrongly separated Ἀφροδίτη Οὐρανία and Ἀφροδίτη Πάνδημος). God's *other* (i.e., the universe) has, from all eternity, the image of perfect femininity, and He wills that this image should not exist for Him alone, but that it should be realized and embodied for every individual being capable of uniting with it. The eternal feminine itself strives for such realization and embodiment, for it is not a mere passive image in the divine mind but a living spiritual being possessing the fullness of powers and activities. The whole cosmic and historical process is the process of its realization and incarnation in an endless multiplicity of forms and degrees.

In sexual love, rightly understood and truly realized, this divine essence finds a means for its complete and final embodiment in the individual life of man, for the deepest, and at the same time most outwardly sensible and real union with him. Hence those glimpses of unearthly bliss, that breath of heavenly joy, which accompany even imperfect love and make it the highest felicity for men and gods—*hominum divumque voluptas*. And hence, too, the deep suffering of love that is incapable of holding its true object and recedes from it further and further.

A legitimate place is thus provided for the element of adoration and infinite devotion which is so characteristic of love, but so meaningless if it refers solely to its earthly object apart from the heavenly.

Immediate, instinctive feeling reveals to us the meaning of love as the highest expression of the individual life which, in union with another being, finds its own infinity. But is this momentary revelation enough? . . . A *momentary* infinity is a contradiction intolerable to the intellect; a bliss that is only in the past is pain for the will. . . . If that infinity and that bliss are merely deceptions, the very memory of them brings with it the shame and bitterness of disillusionment; but if they are not an illusion, if they reveal to us a reality which afterwards is hidden from us and disappears, why should we resign ourselves to its disappearance? If that which is lost is real, the task for our mind and will is to understand and remove the cause of the loss, and not to accept it as irretrievable.

The immediate cause, as already pointed out, is the distortion of the love relation itself. This begins very early. No sooner has the first exaltation of love shown us a glimpse of another, and a better reality, with a different principle and law of life, than we immediately try to utilize the access of energy brought about by this revelation not in order to go where it calls us but to settle more firmly and securely in the old reality above which love had just raised us. We take the good news from the lost paradise—the news of being able to return to it—for an invitation to be finally *naturalized* in the land of exile, and hasten to enter into full hereditary possession of our little plot with all its thorns and thistles. The breakdown of the limits of selfhood, which is the sign and the essential meaning of the love-passion, leads, in practice, merely to egoism *à deux*, then *à trois*, and so on. It is, of course, better than solitary egoism, but the dawn of love opened up quite different horizons.

As soon as the vital sphere of the love-union is transferred to the material reality in its present state, the order of union is at once distorted accordingly. Its "unearthly," mystical basis, which made itself so strongly felt in early passion, is forgotten as a fleeting exaltation, and that which ought to be merely the last and conditional expression of love is recognized as its first condition, its final and most desirable purpose. When this last thing —the physical union—is put in the first place, thus being deprived of its *human* meaning and restored to the animal, it not only makes love powerless against death but inevitably becomes the moral grave of love long before the physical grave receives the lovers.

Direct personal counteraction to this order of things is more difficult to carry out than to understand: it can be indicated in a few words. To abolish this order we must first of all recognize it as abnormal, affirming thereby that there is another, normal order in which everything external and accidental is subordinated to the inner meaning of life. Such affirmation should not be merely verbal; the experience of the outer senses must be countered not with an abstract principle but with another kind of experience—*the experience of faith.*

... But if faith is not to remain dead faith, it must constantly defend itself against the environment in which meaningless chance builds its rule on the play of animal passions and, still worse, human passions. Against these hostile forces, believing love has but one weapon—endurance unto the end. To deserve its bliss, it must take up its cross. In our material environment, it is impossible to preserve true love except through understanding and accepting it as a moral task. It is not for nothing that the Orthodox Church remembers holy *martyrs* in the marriage service and compares the bridal crowns to theirs.

Religious faith and moral endeavor preserve the individual man and his love from being engulfed by the material environment while he lives, but they do not give him triumph over death. The inner regeneration of the love-feeling, the correction of the perverted love relation, do not correct or cancel the law of physical life either in the external world or in man himself. *In fact,* he remains limited and subject to material nature. His inner, mystical, and moral union with the personality that completes his own cannot overcome either their mutual separateness and impenetrability or their common dependence upon the material world. The last word belongs, not to moral achievement but to the merciless law of organic life and death; and people who have championed the eternal ideal to the end die with human dignity but with animal helplessness.

... It is only together with all other beings that the individual man can be really saved, that is, can regenerate and preserve forever his individual life in true love. It is his right and his duty to defend his individuality against the law of life in general, but he must not separate his own good from the true good of all that lives. The fact that the deepest and strongest manifestation of love is to be found in the relation between two beings complementary to each other by no means implies that this relation should be isolated and separated from all else as something self-sufficient. On the contrary, such isolation is the ruin of love, for the sexual relation as such, in spite of all its subjective importance, proves (objectively) to be only a transitory empirical event. Nor does the fact that the perfect union of two particular beings will always be the basis and the true form of individual life by any means imply that this form must remain empty and isolated in its individual perfection. On the contrary, owing to the very nature of man, it is capable of being filled with universal content and is so destined. Finally, if the moral meaning of love requires the reunion of that which has been wrongly separated and demands the identification of one's own self with the other, it would be contrary to this moral meaning to separate the attainment of our individual perfection from the process of universal unification, even if it were physically possible to do so.

If the root of false existence is impenetrability, that is, mutual exclusion of one another's being, true life means living in another as in oneself or finding in another positive and absolute completion of one's own being. The foundation and pattern of this true life is and always shall be sexual or conjugal love. But as we have seen, that love cannot be realized without a corresponding transformation of the whole external environment; the integration of the individual life necessarily requires the same integration in the domains of social and of cosmic life.

The distinction between the different spheres of life, both individual and collective, will never, and should never be abolished, for if it were, the universal mergence would lead to uniformity and emptiness and not to the fullness of being. True union presupposes true difference between its terms, in virtue of which they do not exclude but mutually affirm each other, each finding in the other the fullness of its own life. In individual love, the two different beings, equal in rights and value, are not a negative limit, but a positive complement to each other, and it must be the same in every sphere of collective life. Every social organism must be, for every one of its members, not an external limit to his activities but his positive support and completion. Just as in sexual love (in the domain of personal life) the individual "other" is at the same time "all," so the social *all*, in virtue of the solidarity of all its elements, must appear to each of these elements as a real unity, as, so to speak, another living being completing him (in a new and wider sphere of life).

The relations between the individual members of society must be brotherly (and filial with respect to past generations and their social representatives), and their connection with different social wholes—local, national and, finally, universal—must be still more inward, many-sided, and significant. The bond between the active, personal, human principle and the all-embracing idea embodied in the social physico-spiritual organism must be a living *syzygic* relation.[8] Not to submit to one's social environment and not to dominate it, but to be in loving interaction with it, to serve it as an active fertilizing principle of movement, and to find in it the fullness of vital conditions and possibilities —that is the relation of the true human personality not only to its immediate social environment and to its nation but to humanity as a whole. In the Bible, cities, countries, the people of Israel, and then the whole of regenerated humanity or the universal Church are represented in the form of feminine beings, and this is not a mere metaphor. The image of the unity of social bodies is not perceptible to our outer senses, but this by no means implies that it does not exist. Why, our own bodily image is utterly imperceptible and unknown to a particular brain cell or blood corpuscle. If we, as personalities capable of attaining fullness of being, differ from these elementary entities both by

---

[8] From the Greek συζυγία, conjunction. I have to introduce this new term, for I cannot find a better one in the existing terminology.

greater clarity and breadth of rational consciousness and by a greater power of creative imagination, I do not see why we should renounce this privilege. But in any case, whether with or without images, what is needed in the first instance is that we should treat our social and cosmic environment as an actual living being, with which we are in the closest and most complete interaction without ever being merged in it. This extension of the syzygic relation to the domains of collective and universal existence perfects our individuality—imparting to it unity and fullness of vital content—and thereby uplifts and perpetuates the fundamental individual form of love.

. . . As the all-embracing idea becomes actually realized through the strengthening and greater perfection of its individually human elements, the forms of false separation or impenetrability of beings in space and time inevitably grow less pronounced. But in order that they should be abolished altogether and that all individuals, both past and present, should finally become eternal, the process of integration must transcend the limits of social or strictly human life and include the cosmic sphere from which it started. In ordering the physical world, the divine idea threw the veil of natural beauty over the kingdom of matter and death; through man, through the activity of his universally rational consciousness, it must enter that kingdom *from within* in order to give life to nature and make its beauty eternal. In this sense it is essential to change man's relation to nature. With nature, too, he must enter into the same relation of syzygic unity which determines his true life in the personal and social spheres.

Nature has so far been either an omnipotent, despotic mother of the child man, or a slave, a thing foreign to him. In that second epoch poets alone preserved and kept up a timid and unconscious love of nature as a being possessing full rights and having, or capable of having, *life in itself.*

. . . To establish a truly loving, or syzygic, relation between man and his natural and cosmic, as well as his social, environment is a purpose that is quite clear in itself. But the same cannot be said about the ways in which this relation can be attained by an individual man. Without going into premature, and therefore dubious and unsuitable details, one can confidently say one thing on the basis of well-established analogies from cosmic and historical experience. Every conscious human activity, determined by the idea of universal syzygy, and having for its purpose the embodiment of the all-embracing ideal in some particular sphere, actually produces or liberates spiritual-material currents which gradually gain possession of the material environment, spiritualize it, and embody in it certain images of the all-embracing unity —the living and eternal likenesses of absolute humanity. And the power of this spiritual-material creativeness in man is merely the transformation or the *turning inward* of the creative power which, being turned outward in nature, produces the infinity of the physical reproduction of organisms.

Having connected, in the idea of universal syzygy, individual sexual love with the true essence of universal life, I have fulfilled my task and have defined the meaning of love.

Pavel Aleksandrovich Florensky

1882-1952?

Father Pavel Florensky stands at the very center of that theological and cultural renaissance that so deeply marked the first decades of the twentieth century in Russia. For no one reflects better the peculiar combination of spirituality and aestheticism, mysticism and scientific preoccupation, traditionalism and modernism that were typical of that time. Florensky began as a *wunderkind* in mathematics but, instead of continuing his highly successful theoretical studies in that field, he turned to theology and enrolled at the Moscow Theological Academy. In 1908 he was appointed to its faculty as a lecturer in philosophy and in 1911 was ordained to the priesthood. In 1914 he published his famous book *Stolp i utverzhdenie istini*, "The Pillar and Ground of Truth: An Essay on Orthodox Theodicy in Twelve Letters," which, according to N. Zernov, "marked the beginning of a new era in Russian theology" (*The Russian Religious Renaissance of the Twentieth Century*, p. 101). Everything was strange in this book: its unusual type face (which was made to order), the sophisticated vignette at the beginning of each chapter, the peculiar mixture of lyricism and scientism in its style, the footnotes referring to every imaginable area of human knowledge. The book raised controversies that have not come to an end even today. Like many other Russian religious thinkers, Florensky remains controversial, although no one denies the influence he had and the seriousness of the problems he discussed.

Florovsky characterized Florensky as a "lonely" writer. And indeed, although his indebtedness to Khomyakov and Solovyov is clear, he criticized both of them as well as his own contemporaries, the representatives of the "new consciousness" in the Church. His life after the Revolution was tragic: deprived of his teaching post at the Theological Academy, he worked for a short time at the Institute of Physics, but was soon deported to Siberia and never returned.

We have selected for this anthology one of the most typical and significant chapters of his "The Pillar and Ground of Truth."

Bibliography

Stolp i utverzhdenie istini ("The Pillar and Ground of Truth"). Moscow: Mamontov, 1914.

For an evaluation, see:
Lossky, N. O., *History of Russian Philosophy*, pp. 89 ff. New York: International Universities Press, 1951.

Sabaneyev, Leonid, "Pavel Florensky—Priest, Scientist and Mystic. Reminiscences," in *The Russian Review*, Vol. 20 (October, 1961), Hanover, N.H.

Zenkovsky, V. V., *A History of Russian Philosophy*, Vol. II, Ch. VI. New York: Columbia University Press, 1953.

On the Holy Spirit[1]

Do YOU REMEMBER, my quiet one, our long walks through the forest—through the forest of that dying August? The silvery trunks of the birch trees stretched up like palms, with their gold-green crowns fresh-dipped in blood pressed close to the red and purple aspens. And the fine-textured hazels branching over the surface of the land like green gauze. A holy solemnity breathed beneath the vaulted arches of that cathedral.

Do you remember our deep-searching conversations, my distant but always present friend? The Holy Spirit, and religious antitheses—that was what interested us most. And we walked along through the cornfield near that forbidden grove, intoxicated by the blazing sunset, rejoicing that the question had been settled, that we had both arrived separately at the same conclusion. Then our thoughts flowed like the blazing streams of the firmament and we caught each thought with half a word. The roots of our hair tingled with an inspired, cold, yet flaming rapture; shivers ran up our spines.

Do you remember, my like-minded brother, the bulrushes in the black creeks? We stood silently on the steep bank and listened to the mysterious whispers of the evening. An unspeakable, exultant secret grew in our souls; yet we did not say a word

[1] Translated from Pavel Florensky, *Stolp i utverzhdenie istini: opit pravoslavnoy feoditsei v dvenadtsati pismakh*, Moscow, 1914, pp. 109–142.

about it, speaking to one another only by our silence; and then . . .

Now it is winter outside. I am working beside a lamp and the evening light in the window is blue and grand, like Death. And as if faced by death I am tracing the whole past once more; once more I am stirred by an otherworldly joy. But now that I am alone there is nothing for me to treasure. Here I am, writing my petty, fragmentary thoughts to you. But still . . . I am writing. So many hopes are bound up with the question of the Holy Spirit, that I will try to write down something . . . in memory of you. Let the pages of my letter be the withered flowers of your autumn.

The understanding of Truth (the understanding of the consubstantiality of the Holy Trinity) is perfected by the grace of the Holy Spirit. All ascetic life (life in the Truth) is directed by the Holy Spirit. The third hypostasis of the Holy Trinity appears infinitely near, infinitely true for the one who is zealous for Truth. It is He, "the Spirit of Truth" (John 12:26), Who bears witness to the Lord (and to consubstantiality) in the believer's soul; it is He Who teaches him "what he ought to say" to all who are external to him and therefore who tend to drive the Lord and the idea of consubstantiality away from him (Luke 12:11–12). And yet knowledge of the Spirit as the Comforter—the joy of the Comforter—adorns only the supreme points of affliction, just as the rosy light of the sun, when it has earned its rest, smiles only upon the snow-tipped peaks of the Caucasus. The rosy clouds of purified created being and the snowy-white radiance of a holy, transfigured body are to be seen only at the end of the thorny path.

Only at the end . . . As it is in each person's life as an individual, so it is also in the life of mankind as a whole. So long as man could not stand with firm feet on the path of salvation, the Lord sustained him. Then afflictions were forgotten, though they were already prepared and about to begin. "Can the members of the wedding household mourn as long as the bridegroom is with them? But the days will come, when the bridegroom will be taken away from them, and then they will fast" (Matthew 9:15).

It is true that the Bride met the Bridegroom with a tender kiss at the beginning of the exploit of their life together. It is true that apostolic Christianity throbbed with the fullness of joy. But this kiss—this joy—was only the token of something promised. It was given for the long road, for the many torments ahead, not because it was deserved, but as an encouragement.

The wonderful moment flashed blindingly and then . . . it was as if it had never been. The Lord was separated from the earth and from all that He had, by His radiancy, immediately and visibly overcome. He is with us now; but He is not with us as a man—after the manner of this world. It is the same in the life of the individual at the beginning of the ascetic path, when an unmerited, unspeakable, tremendous joy fills the soul. Like the Most Pure Body and Sacred Blood of Christ which are given for strength and nourishment, this joy is "in token of the Kingdom to come," in token of the future spiritualization and enlightenment of his whole being.[2]

It is like this, I repeat, at the beginning of the path. And this beginning is endlessly joyous; it is so inexpressibly good that man finds power to overcome obstacles later in remembering his fleeting vision and the sweet parting. The ascetic drives away the black thoughts of future difficulty and tedium and the melancholy of everyday life by his dreams of the rapture of his first love.

But in general, on the average, usually, both in the personal life of the Christian (apart from his highest ascents) and in the everyday life of the Church (with the exception of Heaven's chosen ones), people hardly know the Holy Spirit as a Person, and then only dimly and in a confused way. The feeble and fragmentary knowledge of the divine nature of created being is also connected with this fact.

2 "In token of the life and kingdom to come"; St. John Damascene, Fifth Prayer for the Holy Communion.

It could not be otherwise. A vision of the Holy Spirit would give the full property of spirit-bearing, a full deification, a full enlightenment, to all Created Being. Then history would be ended; then the fullness of time would be at hand; then there would indeed be no more Time. I repeat, this would be the fulfillment—which the Mystery-contemplating Eagle (St. John the Divine) was deemed worthy to see: "And the angel whom I saw standing on the sea and on the land," he proclaimed, "raised his hand to heaven and swore by Him who lives forever, Who created heaven and all that is in it, the earth and all that is on it, the sea and all that is in it, that time will be no more; but in those days when the seventh angel shall proclaim, when he shall sound the trumpet, the mystery of God shall be fulfilled, as He announced to His servants the prophets" (Revelation 10:5-7). This is what will happen at the end of history, when the Comforter will be revealed.

But history has reached that point where only moments or instants of illumination by the Spirit are possible; where the Spirit is known only by separate people in separate moments and instants, when they are lifted up out of time into Eternity—"for them there is no time," and for them history is ended. The fullness of possession is inaccessible to the faithful as a whole, and inaccessible to the separate believer in the entirety of his life. Christ's victory over Death and the Flesh is not yet appropriated by Created Being, not entirely appropriated; which means that there is also no fullness of vision. Just as the holy, noncorporeal powers of ascetics are pledges of victory over Death (revelations of the Spirit in corporeal nature), so also holy spiritual illuminations are pledges of the victory over reason (revelations of the Spirit in spiritual nature). But to the extent that resurrection has not yet occurred, there is also no full rational illumination by the Holy Spirit. To assert that a full vision or a full purification of the flesh is attainable is presumptuousness, the presumptuousness of Simon the Magician, Manes, Montanus, of the sectarians, and of thousands of other false spirit-bearers like them, who have lied, and are lying, against the Spirit. This is also that perversion of the whole of human nature which is called "seduction" or "enticement."

Yes, the Holy Spirit does operate in the Church. But knowledge of Him has always been a kind of pledge, a kind of reward— in special moments and in exceptional people; and this is the way it will be until "all is fulfilled." This is why one thing cannot fail to attract attention in the reading of the Church's writings, something which seems strange at first but which later, in the light of pre-existing factors, manifests its inner necessity. It is this: that all the holy fathers and mystic philosophers speak of the importance of the idea of the Spirit in the Christian world view, but hardly one of them explains himself precisely and exactly. It is quite evident that the holy fathers know something from their own experience; but what is even clearer is that this knowledge is so deeply hidden away, so "unaccountable," so unspeakable, that they lack the power to clothe it in precise language. For the most part this applies to the dogmatists, since they must speak definitely and this is the nature of their work; they express themselves almost like dumb persons, or else become obviously confused. One need only recall the second-century "binatural system" of Ermos or the author of the second pseudo-Clementine Epistle to the Corinthians; in both cases the Holy Spirit is directly confused with the Church. Or we may recall the system of Tertullian in the third century, where the Spirit is so poorly distinguished from the Word that He is almost identified with Him and is not infrequently referred to instead of Him.

This inner contradiction struck me for the first time in reading Origen's *On First Principles* (written c. 228–229). In expounding the Christian dogma, Origen expresses the firm conviction that the idea of the Holy Spirit is strictly a Christian idea, the shibboleth of Christianity, so to speak.

All those who in any way acknowledge Providence confess that an uncreated God exists Who has created and ordered everything; they all acknowledge Him as the Father——*parentem*—of the universe. We are not alone in preaching that He has a Son. Thus, even though this doctrine seems rather surprising and improbable to Greek and barbarian philosophers, still some of them express a belief in the Son when they confess that everything is created by the word or by the reason of God. As for the hypostasis (*subsistentia*, i.e., a literal translation of ὑπόστασις) of the Holy Spirit, no one can have any concept with regard to it except those who are familiar with the Law and the Prophets, or those who confess the faith in Christ (*On First Principles*, I 3:1).

Of course one may doubt if this is really so. St. Justin the Philosopher, in his *First Apology* (dated probably about A.D. 150 or even 138–139, and therefore written eighty or ninety years before Origen's *Principles*), no less definitely ascribes knowledge of all three hypostases to Plato. But whether Origen's affirmation is essentially correct or not, it is an extremely typical one in the history of spiritual knowledge. Indeed, one might think that in saying this Origen was only using, for the idea of the Holy Spirit, a deduction which he himself had made earlier for the idea of the Father and the Son. But then "this task of giving a speculative foundation to the fact of the existence of the Holy Spirit, the task of indicating the logical necessity precisely of the three-fold existence of the Divinity, was not completed by Origen." Such is the verdict of a most dispassionate historian and a most scholarly dogmatist (V. V. Bolotov).

In any case, Origen had agreed with this harsh judgment in advance. For that which Bolotov demands of him, that which a natural movement of thought demands of him, is—according to Origen himself—impossible (cf. *Principles* I 3:1). Yes, the deduction is impossible. So be it. But surely the impossibility of speculation is not then a justification for irresolution and indefiniteness in the exposition of dogmatic material. And yet by the interrogative form of his exposition, Origen sometimes simply evades an answer and sometimes obviously forgets altogether about the idea of the Holy Spirit. This forgetfulness is indeed easily explained! The Holy Spirit is in fact not necessary to the profound metaphysical analysis of Origen's system; it is, so to speak, a "false window" for the sake of the symmetry of the structure, and nothing more. Giant Origen, who stepped out boldly and firmly on the field of dogmatics, who was not afraid to develop his own theological concepts (sometimes striking in the audacity and impetuosity of their upward flight), unexpectedly sidesteps what he had himself called the really essential element in the Christian view, and, turning into some kind of little creature, into a stooped and wrinkled dwarf, this same Origen mumbles confusedly and unintelligibly about what is essential.

This change from the great to the puny is so striking that it has long caught everyone's attention, from Basil the Great, in whose opinion Origen was a man who did not have an altogether sound understanding of the Holy Spirit (cf. *On the Holy Spirit* 29:73), to Origen's present-day defenders. The latter try to justify him either by the primary interest of his time in explicating the idea of the Son and the Father, or by citing the lack of definition in the councils' decisions concerning the Holy Spirit. Or they argue that Origen intended to explain himself more fully in some later work on this incriminating question. Whether this is true or not, the clear first impression remains that the idea was somehow indefensible in the inner consciousness of Origen himself. The same can be said of others, for they, too, speak of the Holy Spirit either indistinctly and with many interruptions, or cautiously and with great wariness.

This inability to defend the idea of the Holy Spirit, an inability proceeding from the exceptional nature of intellectual encounters with the Holy Spirt, is apparent also from the fact that in the works of ecclesiastical literature it is not uncommon (as has been partly indicated above) to find a certain lack of differentiation between the idea of the Holy Spirit and the idea of Sofia or Wisdom, as well as between both of these and the Logos. This is all the more striking in that the notions of the Father and the Son were investigated with the utmost subtlety and were, so to speak, etched out in detail. The first impression gained from a reading of the Church's literature is inevitably the same as that gained from her painting—part of it complete, the rest left only in vague outline. Of course, it would be possible to cite particular passages and excerpts from the works of the holy fathers. One simply must agree that in general it is as I have indicated. This impression can be demonstrated easily if one attempts to compare the doctrine of the Father and the Son with the doctrine of the Holy Spirit.

It is true that disputes arise and different allegations are made with regard to the Holy Spirit. But they all have a formal and schematic quality; they are all distinguished from corresponding affirmations concerning the Father and Son as the pencil outlines of a painting are distinguished from the canvas after it is filled with colors. While the hypostatic existence of the Father and Son is apprehended by every nerve of the spiritual organism; while heresy in regard to the Father and Son is organically and immediately unacceptable to the whole of one's inner being; while the nature of the Father and Son is presented in crystal clear and geometrically harmonious formulae having a religiously axiomatic quality; the doctrine of the Holy Spirit is either almost or altogether unnoticed, or is presented by way of a deductive or circuitous route, like a rational theorem, according to plan: "Since such-and-such is said of the Son, so by the same token we are compelled to say such-and-such about the Spirit." The veracity of a statement about the Son is immediately evident for the man of faith; but the veracity of a statement about the Holy Spirit is explained in a circuitous way, is established through the formal accuracy of intermediary arguments. These proofs and arguments of logic could and do appear as naïve, inadequate, preliminary constructions, whereas the building of dogmatic theology has rested on the great word ὁμοούσιος, which was immediately valid for the conscience and life attuned to faith in Christ Jesus, upon which the building has been maintained, and by means of which the building has supported the whole superstructure. The consubstantiality of the Word for spiritual people was something given in the experience of life, and they acknowledged consubstantiality and confessed it in spite of weak argumentation and in the teeth of contrary proofs. Argumentation in the doctrine of the Word was no more than a tiny supplementary activity. But in the doctrine of the Holy Spirit argumentation was almost all there was, and without it the dogma is deprived of its persuasiveness. That which steadfast Origen says about the existence and origin of the Holy Spirit is a doctrine invented *ad hoc,* a deliberate sophistry, created in order not to come into conflict with ecclesiastical tradition; really it would have been far more natural and convenient for Origen, if only it had been possible, simply to remain silent about the Holy Spirit. The Spirit "proceeds" from the Father, since otherwise, as Origen put it, He would either have had to be begotten of the Father—and then the Son would have a "brother" (just as the deniers of the Spirit proclaim), or else begotten of the Son— and then He would have been a "grandson" of the Father (the view of Tertullian and others). Origen thinks so confusedly about the Spirit that in his *Commentary on John* he wavers between the creation of the Spirit by the Father and procession from the Father, speaking now in one way and now in the other.

You will say, "What is it to us that Origen thought in this way?" It affects us, first, because he was a great theologian and a powerful, independent mind; and second, because he exercised an immeasurable influence on all later theology. What has been said about Origen can be said *mutatis mutandis* about others.

Athanasius of Alexandria himself (not just "the Great," but also genuinely great), in his three epistles on the Holy Spirit to Serapion (actually the first, second, and fourth), having made what one scholar calls an "exhaustive investigation of the Spirit which set a pattern for later writers," argues exclusively *ad personas*. He bases himself primarily on just this point: that those who acknowledge the createdness of the Spirit "divide and sunder the Trinity," and in so doing, expose the doctrine of the Son to danger. It is in this way that Athanasius arrives at an acknowledgment of the consubstantiality of the Holy Spirit; any other teaching would mean a rejection of all that had been said of the Son. But then even Athanasius does not make clear the meaning of ἐκπόρευσις, the procession of the Spirit, as distinct from γέννησις, the begottenness of the Son. Of the three individual essences of the Divine hypostases, namely, ἀγεννησία, γέννησις, and ἐκπόρευσις, the first two are spiritually fully understandable, while the latter represents only the sign of some still pending spiritual attempt to comprehend.

In an equally formal way, Gregory of Nyssa and Basil the Great refuted the deniers of the Holy Spirit; and in spite of their love of intellectual flights, they were unable to fly up to the level of the question of the Holy Spirit. With them too, the Spirit is examined only in connection with the Father and the Son, and not independently.

St. Basil the Great, probably more than anyone else, assisted in preparing mens' minds for the second Ecumenical Council, that is, for an awareness of the dogma of the Holy Spirit. Nonetheless the distinction between the renowned patience of St. Basil the Great in his polemic with the Macedonians and, in general, in all questions of pneumatology, as compared with the intemperance of the whole spiritual atmosphere during the consideration of questions touching the Logos is perhaps, in the last analysis, determined by the difference in inner persuasiveness of the defense of one or the other position. One involuntarily suspects that this is not just patience but a certain personal coolness toward the question, his own insufficiently keen penetration into the heart of it. Basil the Great studied the consubstantiality of the Holy Spirit by looking at the question out of the corner of his eye, while his clearest sight was fixed on the consubstantiality of the Son. His willing, free confession and defense of the Son drew him, as it were, into an involuntary, unavoidable confession and defense of the Spirit.

I repeat, this is not an incidental feature of the history of theology, but the unfailing result of the fulfillment of the hours and days, an inevitable and certain indication of the comparatively unclear revelation of the Spirit as a hypostasis, an imperfection of life itself. Our assertion is easily verified. For where is the immediate expression of spiritual experience? Where is spiritual experience analyzed least of all? In prayers and chants, in divine worship. Divine worship is the most significant and essential function of the life of the spiritual body. The witness of divine worship is a most reliable witness. Where should one look first of all for an indication of the place which the Holy Spirit occupied (as compared with the other hypostases) in the hearts and minds of the members of the early Church? Well, of course, at the point where the feast was dedicated to all three hypostases.

The divine worship on the Day of the Trinity, i.e., the day expressly consecrated to the Most Holy Trinity, will give us a definite indication of how much the hypostatic nature of the Holy Spirit was a property of the living experience of the Church and not just a theorem of dogmatic theology. And this indication is all the more valuable in that the basic section in "The Ritual of Pentecost"—I am thinking of the three prayers at the solemn genuflections—was composed (more than probably) just at the time of Basil the Great.

What then do we find here? The first prayer of genuflection begins with the words:

O most pure, spotless, unbegotten, incomprehensible, invisible, untraceable, invincible, unaccountable, gracious Lord; Who alone art immortal, living in unapproachable light, creator of heaven and earth, and the sea, and all that is in them; Who givest forgiveness to all before it is asked. We pray Thee and beg Thee, O Lord the lover of mankind, the Lord God and Father of our Saviour Jesus Christ. . . .

It begins, that is, with an obvious address to God the Father. The second prayer of genuflection is addressed to the Son:

O Lord Jesus Christ our God; Who hast granted to men Thy peace and the gift of the Holy Spirit; Who art still with us in life; Who ever givest to the faithful as an inalienable heritage. . . .

Finally, the third prayer of genuflection, occupying a position in the ritual exactly corresponding to the positions of the two previous prayers (i.e., the liturgical analogy of the first two prayers), begins with the address:

O ever-flowing, life-giving and radiant Wellspring, coexistent with the Father; O enabling Power, Who executeth ever-watchfulness for the blessed salvation of men . . .

But precisely to Whom is this prayer addressed? What comes next? According to the meaning of the feast itself (The Day of the Trinity), according to the liturgical position of this third prayer, and, finally, according to the epithets used in it for the Person to Whom it is addressed, it would be natural to expect the continuation: "O Holy Spirit," or "Holy Comforter," or "King of Truth," or at least some name of the third hypostasis of the Most Holy Trinity; so natural in fact, that when you hear this prayer you involuntarily hear something of this sort and remain convinced that it is addressed to the Holy Spirit. But in fact there is no such thing. Here is what follows in the prayer which we have interrupted:

. . . O Christ our God; Who hast broken the unbreakable bonds of death and the bars of hell; Who hast healed a multi-

tude of evil spirits; Who hast taken upon Thyself for our sakes
an innocent death . . .

—all this being addressed to our Lord Jesus Christ and not at all
to the Holy Spirit.

The age of stereotyped and more or less widespread religious
doctrines, when the dogma of the Holy Spirit had been set forth
in words only superficially, and then only to the extent that the
economical activity of the Spirit was tied to that of the Father
and the Son, was followed by an age which applied to the Holy
Spirit concepts invented for the Son. But it is significant that
the personal individuality of the third hypostasis was still represented only formally, by the word ἐκπόρευσις, "procession," a term
without any concrete meaning.

And so it went on. The theological recipe for speaking of the
Spirit on the model of what had been said of the Word (the
recipe, really, for creating simply a shadowy outline of the Word)
held sway in one way or another in Orthodox thought. Yet at the
same time, in the deserts of Thebes and Palestine, the Spirit was
manifesting Himself to individual saints—to those almost supra-
human pinnacles of the Church—and through them, through
their souls and bodies, was manifesting Himself also to the people around them. But the non-Orthodox fell into obvious false
doctrine when they attempted to understand the Comforter by
force, to contain Him (the Spirit of Freedom) by force within
the cage of philosophical concepts. Instead of the Spirit they
laid hold on the seductive, pseudomystical experience of the
soul, which is plunged in the gloomy underworld of this life, and
which clutches at the forces of darkness as if they were the angels of light. This proves once more that the Spirit is known
only negatively outside asceticism and discipline.

The mystics of recent times (who have always had a lively interest in pneumatology) were in no better position. Having ver-
bally differentiated the hypostases of the Spirit and the Son they
usually treated them as identical in fact, ascribing to the Holy

Spirit everything that had already been said about the Son, and in addition, confusing the Spirit with Sofia.

Wherein lies the personal uniqueness of the Holy Spirit? People have talked about this a great deal but nothing much has been said. Basil the Great concedes that "the figure of 'procescession' remains inexplicable," and consequently makes no effort to throw light upon it. It is notable that even Mark of Ephesus, the remarkable defender of Orthodoxy against Catholic leanings (against attempts to rationalize dogma and to forcibly explain— as if to a philosopher—that which does not come within the realm of philosophy), the man on whose tombstone George the Scholar inscribed the following epitaph:

Bishop of Ephesus, the sun of the whole land, a fire which consumed heresy, the guiding light of devout souls . . .

—this same Mark of Ephesus writes "to the Orthodox Christians": "We then, together with Justin the Philosopher and Martyr, say that as—ὡς—the Son is from the Father, so also— οὕτως—the Holy Spirit is from the Father; but they—the Greco-Latins—do say with the Latins that the Son proceeds without mediation—ἀμέσως—but the Holy Spirit mediately—ἐμμέσως— from the Father; we, together with John Damascene and all the holy fathers, know no difference between origin and procession; but they, together with Thomas, distinguish two kinds of procession—mediate and without mediation." Moreover this is not the only testimony; it would be possible to cite many similar assertions. I will only mention Gregory of Nyssa, who speaks of the "incomprehensibility of the procession of the Holy Spirit" (*Catechetical Instruction*, 3).

Theosophical speculation either has not said all that it has to say, or else it has become confused in its distinction of origin and procession; that is, if it has not resorted to the Catholic "Filioque"—that naïve invention of superfluous devotion and abortive theology. Need we name names? Let us leave them alone; let the inventors of various theories about the Holy Spirit sleep peacefully in the earth until the time when these questions will have resolved themselves without our efforts. It would be too naïve to seek the reason for this two-thousand-year-old silence in a lack of theological perspicacity. And does perspicacity really count when it is a matter of faith? *"Ex nihilo nihil"* applies more than anything to theology, as an experimental science. If now there is no full understanding of the Holy Spirit as a hypostasis, if there are no personal pneumatic manifestations (except in exceptional cases with exceptional people), then it is also impossible to work out a formula. Formulae grow on the soil of ordinary, everyday ecclesiastical life, on the basis of common, as it were permanent elements, and not out of an adaptation to isolated, special points in the spiritual life. Of course, everything in the Holy Church is a miracle: the Sacrament is a miracle, the prayer for holy water is a miracle, every icon is a miracle, and every chanted canticle is nothing but a miracle. Yes, everything is a miracle in the Church, for whatever is a part of her life is blessed, and the blessing of God is the one thing worthy of the name "miracle." But all this is a constant miracle. Then there are also in the Church less frequent signs (or "wonders," in the more usual sense of the word), and the rarer they are the further removed they are from verbal expression. A formula cannot be created for such wonders, since every formula is the formula for something repeated. Except for certain separate moments when believers were all united (and this is the whole point) in the Holy Spirit or were about to enter into Him, this state did not become the mainstream of the Church's life.

But in associations or groups where the experience of the Spirit appeared as a norm, sectarianism inevitably arose—taking the term sectarianism in the broad sense as including every pseudospiritual enthusiasm and pseudomystical, mental (not spiritual) excitement in gatherings of rejoicing people.

Let us begin to look at the writings of the holy fathers, especially the ascetic writings, where the spiritual life is more clearly expressed. Then we will see something quite typical: Little is said of the Father, rather more is said of the Son of God, while the Holy Spirit is mentioned most of all. And in all this it is impossible to dismiss the impression that the holy ascetics have a very keen apprehension of the Son of God as an independent hypostasis; He is so close to their understanding that He even tends to obscure the Father; they also know about the Father; but they know little or nothing about the Holy Spirit as a hypostasis. If by their indecisiveness and silence, the dogmatic fathers reveal an inner want of confidence in the question of the Holy Spirit as well as their inadequate knowledge of Him as a hypostasis, then by their abundance of words, the ascetic fathers reveal the same state of mind even more clearly. For them, in a practical, living way, the Holy Spirit is "the Spirit of Christ," the "Spirit of God," a sanctifying, purifying, and impersonal power of God. Not for nothing did they gradually and imperceptibly begin later to speak of "grace" (i.e., of something completely impersonal) instead of the Holy Spirit. Usually it is not the Holy Spirit that is known, but His gracious energies, His powers, His acts and activities. "Spirit," "spiritual," "spirit-bearing," "spirituality," are sprinkled all through the works of the holy fathers. But it is also evident that these words, "Spirit," "spiritual," etc., are related to special states initiated in the believer by God, and rarely, if ever, do they indicate a personal independent existence of the third hypostasis of the Most Holy Spirit. Essentially, the holy fathers speak at length not about the Holy Spirit but about a holy spirit, and it is hard to draw the line and distinguish when they are speaking of the Spirit or when of spirit. The general impression is that there is an unperceived transition from the Spirit, through Spirit, to spirit. At best there is an inference of the Spirit from the spirit of God. It is true that our spirituality is from the Spirit, just as our adoption by God is from the Son and our creative personality is from the Father. But could it ever enter the head of anyone reading the works of the holy fathers—let alone the heads of the fathers themselves—to doubt or be confused about whether the Son or just a son was being considered? the Creator or just a creator?

Furthermore, in trying to prove the consubstantiality of the Spirit with the Father and the Son, the fathers pointed to the similarity of the sin-propitiating activity of the Holy Spirit and the Son. This means that even in their understanding of the grace-bestowing activity of each hypostasis, there was no precise line of demarcation in the thought of the holy fathers. Here Macarius the Great differs little from Isaac of Syria, John the Ascender differs little from Ephraim of Syria. Of course I am generalizing and simplifying; of course I am only sketching in outlines, and then not with a fine point but with a broad brush; of course what has been said here is by no means the whole story. Unquestionably from time to time elements of another sort of understanding—of the acceptance of a personal Holy Spirit— come to the fore; but these elements are preliminary, they are not spelled out. Moreover, it would be ridiculous to see in this silence a personal shortcoming on the part of the holy fathers, or to see it as a consequence of their insufficient depth or purity. The holy fathers shine out of the murky abyss of the ages, out of the obscurity of history, like living, incorporeal stars, as the God-contemplating eyes of the Church. But the time has not yet come for us—just as it had not come even for those bright eyes— to see that One by Whom all Created Being will be comforted and cheered. The "fullness of time" had not come then, just as it has not yet come. The holy fathers were longing and wait-ing for it, just as the righteous ones of the Old Testament were waiting for knowledge of the Son of God. The whole life of pre-Christian antiquity—religion, science, art, society, even in-dividual states of mind—all were based wholly upon the revela-tion of the Father, upon experiences of the Father, the Creator of all, upon the conscious or half-forgotten Covenant with Him. The whole concept of the world and life was the development of a single category of thought, the category of fatherhood, genesis, parenthood, whatever it may have been called (cf. V. V. Rozanov). It is just as impossible to clarify the vague features of their knowledge as it is to force an underexposed photographic negative to become clear; if we hold it in the projector for more than a certain length of time, then the whole picture begins to be "veiled," to be covered over with a gray haze, a shroud. In wishing to comprehend the Spirit without holiness, our thought is "veiled" in the same way. The same thing happens, incidentally, with the school of "new understanding."

The closer we come to the End of History the more new, hitherto almost unnoticed rosy rays of the coming Undarkening Day appear on the summits of Holy Church. Already Simeon the New Theologian speaks in a new tone, somehow in a different way than the ascetics of antiquity. These tones are "playing" on our terrestrial Church just as the rising sun plays on the Feast of Feasts. St. Seraphim of Sarov and the great ones of the Optino Monastery (the startsi Leo, Leonid, and Macarius, and especially Ambrose) concentrate in themselves, as in a fiery focus, the whole of popular sanctity. And half of these saints are not monks in the strict sense of the word. The Coming Day is seen through them as through a telescope. Their whole coloring is something new, special, apocalyptic. Only the blind could fail to see this. To go further without them, instead of in their footsteps, would be rashness and stupidity; it would mean to try willfully to dismiss the established course of history from our own age. It would mean to reject the word of the Lord Jesus: "Which one of you, if he tried, could add even one cubit to his own growth?" (Matthew 6:27; Luke 12:25)

But now consider: the whole of our life-understanding, the whole of our science—and I am speaking not of our theological science but of science in general, of the scientific spirit—the whole of it is built on the idea of the Logos, on the idea of the God-Word; and indeed, not science alone, but all of life, the whole make-up of our souls. We all cogitate under the category of law, under the standard of harmony. This idea of logicality, of logism (derived from Logos), of "letters," frequently perverted beyond recognition, is the basic nerve of every living thing, of everything genuine in our intellectual and moral and aesthetic life. The religious premise of our knowledge is the single, universal, all-embracing common "Law" of the world, the hypostatic name of Father, the Divine Providence without Whose will not even a hair falls from the head, Who cultivates the lilies of the field and feeds the birds of the heavens; the God Who exhausts Himself in the creation of the world and in His care of it. Without this premise, formulated here in a more or less abstract way, there is no science. "The uniformity of the laws of nature": this is the postulate without which all science is empty sophistry. But this postulate can become a psychological reality only by faith in that Word Whom the Mystery-contemplating Eagle (St. John the Divine) proclaims in the first verses of the Easter Gospel: "In the beginning was the Word, and the Word was with God, and the Word was God. He was with God from the beginning; all things through Him were made, and without Him nothing was made; in Him was life, and the life was the light of man; and the light shines in the darkness, and the darkness does not overcome it" (John 1:1–5). Here are the "fundamentals of science"; and if we reject them, then a cruel reward is inescapable. The science that is built on shifting and marshy sands will fall.

The realm of science is worldly lawfulness, the good order and fitness of the world, the κόσμος of creation. This law of the universe, this worldly number, this harmony of spheres bestowed upon created being, is entirely rooted in the God-Word, in the unique Person of the Son, and in the gifts which are His.

But everything which rests not on this one Person, everything which is connected with the express gifts of the Holy Spirit, is not a subject of knowledge for our science—the science of the Logos taken alone. Inspiration, creativity, freedom, asceticism, beauty, the value of flesh and blood, religion, and much else only dimly sensed is from time to time described, arranged in order.

But these things stand outside the ways and means of scientific investigation, because the basic premise of science is, of course, the premise of relatedness, the premise of uninterruptedness, of progression. The idea of lawfulness in its essential form is absolutely inapplicable to these manifestations of the Spirit. Here there is interruptedness, and interruptedness goes beyond the boundaries of our science, is not connected with the basic ideas of our contemporary world view and abolishes it. Perhaps the latest investigations and studies in the area of the idea of interruptedness (especially in mathematics and logistics) are a hint of the nearness of the End.

One-sided knowledge of the first hypostasis created the religion and life of antiquity, created its "substantial," organic world view, in the light of which the immediate generation of the phenomenal result by its metaphysical cause came to be known.

One-sided knowledge of the second hypostasis gave birth to the religion and life of the new age, gave birth to its "lawful," logical world view, having as its goal the regulation of phenomena by their ideal form.

And, finally, the free striving for beauty and love for the Whole are deviations from science, typologically foretelling an immortal life and a holy, resurrected body. Holy fasts are tokens of the transfiguration of the body; the holy relics which we kiss are gleams of resurrection; the holy sacraments are the sources of deification. Here are the pledges and revelations of the Kingdom to come. But this Kingdom is coming to individuals, and will come universally only when the Comforter is known and will be known as a hypostasis, only when, by this knowledge, the "Threefold Unity" which illuminates the soul is apprehended and will be apprehended; only when

> Each soul is enlivened by the Holy Spirit
> And is elevated by purity—
> Is transfigured by the Threefold Unity
> Into a sacred mystery.

First, the sacred, white-haired mysteriousness of ancient science; then the moral, serious strictness of the new; finally, the joyous light wingedness of the future "science of happiness." . . .

My winged one! I am scribbling down thoughts which I feel more than I can express. As if some fabric, as if some substance was being woven out of the tiniest rays of the stars into the warp of the world . . . we are waiting for something. Here lies the lack, here lies the reason for the languishing of the soul longing to be finished and to be with Christ. And something will come; but "it does not yet appear what we shall be." But the more keenly that which is being prepared is felt, the closer and more real becomes the bond with Mother Church, the lighter and simpler it is to endure out of love the dirt that is flung at her. That which will come to be will come in her and through her and not otherwise. With quiet joy I am waiting for that which will be, and the Nunc Dimittis is chanted and resounds for days at a time in the heart that is reconciled. When that time begins, when the Great Easter of the world dawns, then all human disputes will end. I do not know if this will be soon, or if there are still a million years to wait, but my heart is calm, because hope leads me wholly to this faith. The efforts of people of "the new religious understanding" (Merezhkovsky, Gippius, also A. Byely and N. A. Berdyaev) to seize the Holy Spirit by force are utterly alien to me. In their fixed desire to abolish time and end the period of grace, they cease to see that which is in front of their eyes, which is given to them, and which they do not know and do not understand inwardly; in pursuing everything they are deprived of that which is. And more than this we are not in a position to assimilate, because our heart is not yet pure, the heart of created being is not yet pure, and being impure it would burn up in proximity to the Most Pure and Holy One. If only for a short time a calm sobriety would return to them, then perhaps they would see—these people of false understanding—that they have no solid ground under their feet and that they are speaking sterile words, words which they themselves are beginning to believe. Something of this sort happened with Leo Tolstoy; he himself created a scheme for an unblessed, pretended Church order and then later on destroyed it; which was easy enough for him to do, of course. Satisfied by the victory over the chimera which he had created, he left the blessed though dirty soil and (wholly by way of rational, self-asserting intelligence) went into the wilderness of "pleasant" words, which he himself was unable to fulfill and which simply disturb others. But then Church order is so beautiful that even the aesthetic participant, by an immediate sense of taste, can not bear the stench of a project like Tolstoy's. To compose one's own "fifth Gospel" . . . is it really possible to think of anything more tasteless!

Nevertheless, a true idea lies at the base both of Tolstoyism and of the "new understanding." Take only the fact that the ancients prayed to the Father, while in the whole course of our epoch people pray for the most part to the Son. And if they pray at all to the Spirit, then it is more an expectation of Him than having Him face to face, more a grieving for the Comforter than a rejoicing by Him before the Father in the Son. I know that it is possible to collect all sorts of quotations which assert just the opposite; I could even cite them myself. But I am speaking about the typical, if also about something which is almost undemonstrable. It is for just this reason that I am writing "letters" to you instead of composing an "article"; I fear the making of assertions and prefer to question. But the typical attitude to the Holy Spirit, it seems to me, is precisely an expectation, a hope; a gentle and conciliatory hope.

Undoubtedly the Old Testament also has its Word-manifestations and Spirit-manifestations—logophanies and pneumatophanies; there, especially in the Pentateuch, it is possible to find hints of the Word and the Spirit. But they are so imprecise and are so inconsistent with the general background of the Old Testament that only in the light of the Incarnate Word can we find their meaning; only by having in mind the dogma of the Trinity

can we see, through this "eye," the first glimmerings in the Old
Testament of the knowledge to come. Just try to convince a
Chinese of the dogma of the Trinity on the basis of the Old
Testament alone! I am not at all sure that it would be possible
to explain to him when the hypostatic Word and Spirit are being spoken of and when the writer is speaking of the activity
of the Father alone. In any case it is certain that for any un-
prejudiced reader the doctrine of the Word and, even more, the
doctrine of the Spirit stand out in the Old Testament books far
less prominently than the doctrine of God the Father. And this
is understandable, for the prophets did not have the fullness
of concrete experience of the Word and the Spirit. At best a
new revelation was expected. But look now at the New Testament. How solidly does the doctrine of the Father and the Son
appear here before everyone, and in comparison how little developed is the doctrine of the Spirit. The idea of the Spirit is
occasionally almost dissolved into the idea of spiritual gifts. The
powers and gifts of the Holy Spirit, which dwell within people
(isn't this significant?), obscure the Spirit Himself as a hypostasis. We are spirits, but only if we are in the Spirit. This "but"
is often forgotten, however. Yet is it ever possible to say that
the God-sonhood of men in the Son of God can be compared
to the Son's own existence? While only fools or those who are
spiritually seduced (sectarians of all sorts) can confuse "son"
with "Son," it is sometimes very easy to confuse "spirit" with
"Spirit." Quite often the same passage may be read as referring
either to spirit or to the Spirit.

Of course, other passages in the epistles of Paul the Apostle
reveal the hypostatic existence of the Holy Spirit to the conscience in a flash of lightning. "All who are lead by the Spirit of
God," the Apostle testifies to the Gentiles, "are the sons of God,
—and when we cry out 'Abba, Father,' it is the Spirit Himself
bearing witness with our spirit that we are the children of God"
(Romans 8:14–17). And again, "And because you are sons, God
has sent His Spirit into your hearts, crying out 'Abba, Father' "

(Galatians 4:6), and ". . . the Spirit strengthens us in our weakness. We ourselves do not know what we should pray for, but the Spirit Himself intercedes for us with sighs too deep for words" (Romans 6:26–27). It is certain that these "intercessions" of the Spirit, these "sighs too deep for words," these exclamations of the Comforter, these "Abba's," were known to the apostles and have been known also to other holy men and women. But it is equally certain that these insights, these instants and moments of spiritual fullness, these flashes of light from a distant, complete knowledge, remain, so far, as something special, as something accessible only to exceptional people in exceptional circumstances, rather like the messianic insights of the Old Testament. Just as Christ-bearers existed before Christ, so also Spirit-bearers exist before the full descent of the Spirit. The righteous ones of old "died in faith, not having received what was promised, but only having seen it from afar, and having rejoiced and said to themselves that they were strangers and aliens on earth. For those who speak thus show that they are seeking a homeland" (Hebrews 11:13–14). This was what the ancient Christians were like. "By faith they conquered kingdoms, established justice, received promises, stopped the mouths of lions, quenched the force of fire, escaped sharp swords, strengthened themselves in weakness, were mighty in war, drove off foreign armies. Women received their dead by resurrection. Some were tormented, refusing to accept release, that they might rise again to a better life. Others suffered insults and beatings, even chains and imprisonment. They were stoned, they were sawn in two, they were subjected to torture, they died by the sword. They wandered about in sheepskins and goatskins, suffering want, affliction, and abuse. Those of whom the whole world was not worthy wandered over deserts and mountains, and lived in dens and caves of the earth. And all these, having borne witness to the faith, did not receive what was promised, because God foresaw something better for us, that apart from us they should not be made perfect" (Hebrews 11:33–40).

Knowledge of Christ flickered before them, they almost touched Christ. They saw their salvation in their hope (cf. Romans 8:24). But the days must be fulfilled before their hope can be realized and the invisible become visible. They knew how to wait and endure. "Hope which already sees before it that which it is expecting is not hope, for if something is already visible to someone, how can he then be expecting it? But when we hope for that which we do not see, then we wait patiently" (Romans 8:24-25). They, the great and holy ones, did not see Christ so that "apart from us they should not attain perfection," but He was almost known by them—at special times and by the purest minds. The tremor of Eternal Life quivered on their faces at such times; the Spirit-Dove had brushed their hearts with its snowy wing. Just as the concept of God the Word trembled before the forefathers and prophets, so also the knowledge of the Holy Spirit trembles before the holy ones of our own day, and almost touches them. But here too the fullness of time must be accomplished; here too the high points of mankind have to wait in order "not to attain perfection apart from us." Their hearts are purified, their chambers swept and made ready for the reception of the Comforter. But ours are full of filthiness. And so the higher await the lower, the seers await the blind, the holy await the sinful, the living await the dead, the spiritual await the carnal, the people who go before and even warn the rest await the tardy and the stragglers. Only in isolated moments is the curtain of the future folded back before them.

"So that apart from us they should not attain perfection . . ." This, too, explains why, in spite of their depth, the doctrines of the Holy Spirit which have appeared in the history of the Church have found no response and have remained isolated. It also explains why those sides of Christian life which are pre-eminently connected with the Holy Spirit—Christian freedom, adoption as sons, creativity, and spirituality—have been changed or perverted as soon as some heresy has tried to bring them into life prematurely or willfully. Indeed the wordy people of "new religious understanding," from the first century to the twentieth, have always brought condemnation on themselves; the rose bushes which they have planted have always brought thorns and thistles; the "new" understanding has always turned out to be not supra-ecclesiastical, as it has claimed to be, but antiecclesiastical and anti-Christian, i.e., ecclesiastically rebellious. Whoever possesses the Holy Spirit as the saints have possessed Him will see the obvious foolishness of claiming anything beyond this. But in case of complete unspirituality it is all too easy for people to fall into seductive self-magnification and to replace their spirituality (the spirit-bearing characteristic) by a subjectively human, mental creativity, and then, by a diabolical hallucination. Ecstasy and enthusiasm, dreamy prophesying and a sombre exaltedness have been accepted as the joy of the Holy Spirit; and in addition, sin, when left to itself, has acquired "freedom." The quest for the "two infinities" begins, and after the quest—submersion in "both abysses": in the upper abyss of gnostic theory and in the lower abyss of sectarian practice. Yet this has been given out as the fullness of the blessed life. I repeat, this thread of pseudoreligious thought, always claiming to be "new," runs parallel to the whole of Church history.

A dispassionate study will show that in general there is no firm ground for speculation about the Holy Spirit, nor for assertions about a new understanding in man. And if there were ground for such speculation, if there were a real experience of life with the Holy Spirit, could what is happening now in Created Being take place? Hope in the Comforter has not come to an end in the depths of the Church's understanding. But beside ecclesiastical exotericism there is a kind of ecclesiastical esotericism—there is a hope which must not be spoken about too openly. Others do not understand or feel this because they are not in the Church and because they do not understand the spirit of the Church. They lay bare the undemonstrable—because they are without shame. An unbroken chain of shameless heretics of "new under-

standing" runs through the whole of Church history. This unbroken chain of heresy also helps to clarify the hidden main
artery of the Church's life.

But within the Church, too, there have been attempts to speak
clearly about the Holy Spirit. Here is something which seems
very instructive to me: St. Gregory the Theologian, in his *Dogmatic Poems*, speaks of the gradualness of the revelation of the
Trihypostatic Divinity and sees in this a pledge of new revelations:

> Whoever wishes to find the Divinity of the heavenly Spirit
> in the pages of the law inspired by God will see many paths
> joining together, if only he wishes to see them, if only he has
> in some way pleased the pure Spirit in his heart, and if his
> mind is keenly perceptive. But if anyone demands plain words
> of the all-loving Divinity, then let him know that his demand
> is unreasonable, since until the Divinity of Christ was mani-
> fested to the greater part of mortals it was not deemed neces-
> sary to impose such a burden on hearts so feeble. The perfected
> word was not appropriate for beginners. After all, who begins
> by showing the full glare of fire to eyes that are still weak, or by
> filling them with excessive light? It is better gradually to ac-
> custom them to the bright glare in order not to harm the in-
> struments of light themselves. So also the word, having re-
> vealed the whole Divinity of our God and King, began to
> shine its light upon the great glory of Christ, manifesting it
> first to a few wise ones among the people, and later, having
> revealed the Divinity of the Son more clearly, illuminating for
> us also the Divinity of the radiant Spirit. Even for these revela-
> tions the word poured out little enough light, leaving the
> greatest part up to us, to whom the Spirit was later imparted
> abundantly and in fiery tongues, revealing the manifest signs
> of His Divinity, when the Saviour ascended from the earth
> (*Third Word on the Holy Spirit*, Gregory the Theologian).

The same thought is expressed still more powerfully in the *Thirty-first Word on the Holy Spirit*:

> In the course of the ages there have been two significant conversions—μεταθέσεις—in the life of man, called the two Testaments, or, according to the well-known saying of Scripture, the Shakings of the Nations—σεισμοῖς (Haggai 2:7). One led from idols to the Law, the other from the Law to the Gospel. I preach the good news of a third Shaking—of a death from this world and an entry into that other firm and enduring world beyond. But the same thing happened with both Testaments: neither of them was introduced suddenly or accepted on first sight. Why? It was necessary for us to know that we were being persuaded, not compelled. For what is involuntary is also unstable. A stream or a plant cannot be long restrained by force. But what is accepted willingly is both more stable and more reliable. What is done involuntarily is the work of one who is exercising force; what is done voluntarily is our own work. The former is a sign of compulsive authority, the latter is a sign of the justice of God. Thus God has commanded that good need not be done to those who are unwilling to receive it, and has commanded us to be good to those who wish good.

Thus St. Gregory the Theologian explains the gradualness in the replacement of idols, sacrifices, and circumcision. The holy father continues:

> I also wish to compare Theology with this gradual process, only in the opposite way, since in life conversion is achieved through change, but in theology perfection is achieved through augmentation. The Old Testament clearly preached the Father, but did not speak with the same clarity about the Son; the New Testament revealed the Son and gave some indication of the Divinity of the Spirit; now the Spirit dwells within

us, giving us the clearest knowledge of His being. It was not safe to preach the Son clearly before the Divinity of the Father had been confessed, nor was it safe—I express myself somewhat boldly—to burden us with the teaching about the Holy Spirit before the Son had been acknowledged, and to subject us to the danger of losing all our capabilities, like people who are stuffed with food eaten immoderately, or who fix eyes that are still too weak on the light of the sun. It was necessary that the light of the Trinity illumine those enlightened by gradual increments—ταῖς κατὰ μέρος προσθήκαις—as David says "by ascents," by transitions from glory to glory, by successive stages. For this very reason, I think, the Spirit descended gradually on the disciples, accommodating Himself to their strength. At the beginning of the Gospel, through the Passion and the Ascension, He first achieves manifestations through them (Matthew 10:20), then He gives Himself to them through a breathing upon them (John 20:22), and then He appears in tongues of fire (Acts 2:3). Even Jesus expounds Him gradually, as you will see yourself in an attentive reading. "I will pray to the Father," he says, "and He will send another Comforter to you" (John 14:16), so that they would not consider Him a rival of God speaking by some other authority. Then, even though he uses the phrase "He will send" He also adds "in my name" (John 14:26), and, setting aside the phrase "I will pray," He retains the phrase "He will send." But then He says, "I will send" (John 16:7), revealing His own nature. And then he says: "He will come," indicating the power of the Spirit. You see here a series of illuminations that gradually shine upon us, and that is the form of Theology—φωτισμούς κατὰ μέρος ἡμὶν ἐλλάμποντας καὶ τάξιν θεολογίας—which it is best for us to observe, neither suddenly putting everything into words nor concealing everything to the end; since the former is imprudent and the latter godless. While it is possible to strike others in the first way, we only alienate ourselves in the latter. I will also add to what I have said something which, even

though it may have already occurred to others, I still consider
as the fruit of my own mind. Even after the Saviour had taught
much to the disciples, there was still something which, as He
Himself said, the disciples (perhaps for the reason which I
gave above) could not then "bear" (John 16:12) and which
therefore He was hiding from them. Again, the Saviour says
that we will be instructed in all things by the Spirit when He
has come (John 16:13). From this too I deduce the Divinity
of the Spirit, which was clearly revealed after the Restoration
of the Saviour to life—ἀποκατάστασιν—when this knowledge
had become timely and appropriate, when they had begun to
receive the miracle with disbelief.

St. Gregory the Theologian asserts a gradualness in the historical manifestation of the Spirit; but still another side of the
question must be considered. The subsequently interrupted historical revelation of the Spirit, as well as the interrupted revelation of the Kingdom of God, both have a historically gradual as
well as an eschatologically delayed manifestation. Otherwise it
would be impossible to understand precisely how the final state,
the illumination of created nature, the casting out of death, in a
word, the "age to come," is to be distinguished from the preliminary and expectant state, i.e., from "this age," in which
death still reigns supreme.

Thus the ideas of the Kingdom of God and the Holy Spirit
have a formal similarity. But the similarity is not only formal.
The doctrine of the Holy Spirit and the doctrine of the Kingdom
of the Father (as common ideas) certainly have their roots in
the Gospel, but with the apostle Paul they receive also a verbal
identification. "The Kingdom of God," he writes to the Romans,
"is righteousness and peace and joy in the Holy Spirit" (Romans
14:17)—'Εν Πνεύματι 'Αγίῳ—"in" or "concerning the Holy
Spirit," i.e., in the righteousness, peace, and joy which are produced by the Holy Spirit. The subjective state of righteousness,
peace, and joy produced by the Holy Spirit is that same Kingdom

of God which is "within us" (Luke 17:21)—the almost visible mustard seed of faith sown in the soul. But in germinating and growing in the field of what is mine and only mine, in the region of subjectivity, the sprout of the seed of faith also becomes objective, cosmic, universal. Divine worship and the sacraments are the external manifestations of the Kingdom of God in ecclesiastical life, while the working of miracles and the recovery of sight reveal that same Kingdom in the personal life of the saint. And we all invoke the final coming of the Kingdom—of the Holy Spirit—every day. For according to St. Gregory of Nyssa, the Lord's Prayer in St. Matthew 6:10 and St. Luke 11:12 had an important variant—which does not exist in the modern text. It was read both as: "Our Father . . . thy Kingdom come . . ."— ἐλθέτω ἡ βασιλεία σου—and as: "Our Father . . . thy Holy Spirit come upon us and cleanse us . . ."—ἐλθέτω τὸ ἅγιον Πνεῦμα σου ἐφ' ἡμᾶς, καὶ καθαρισάτω ἡμᾶς.

From a comparison of these variations of the same passage, Gregory of Nyssa concludes that there is an identity of meaning in the phrases "Holy Spirit" and "Kingdom of God," i.e., that "the Holy Spirit is the Kingdom"—Πνεῦμα τὸ ἅγιον βασιλεία ἐστί. And later, basing his thought on this last conclusion, St. Gregory develops the remarkable doctrine of the Spirit as "the Kingdom of the Father and the Unction of the Son."

A kingdom must have a king. The Father is the King and this means that within the Holy Spirit there resides the kingly might of the Father Himself. And furthermore, the Son, eternally begotten of the Father and consubstantial with Him, also eternally receives in the Holy Spirit the kingly glory belonging to the Father. The Spirit crowns the Son with glory. This is the anointing activity of the Spirit, and if in relation to the Father He is the Kingdom, then in relation to the Son He is the Unction, the Chrism. Gregory of Nyssa once more verifies this conclusion by an examination of the well-known messianic psalm: "God, thy God, hath anointed thee with the oil of gladness more than thy associates" (Psalms 45:7). The Anointing One is the Father; the Anointed is the Son; the Unction itself, or Oil of Gladness, is the Holy Spirit (Gregory of Nyssa, *Against Apollinarius*, 52).

Oil was always a symbol of gladness, and the Holy Spirit is the Comforter, Paraclete, the One Who gladdens. He is the True Chrism—the Chrism of chrisms—the Chrism which softens the pain of the wounded, exhausted, and broken heart.

The very name "Christ" ($X\rho\iota\sigma\tau\acute{o}s$ = Messiah = Anointed) contains, therefore, a hint of the hypostatic triunity of the Divinity. "The confession of this Name," says Gregory, "contains the doctrine of the Holy Trinity, because in this Name each of the Persons in Whom we believe is suitably represented. In it we recognize the One Who has anointed, the One Who has been anointed, and the One through Whom the anointing has been accomplished" (Gregory of Nyssa, *Against Apollinarius*, 52). The relationship of the Spirit to the Son as Anointer is indicated still more definitely in the speech of the apostle Peter to Cornelius: "God anointed Jesus of Nazareth with the Holy Spirit and with power" (Acts 10:38). By virtue of this anointing He, being from eternity both Christ and King, is "eternally arrayed in the kingly glory of the Spirit, which also constitutes His anointing" (*Against Apollinarius*, 53).

Thus if previously the mutual relations of the hypostases had been defined through love, through the giving up of self, through the intradivine self-emptying of the hypostases, through eternal humility and kenosis, so now, on the contrary, they are defined as an eternal mutual restoration and affirmation, or as a glorification and kingly rule. "Eternally glorious is the Father, Who existed before all ages, and the glory of the Father is the everlasting Son (in giving Himself to the Son the Father finds His glory in Him), just as the glory of the Son is the Spirit of Christ" (*Against Apollinarius*, 53).

The first moment of the Divine inner life (as considered above) consisted in the mutual exchange of tragic, sacrificial love, in the mutual self-emptying, self-impoverishment, and self-abnegation of the three hypostases; the second moment, (being considered now) is, as it were, the current running in the opposite direction, almost inconceivable in visual terms to those of us who have not received the Spirit and who know intimately only the God of Sacrifice. Restoration has not yet begun for created being, nor the glory for which it is waiting, groaning and travailing (cf. Romans 8:19-23). But in the supratemporal order of the life of the Trinity this moment of responsive love, of a triumphant love which glorifies the Beloved and restores Him, is eternal. It is the transmittal of glory from hypostasis to hypostasis. "The Son is glorified by the Spirit, the Father is glorified by the Son. On the other hand the Son receives glory from the Father, and the Only-begotten becomes the glory of the Spirit, because how is the Father glorified, if not by the true glory of the Only-begotten, and in what way is the Son glorified, if not in the glory of the Spirit?" Thus the Holy Spirit is Χρίσμα βασιλείας— the Unction of the Kingdom; He is ᾿Αξίωμα βασιλείας—of Royal Rank. But these titles are applied to Him for His activity within the Trinity; He is not a symptom of the Divine existence, not the nature or an attribute of Divinity, but a "living, real, and personal kingdom," βασιλεία δὲ ζῶσα καὶ οὐσιώδης καὶ ἐνυπόστατος, πνεῦμα τὸ ἅγιον—a Personality, having His own unconditional functions —as the third Person of the Holy Trinity, i.e., as the Kingdom of the Father and the Unction of the Son.

A similar doctrine of the anointing activity of the Spirit was developed by St. Irenaeus of Lyons. But I shall pass over Bishop Irenaeus and go on to St. Maximus the Confessor.

According to St. Maximus the Confessor, the first words of the Our Father

contain references to the Father, to the Name of the Father, and to the Kingdom of the Father, so that from the very beginning of the prayer we might be taught to honor the Trinity, to invoke It, and to worship It. For the Name of God the Father, which exists essentially and hypostatically, is the Only-begotten Son of the Father. And the Kingdom of God the Father, existing essentially and hypostatically, is the Holy Spirit. For that which Matthew calls here the Kingdom another evangelist calls the Spirit, saying: "thy Holy Spirit come and cleanse us." For the Father has this Name not as something acquired recently, and we understand the Kingdom not just as a quality perceived in Him. He did not ever begin to be; nor does He begin to be a Father or a King. Eternally existent, He is eternally both Father and King, there being no beginning whatsoever either to His existence or to His Fatherhood or Kingship. But if He is eternally existent and is eternally both Father and King, then this means that both the Son and the Holy Spirit dwell eternally with the Father essentially and hypostatically; they exist by Him and in Him by nature, above motivation and command; they did not come into being after Him according to the law of causation. The Persons of the Divinity coexist; we are not permitted to think that any one Person within the Trinity came into being after the others.

Such is the doctrine of St. Maximus the Confessor.

All the perplexities, difficulties, and torments of our life are gathered around the Holy Spirit; yet all our hopes are found in His revelation. So then let us pray together for the manifestation of the Holy Spirit, let us entreat Him together, using the mysterious invocation of Simeon the New Theologian:

Come, true light. Come, life eternal. Come, hidden mystery. Come, nameless treasure. Come, that which is beyond words. Come, Person Who flees from human comprehension. Come, unceasing courage. Come, true hope of all the saved. Come, resurrection of the dead. Come, O mighty One; thou Who art eternally creating, reforming, and changing all things by a mere sign. Come, thou wholly invisible, sacred, and intangible One. Come, thou Who dwellest eternally immovable even though thou dost bestir thyself hourly to come to us who languish in hell while thou livest above all heavens. Come, Name that is most longed for and met with more often than any other; even though we are strictly forbidden to speak about thee and what thou art or to know what thy nature is and who thou art. Come, eternal joy. Come, garland unfading. Come, great God and Lord of our realm. Come, bond that is transparent as crystal and adorned with a precious stone. Come, impregnable refuge. Come, royal vesture and the right hand of sacred might. Come, for my wretched soul has need of thee. Come, O solitary One, to the solitary; for I am alone, as thou seest. Come, for thou hast separated me and made me alone on the earth. Come, for thou art become my need and hast caused me to have need of thee—of thee, Who art accessible to no man. Come, my life and breath. Come, consolation of my mean soul. Come, my joy, my glory, my perpetual delight. I give thanks to thee, for here, midst confusion, change, and turmoil, thou art become one with my spirit, and though thou art God above all, yet thou art become for me all in all. Inexplicable food, thou canst never be taken away. Thou art perpetually pouring thyself into the lips of my soul, and flowing abundantly in the springs of my heart. Radiant vesture that destroys demons! Purifying sacrificial offering! thou dost wash me with perpetual and holy tears, plentifully shed as a result of thy presence. I render thanks to thee, for thou art become a day without end for me and art become a sun that eclipses the sun; there is no place where thou art able to hide, thou fillest the universe with thy glory. Thou hast never hidden thyself from anyone, yet we are always hiding from thee— as long as we do not wish to come to thee. But where couldst thou hide thyself, when for thee there is no place of repose? Or why shouldst thou hide thyself, thou, Who hatest no one and fearest no man? Create in me now a tabernacle for thyself, kind Lord, and dwell in me, and do not tear thyself away from me as long as I live; do not withdraw from thy servant, that I may be found in thee both at my end and afterwards, and that I may reign with thee, O God, Who reignest over all. Stay, O Lord, do not leave me alone, so that when my enemies come, who constantly seek to devour my soul, they may find thee dwelling within me, and may be utterly routed and not gain a victory over me; for they will see thee within me, they will see that thou, Who art more powerful than all, hast settled in the humble dwelling-place of my soul. Truly as thou remembered me, O Lord, when I was in the world, and as thou thyself chose me without my knowledge, and separated me from the world, and placed thy glory before my eyes: so now also, preserve me through thy presence bestowed fully and forever, so that in contemplating thee from day to day I may be immortal, even though I am mortal, and that in possessing thee I may be eternally rich, even though I am poor. Then I will be more powerful than any king; in feeding and drinking on thee and in clothing myself in thee every hour, I will enjoy an unspeakable, glorious rapture. Since thou art every good, and every adornment, and every solace, and thou also art worthy of glory, as is the Holy and Consubstantial Trinity, glorified in the Father, and the Son, and the Holy Spirit, and confessed, honored, and adored by the whole assembly of the faithful now and ever, throughout all ages. Amen (Simeon the New Theologian, *Divine Love*, 1).

Amen. Amen. Amen.

Translated by Asheleigh E. Moorhouse
August, 1963

Nikolai Fyodorovich Fyodorov

1828 - 1903

When Fyodorov died, at the age of seventy-five, not many people knew even his name. And today, sixty-two years later, he remains almost totally unknown not only in the West but also among Russians themselves. But there was something unique in the admiration he provoked among the very few who were informed of his thought. Leo Tolstoy was "proud to be his contemporary." Vladimir Solovyov wrote to him: "Your project is the first movement of the human spirit along the path of Christ. I can only recognize you as my teacher and spiritual father." Finally, Dostoevsky declared himself "in complete agreement" with Fyodorov's ideas.

He was a natural son of a Russian prince and a simple peasant woman. After completing his secondary studies in Tambov, he attended the Richelieu Law School in Odessa. For fourteen years, he taught history in the elementary schools, moving from one city to another seven times. In 1868 he joined the staff of the Rumyantsev Library in Moscow and worked there until his retirement in 1893. His erudition and his knowledge of everything related to the printed word soon became legendary among the library's visitors. He lived in almost complete poverty, distributing his meager salary among the poor. His prolific but unpublished writings were known only to a small circle of devoted friends and disciples. It was only after his death that two of them, V. Kozhevnikov and N. P. Peterson, collected and edited the amorphous mass of his manuscripts and published them in two volumes. In accordance with Fyodorov's will, the volumes had to be distributed free and not sold.

No serious study of Fyodorov's work has yet been written, and he remains a controversial figure, heretical to some, deeply Orthodox to others. George Florovsky in his *Ways of Russian Theology* defined Fyodorov's ideas as "not Christian at all." According to Zenkovsky, however, "Fyodorov's fundamental inspiration, the struggle against death, reflects so deeply the light of Christian revelation of Resurrection that this light cannot be obscured by the naïve forms" in which he sometimes expressed his views. Obviously no final word has been said about this strange "project" and it deserves further study. Above everything else, it requires an effort of understanding, for Fyodorov's writing is heavy—he had no gift of style, no philosophical clarity. But his fundamental themes—death and resurrection, cosmos and history, science and faith—are so essential, and indeed so "actual" (cf. Teilhard de Chardin) that before any judgment is passed, Fyodorov must be given a hearing.

The chapter published here is from the first volume of the "Philosophy of the Common Task."

Bibliography

Fyodorov's works are available only in Russian, in *Filosofia obshchevo dela* ("Philosophy of the Common Task"), edited by V. A. Kozhevnikov and N. P. Peterson, Vol. I, Verny, 1906; Vol. II, Moscow, 1913.

In English, nothing has been written about Fyodorov, except general evaluations of his philosophy in Zenkovsky, Vol. II, Ch. V, and Berdyaev, *The Russian Idea*, Ch. IX. London: Centenary Press, 1947.

The Restoration of Kinship
Among Mankind[1]

The cult of ancestors

EACH YEAR Christmas is a reminder to citizens and men of their sonship; this childlike feeling must govern the common task of adults. The condition of majority[2] consists in the guiding or directing of the common task by precisely this feeling of *sonship*. Orthodox baptism is the beginning of adoption, while transfiguration, before the accomplishment of the duty of executor of God's will, is the conclusion of the task of creating brotherhood through adoption. Between these two adoptions (baptism and transfiguration), there is an instruction or catechism, expressed in the parables of the publican and the Pharisee and that of the prodigal son; and there is also a repentance or remorse for the separation of oneself from all others, for the dedication of oneself solely to knowledge of self and not to knowledge of all the living and dead; a remorse, finally, for having separated knowledge from action. If "know thyself" means do not trust your fathers (i.e., tradition), do not confide in your brothers (i.e., in the

[1] Translated and abridged from the text printed in *Filosofia obshchevo dela Nikolaya Fyodorovicha Fyodorova*, ed. by V. A. Kozhevnikov and N. P. Peterson, Vol. I, 1906.

[2] Fyodorov uses this term frequently in his writing as a synonym for "maturity."

testimony of others), but believe only in yourself, know only
yourself, then this remorse will broaden the sphere of knowledge
among all the living, uniting them not just in knowledge about
the dead but also in the task of raising them from the dead. For
Christians, Shrovetide is a warning against the imaginary raising
of the dead, i.e., against the purely intellectual remembering of
the dead. The Resurrection of Christ, together with the general
raising of the dead, is the full expression of the cult of ancestors;
here, too, is the fullness of religion. To honor God and not to
offer what is due to the fathers (to reject their cult) is the same
thing as loving God, Whom we do not see, while not loving the
person nearby who is seen. Estrangement from the fathers or
renunciation of the cult of ancestors involves breaking faith not
only with our fathers but also with the God of our fathers. In our
separation from the fathers infidelity and treachery are concealed
by a professed faith in God. The class in which the cult of ancestors is being replaced by faith in God only is the learned
class, which does not realize that this replacement is a betrayal.
When it asks the question about the origin of faith in God, this
class does not admit or does not guess that the question itself
originates in infidelity to the fathers; to speak about the origin
of faith in God means to assume that in the beginning there was
no such faith, that man was created an unbeliever. One should
speak not about the origin of faith but about the origin of unbelief, which is born out of treachery. Faith by itself, faith
alone, bears witness to the separation of thought from work,
from life.

*The only true religion is the cult of ancestors, i.e., the universal
cult of all fathers considered as one father,* unseparated from the
Triune God yet unconfused with Him, in Whom the inseparability of sons and daughters from the fathers, as well as their
differentiations, is deified. Limitation of universality is already a
perversion of religion, characteristic not only of pagan religions,
which honor only the fathers or gods of their own people, or
which, in the event of political alliance, easily assimilate even

foreign gods, but characteristic also of those Christian religions which limit salvation only to ancestors who have received baptism. The separation of our forefathers from the Triune God is the same perversion as the limitation of a religion's universality. Such a separation is characteristic of Protestants and deists and, in general, of all whose God does not accept the prayers of the sons for the fathers. The cult of ancestors (or of the dead) consists in representing them as alive, or, more accurately, in their revivification through the sons by the undying Father of all. This revivification will not be realized, of course, so long as diversity reigns and knowledge is separated from action.

There is a complete course of education for sons in the annual cycle of Church Feasts. On these holidays those who are learning the obligations of a citizen and a person (i.e., obligations of a juridical and economic nature) are released from their studies, and those who deal with juridical and economic matters are released from their duties. On these holidays there is a turning of the hearts of the sons to the fathers, or to the cult of ancestors, as to the one true religion, the one true life, which releases everyone from weekday labor, replacing it by the work of the fathers, by a meteorological regulation which will be the beginning of universal regulation. In using the witness of God Himself—who calls Himself the God of the fathers—to support this truth (i.e., the fact that religion is the cult of ancestors), we have no right to separate God from our fathers, or our fathers from God; or to confuse them (i.e., to permit their absorption—which would indicate a confusion of God with nature). Not only are separation and schism condemned in the doctrine of the Trinity, but also *deism* (separating God from the fathers) and *pantheism* (confusing Him with the fathers). And both of these, it should be added, lead to atheism, i.e., to the acknowledgment, worship, and service of blind force. Worship of blind force presupposes its deification, it is an acknowledgment that it is living; but if such an acknowledgment or deification exists then this is not

religion but its perversion. A genuine worship of blind force is
the direct negation of religion, and it is expressed in worldly
(industrial) as well as in hellish (military, destructive) technol-
ogy. The negation of religion consists not in the right or good use
of blind force, but in its bad use, in submission to it under the
mask of dominion over it, in submission to it both in the process
of sexual selection (industry) and in the process of natural
selection (the destruction of foreign nations). Worship of the
God of our fathers consists in converting blind, death-dealing
power into life-bearing power by way of regulation. In contrast
with the exploitation and utilization of nature, in contrast with
its depredation by prodigal sons for the sake of their wives (a
process leading to exhaustion and death), regulation leads to the
restoration of life. To regard the earth as a dwelling place and
not as a cemetery means to cleave to one's wife and to forget
one's fathers, turning the whole earth into a snug home (or
nest); i.e., it means to regard it as an earthly and not a heavenly
body. But to regard the earth as a cemetery means to make use
of the forces which it is receiving from the heavenly bodies for
a restoration of life to the fathers, for a conversion of the
heavenly bodies into dwelling places, and for the unification of
heavenly space.

The thousand-year testing or examination of faiths,[3] and the question of the Trinity considered as a precept

The examination of faiths must lead to the cult of ancestors,
and a militantly ethical state must begin by regulation, by
direction of the blind death-dealing power which killed our

[3] The concept of an "examination of faiths" occurs repeatedly in this work.
It was undoubtedly inspired in Fyodorov's mind by the famous legend about
the Christianization of Kievan Russia during the reign of Vladimir in the
ninth century.

fathers and ancestors. The conversion of a fatal power into a vivifying one will signify the restoration of life to the fathers.

This part of my essay on the question of brotherliness can be called a continuation or revival of the age-old examination of faiths, begun even before St. Vladimir and brought about by our very position between the West and the East, by our constant collisions with the neopaganism of the West and the Neo-Judaism of the Moslem East, and also sometimes by the triumph of one or other over us. So then we are unable to reject this examination, unable not to think about it even if we wanted to. The revival of the examination of faiths (which is at the same time also an educational process) is only an attempt to end this examination, so that at last we can get down to our task. Muscovite Russia did not examine foreign faiths because its own faith (inseparable from its life) was being subjected to examination (and stood up to it). Having built a monastery in the name of the Trinity, which promoted its own unification and liberation from the Tatars as well as its renunciation of the West, Muscovite Russia did not realize but only sensed, perhaps, that *the unconfused Trinity* involves an indictment of Islam, while *the indivisible Trinity* is an indictment of the West (and its divisions). The Muscovite state was an ethically vigilant state, strictly maintaining the office of executor while weakly understanding the office of Godfather (the duty to educate) which, when it is not fulfilled, renders the office of executor (even if only in the sense of preserving a memory of the ancestors) unfruitful. The Petersburg state, continuing the work of a guardian, yet indifferent to the office of executor (having abolished the moral obligation of guard duty—cf. the liberties of the nobility), did, however, accept the office of Godfather, i.e., the duty of an educator. But its education destroyed respect for the fathers, eliminated the memory of ancestors, and did away with the office of executor. Between Petersburg and Moscow there is the same contradiction as that which exists between the worldly and the spiritual, between knowledge and faith.

Faith as a uniting in the fathers' task, as a restoration of faithfulness

In speaking about the examination of faiths we are using the word "faith" not in the new, modern scholar-class sense, i.e., not in the sense of certain representations about God, the world, and man; in which case the adoption of a new faith would be a change in thought only, simply the adoption of a new thought. The word "faith" is used here in the old, popular sense, since the Russian people (including Vladimir) were and are looking not for a knowledge or dogma, but for a task, which could not even be adopted without the sense of obligation, without the promise to fulfill it. Such then is the sense and meaning of the word "faith." "Faith" in olden times meant *a sworn promise*. The Symbol of Faith[4] in its shortest form is the last word of Christ spoken on earth, i.e., a covenant. The Symbol of Faith is the covenant of the second Adam, confirming the covenant of the first, and it is preserved in the form of the cult of ancestors. Baptism involves a renunciation of old ways or heresies and a confession of the Symbol of Faith, in which a promise is given (in the form of faith in the Triune God) to fulfill the age-old common task; while chrismation is a consecration to the task itself, i.e., a descent of the Holy Spirit or a revelation to the sons of their relationship to the fathers. The present section of these notes on the question of brotherliness also includes an examination of two extremes (neopagan Western diversity and Neo-Judaistic Moslem compulsion and oppression)[5] and a re-

4 Russians use the phrase "Symbol of Faith," where Western Christians use the word "Creed."

5 Fydorov was obviously fascinated by the political as well as the religious significance of the sorry war between Russia and Turkey in 1853–1855. He found evidence to support his theories about the role of Orthodoxy and the nature of Christianity in the fact that Western European nations (neopagan diversity) should have entered the war on the side of the Moslem Turks instead of aiding the Christian Russians who were, supposedly, fighting to liberate their Christian brothers in the countries under Turkish rule. Much of Fyodorov's thought was constructed on the basis of the opposition of forces in this war.

nunciation of all heresies regarding themselves as special religions and contained between these two extremes, and of
Buddhism, which is an exception, since it is not a faith at all,
or a task, but simply doubt in everything and everybody, in-
action, renunciation, estrangement from everybody and everything, from God, from people, from nature, and one's own self;
in a word: complete annihilation. As deviations from the royal
way both of the above-mentioned extremes (neopaganism and
Neo-Judaism) merge in the end into inactive Buddhism with
its impossible goal, into the Buddhist absurd, the one thing
which we will have to deal with finally, perhaps, i.e., the Buddhism of Indo-China and Tibet.

As for Neo-Buddhism, this doctrine is still less a religion and
still more a philosophy; it dreams of uniting people while it
pays no attention to such trifles as differences of race, religious
belief, sex, color, and way of life. In short, this is one of the
attempts to establish brotherliness without taking into account
the reasons for diversity, the radical causes of nonbrotherliness.

Christianity holds a central position between the above-mentioned extremes, just as Orthodoxy (which is a mourning or
grief for Protestant diversity and the Catholic yoke) holds a
central position within Christianity itself—not a position of
repose, however, but of action, since its grief is not indifference
or indifferentism, neither is it tolerance or tolerantism (the legitimation of diversity), but a nonrevolutionary fanaticism, a call to
the task which will eliminate the very causes of enmity, revolt,
and oppression. Though this grief is a sorrow over the world,
still it is not a Buddhist sorrow that seeks annihilation, but a
Christian sorrow that seeks the restoration of the annihilated.

The criterion indicating the way of the Lord
   and the image of God

An epigraph could be placed above the present section: "Tell
me who your God is, and I will tell you who you are." (The

reverse is also true: "If I know who you are, I can tell who your God is.") But this is only a criterion for knowledge about God, not for His task; for us it is important and necessary to know not only who your God is and who you are, but above all who is our common God and in what way we are to be like Him *in our communality*. If Allah is your God, who is alien to everything human, even to the very best that is human . . . or Jupiter, who is alien to nothing human, even the very worst in man . . . then you will not be a worshiper of the One in whom the divine and human is united, the One for whom there is no Hellas or Neo-Hellas, no Judea or Neo-Judea, the One whom it is impossible to serve in diversity and isolation, who can be served only in communality and harmony. The concept or representation of divinity defines not so much what a man is as what he ought to be, what he must become, and not each man in isolation, but all taken together; if, of course, the concept is true and all-embracing. But if you believe that there is no God, if you deny His existence, then annihilation or Buddhism will be the end. To admit the existence of God without separating knowledge from action or action from knowledge is the first rule in the examination of faiths. But not to separate knowledge from action simply means not to destroy the primitive childlike integrity of human nature. The learned class represents a separation of knowledge from action, and so the knowledge of the learned class is not a whole, complete wisdom. Learnedness is knowledge, but not wisdom.

The second rule requires that knowledge not be limited simply to knowledge of oneself, in the sense of a person, a class, or a people. Pride, division, exhaltation, self-love, selfishness, egoism, and altruism are all repudiated by this rule.

In order to understand the origin of these criteria it is necessary to study people in their primitive state when disuniting causes have not yet begun to take effect. But if, along with the ineffectiveness of disuniting causes, that power begins to operate which brings loss and deprives sons and daughters of their fathers and mothers, then who will be the God of these sons and daughters if not that Being who gives life to beings like Himself in strength, knowledge, and feeling, and in whom there is no disunity or death? Such a Being is the highest expression of kinship, and therefore only kinship in all its power and fullness can be the criterion for the examination of faiths. Every doctrine which does not require the full restoration of relatedness is false. Just as our fathers did not accept them, so now we too cannot accept either Neo-Judaistic Islam or the neopagan West. If we take mankind in that state when only a uniting and death-dealing power is acting upon it and disuniting causes are not yet operative, then we will find in it the purest, childlike feeling, out of which the two rules mentioned above are evolved. Not to separate knowledge from action indicates strength and sincerity of feeling; knowledge in this case will not only not limit itself to knowledge of self but will limit itself precisely to knowledge of the many; and death will drive people more and more toward unity. The childlike feeling of general relatedness is the criterion and starting point for the attainment of ultimate perfection; deviation from this feeling is a fall, creating prodigal sons, making the attainment of majority impossible, turning the feeling into *puerility*, which must be distinguished from *childlikeness*. When we were small, all adults were for us the brothers and sisters of our fathers and mothers, they were our uncles and aunts; indeed our parents spoke to us in this way, compelled to adapt themselves to children's understanding and not suspecting that this compulsory adaptation was turning them toward a primitive truth and blessing. But if for a child all adults are the brothers and sisters of his parents, what is this child himself if not a son of man? It becomes clear from this why kinship is the criterion of the common task (the brotherliness of sons in the task of raising their fathers from the dead, and the brotherliness of fathers in the task of educating their sons). It also becomes clear why the Gospel makes the childlike feeling a condition for entry into the Kingdom of God. For what is Christianity? It is the Gospel of the Kingdom of God, of a general salvation which (according to the Gospel) must be sought first and above all. But to whom does the Kingdom of God belong? It belongs to children and those who, having reached majority, still preserve the childlike feeling. Regeneration ("to be born from above") is a conversion to childlike feeling. According to the second Gospel, the disciples themselves, when they started to quarrel about primacy, knew (perhaps only in a confused way) that this quarrel was a transgression of the purity and holiness of the Kingdom of God. They were ashamed to admit to their Teacher that they had had such a quarrel, and by this very fact witnessed to the childlike feeling still within them. A child who not only does not yet understand ranks, or grades, or any of the distinctions which are set up outside the Kingdom of God, which destroy relatedness and rise up on its ruins, but is also aware of his relatedness to all without any distinction whatever . . . a child who knows nothing outside of relatedness and is ready therefore to be of service to all without thought of benefit or profit, without any partiality . . . such a child will make clear to his pupils why the Kingdom of God belongs to children and in what way they, the adults, must become like children in order to become members of this Kingdom. But to become like children means to become a son of man, or to be born again as such.

The whole morality of the first three Gospels consists in the call to be converted into a child, to be born again as a son of man, utterly ignorant of worldly distinctions and instead deeply conscious of inner relatedness, wishing to serve and not to rule. Being free from the struggle for existence, not yet forced to use his powers in the acquisition of the means of life, a child is able to spend these powers disinterestedly in the service of all, seeing nothing slavish or humiliating in this service, just as Christ Himself saw no humiliation in washing the feet of the disciples who had been quarreling about the question of primacy.

The selection of a child as the pattern is a condemnation first of all of pride, the vice children do not have, the vice so difficult to eradicate among adults, and especially among the learned class. It could be said that this vice is condemned in a truly divine way, by replacing an imaginary value with one that is tremendously real. Pride grows with abstraction and negation; the Buddhist who sees the world as a figure of his own mind (a mirage, unreality) is the proudest nonentity. Christianity is the consciousness of this pride, and its renunciation, and at the same time a restoration of reality by means of work.

Thus, with a child as pattern, there is a renunciation of non-kinship, grades, ranks, of everything juridical and economic, and an affirmation of universal kinship, not just in word or thought, but in action. Kinship is the touchstone and compass of the common task.

The childlike feeling of universal brotherhood involves the fact that each man is a son, a grandson, a great-grandson, a great-great-grandson . . . the descendant of his father, grandfathers, great-grandfathers, ancestors, and finally of all his forefathers. This feeling involves not only the closest uniting of the living sons (in the present) but also a similar and even closer uniting of the present with the past (of the sons with the fathers) as opposed to the teaching of ancient and modern philosophers, whose mistake consists precisely in tearing away the past from the present.

The relationship of son to father, of grandson to grandfather, of descendant to ancestor, involves not just knowledge but also feeling, and feeling cannot be limited to representations (thoughts) but requires also a vision, a personal relationship, a face to face encounter. So then kinship as a criterion involves a command to raise the dead. Nor is this requirement of visibleness limited to external sight, for openness and sincerity necessarily enter into the concept of kinship, so that the whole depth of inwardness is expressed through externality; contemplation becomes intuition. Love is the fundamental characteristic of kinship, and with love there is also true knowledge. There is a secretiveness and insincerity in the relations of a slave to his master, in the relations between citizens; consequently there is no true knowledge and no filial or fraternal love between them. The characteristics of a citizen do not meet the requirements of our criterion. And in spite of its external similarity to kinship, that family ethos in which primitive people lived (traces of which are seen among us down to the present day) also fails to meet the requirements of the Christian criterion and is even a direct contradiction of it. A continual process of education is needed to turn the widely used term "brotherhood" from a word into a task; an external and internal unification is needed for this to happen.

Thus the age of childhood is defined by the external activity of unifying causes and the inactivity of disuniting causes, and by the internal consciousness of brotherhood and the feeling of mortality. The criterion of Christianity is drawn from the beginnings, the roots, the foundation; while the criterion of the present-day neopagan age demands life in harmony, not with innocent nature (not with nature in its beginnings, in its basic forms), but with nature in general, and promises individual happiness as a result (but a happiness that does not exclude death). Christianity promises a shared rather than a separate, individual happiness, i.e., the Kingdom of God. While it admits evil in this world today, Christianity denies evil and does not admit it at the beginning. It is opposed to both optimism and pessimism. The former limits good and refuses to see evil in nature or even in sickness and death. The latter sees evil everywhere, even in the very beginning and origin of things. They are both heading in the same direction: annihilation. But Christianity sees God in the beginning, and the Kingdom of God at the end. The childhood of Christianity (its primitive era) was marked by an expectation of the end of the world and by the feeling of brotherhood. This is true probably also with the childhood of mankind.

Both man and the world are pure only in their origins, in their childhood. Childhood is indeed a return to the beginning. The love of sons and daughters (fraternal love) is transformed later into sexual love. Only when sexual love is replaced by the raising of the dead, when the restoration of the old replaces the generation of the new, only then will there be no return to childhood, since then the whole world will be pure. Our present body is the product of our vices, individual and generic, and the world is the product of blind senseless force, bearing within itself hunger, pestilence, and death. Thus to conform one's actions to the organization of one's body (to follow nature, as ancient pagan wisdom used to teach and as modern pagan wisdom teaches today), to demand submission to the blind force of nature and to make one's own body the criterion for ethics, means to destroy ethics. How can one's behavior be conformed to the organization of one's own body when this body itself is the result of depraved behavior? To accept a child as the norm, to accept as a norm a being in whom enmity and sensuality have not yet appeared, who is governed instead by the greatest devotion to his parents, means to accept the moment of innocence as the norm. Pagan wisdom teaches us to follow nature, but Christian wisdom teaches us to follow innocent nature: the child; and the child is the negative expression of the absence of vice and the positive expression of the kingdom of relatedness. To be conformed to the structure of our organism (to the unconscious product of our vices) cannot be accepted as the rule for our behavior. Our body must be our task, not in egoistic self-organization, however, but a task carried out through the restoration of life to the fathers. The rule, "follow nature," demands the submission of a rational being to blind force. To follow nature means to participate in the sexual or natural struggle, i.e., to contend for oneself and to wage a war for existence, and to accept all the consequences of such a struggle, i.e., senility and death. Senility is a decline, and the senility of Christianity will begin if the preaching of the Gospel does not bring mankind to a unity in the common task.

Conditions for the realization of unity

Filial love is a necessary condition for the realization of unity. Without the Son, neither the unity of God nor the brotherhood of mankind is possible. The first three Gospels contain the teaching of the Son of Man about the God of the fathers, about the God, not of the dead but of the living, who sets Himself as the pattern for mankind. The Gospel of John is the teaching of the Son of God about God the Father, about our Heavenly Father. This Gospel is an expression of the infinite love of the Son for the Father, a love extending to the most profound self-likening to the Father. And the likeness of the Son to the Father consists in the fact that the Son also gives life. The raising of the dead is not just something in the future, it is also present. The Gospel of John is the highest expression of Christianity, and the complete contradiction of Islam and the Koran.

The false unity of Islam consists in the unconditional submission of the self to the blind force of nature, in which it sees the will of Allah, and to uninterrupted conflict with other people. To be a sacrifice to blind force and a weapon of destruction of the force of life—such is the true ideal of Islam. "Islam and holy war." Here is the full name of Mohammedanism. It is not hard to understand that the unity of God is possible only in the event that people cherish a filial love for Him. But if they have only a fear of God, then, no matter how they abase or humiliate themselves, as long as they exist they limit His unity. Like the fanaticism of war, such a God will exist only so long as those who limit His being exist; He Himself will be annihilated with their annihilation. Their God can bear no limitation, but without limitation He cannot exist; this is therefore a false unity. To preserve unity one must either admit an absolute intolerance and all-consuming fanaticism in one's God; or one must acknowledge the striving of all created beings to become loving sons. In the first case obedience to the will of Allah is expressed positively in holy war, in the obligation to become a weapon of destruction in the creation of unity; it is expressed negatively in the command to become a sacrifice to this destruction, not opposing, but rather, painfully accepting sickness and death . . . not even opposing that natural, animal, and destructive passion which appears in polygamy.

The transcendence and immanence of God

The acknowledgment of ourselves (according to the Christian criterion) as sons of all our dead fathers (the acknowledgment of ourselves as mortals) would be an admission of the transcendence of God (His absence from the world) if we, the living, failed to see ourselves as the instruments of God in the task of the restoration of life to the fathers.

One must not remove the Immortal Being from the world and leave the world mortal, imperfect; just as one ought not to confuse God with the world in which blindness and death reign. The problem is to turn this nature itself, these forces of nature, into an instrument for the universal raising of the dead, and in this way to establish the union of immortal beings. The question of the transcendence and immanence of God can be resolved only when all people together become the instruments for the raising of the dead, when the word of God becomes for us the work of God.

Our limited understanding of God

Religion is the task of raising the dead, not in its full form, but in the form of a sacrament. Without knowing it ourselves, as we unite we participate in the task of raising the dead, doing so through participation in the liturgy of Easter and the services preparatory to it. This includes the whole of Easter Day and the whole night preceding; and the Easter Passion, which comes at the end of the Forty Days of Lent (with the weeks preparatory to that); and the Easter of Resurrection, which begins the Fifty Days (with the weeks following that). We are speaking, therefore, of an Easter which includes the whole year. But while we participate in this way in the task of raising the dead, we have transformed it all into a mere ceremony. And until there is a liturgy outside the churches, until there is a solemn and holy celebration of Easter outside the churches, until there is an all day long and all year long (meteorological or tellurian) task, the raising of the dead will remain only a ceremony and there will be no harmony between the work in the churches and the work outside.

A Divine Being who in Himself has revealed the most perfect pattern for society; a Being who is a unity of independent, immortal Persons who in all fullness feel and are conscious of their unity (a oneness unbroken by death and excluding death); such is the Christian idea of God. This means that in the Divine Being there is revealed that which is necessary for the human race if it too is to become immortal. The Trinity is the Church of the Immortal Ones. Such a Church can become the Church of the revivified only by the process of man becoming like the Trinity. There is no cause of death in the Trinity; the Trinity includes all the conditions of immortality.

Does not this idea, or better, this plan, set forth the very law of love, the very essence of Christianity? In the unity or society of immortal Persons their faithfulness to one another, their fatherly and filial love, have no limits in death, as it is now with us in the society of mortals. Or rather it would be truer and more understandable to say that there is no death for them *because* their faithfulness and mutual love are unlimited. Only a raising of the dead which negates the limits placed on our faithfulness by death will make us like the Triune One.

Altogetherness as a condition
   for understanding the Triunity

Human multiunity, or altogetherness, actualized in reality (we say "altogetherness" and not "all-unity" in order to express a unity of persons and not some abstract unity) is a necessary condition for the understanding of the Divine Triunity. As long as the independence of individuals is expressed in life and reality as diversity, and as long as unity is expressed as enslavement, just so long will altogetherness as a likeness of the Triunity be simply a thought, an ideal. But if we do not separate action from thought, then the Triunity will not be just an ideal for us, but a project, not just a hope, but a precept. *Only in working, in actualizing unity in work, is it possible to understand.* The Indivisible Trinity has remained an empty formula because those who have made peace in the world have not given any thought to the conditions for that firm and eternal peace contained in the doctrine of the Indivisible Trinity. The more we enter into unity, the more Divinity is revealed, and vice versa. If our thinking and knowledge are formed by way of experience, but in the meantime experience gives us an understanding only of enmity and domination, then it is clear that only the triumph, the complete triumph of moral law can make the Triune Being fully understandabie to us; i.e., we will understand Him only when we ourselves (all mankind) become a multiunified or, more precisely, a togethered being . . . only when unity is no longer expressed in domination or the independence of individuals in enmity . . . only when there will be full mutuality and mutual knowledge. Won't the Christian idea of God, when it is actualized, be also the actualized law of love? External authority can bring people to silence but not to conviction, not to truth; while diversity leads directly to the negation of truth. Therefore those conditions needed for blessedness are needed also for truth, i.e., the absence of bondage (or external authority in the task of knowledge) and the absence of diversity. There is no truth in the West, due to its diversity, or in the East, due to its oppression.

The first Son of Man

As descendants of the first Son of Man (who did not forsake His parents even in death), we ourselves must not separate Him from His parents in our thoughts, in our commemorations, and in our project of raising the dead. We must consider Him with His parents as one indivisible unit, as our common forefather. Nor will we separate them in our thoughts if, by our task, we form a moral unity as they did, because we must unite them in our thoughts before they (our departed ones) will be restored by our task. But if the son abandons and forgets his parents in their death, having himself become a father, then he is no son of man, since the image of parents remaining after their death in the hearts of the sons constitutes a distinctive feature of man. For the learned, as a special class, these images are only a representation, but for common people they are a project; the latter is something natural, one might even say universal, while the former is something artificial. The son who has not forgotten his parents is the first Son of Man; he who has forsaken his parents is the first prodigal son. The son's abandonment of his parents is the original Fall, while hetaerism and the extermination of parents by the sons is the most terrible fall. Matriarchal and patriarchal states are already a restoration, though not yet a full restoration, just as the "social society" (ancient and modern civilizations) is a new, second, but also not complete fall. Universal hetaerism, or the herd state, would be a complete fall; but this is only the ideal, the dream, the utopia of social society, and then only of those members of society who are called the "leading members." Each of the states indicated has its own religious expression: ancestors are honored in the patriarchal, and partly in the matriarchal states; ancient and modern civilizations honor not the dead but the living, preferring the young to the old and abandoning the latter for the sake of the former; this is the pagan cult of Aphrodite and Ares. Only the herd state, if it ever actually existed in the past or ever will exist (in a strict sense) in the future, is incapable of having a religion. By defining the good as a nonabandonment of the parents, and evil as a falling away or estrangement from them, we are only following the Gospel criterion. If a man can be defined by the term "affection" (love, desire, will), then a child too is "affection," but his love is not sexual or covetous or parental, but filial. While accepting filial love as the essence of the child, taken as a criterion, however, we cannot and must not separate the child from his father; any such separation or abandonment we must consider as evil, and every replacement of love of father by love of things, or love of wife, and so on, we must regard as vice.

Thus He who first, out of love, did not abandon His parents to the end, who did not abandon them in life, even when He could have lived separately by reason of His majority and His ability to lead an independent life, and who did not abandon them after their death: this man may be called the first Son of Man, marking the beginning of family life, family religion (the cult of ancestors) and of human society in general. This first Son of Man was our forefather, having formed with his parents, as it were, one indivisible society or, more accurately, the first ethical unit.

The whole family should have remained as an ethical unit, whatever the number of sons and daughters, and in spite of the rupture of unity by the parents' deaths. All the sons and daughters, no matter how many, are one son, provided there are no divisions between them. But there will be no occasion for divisions only if the obligation to support the parents in their lifetime is converted (at the time of their death) into a sincere effort to restore the life of the parents. Without this effort there is no son (one son in the midst of many) just as there is no brotherhood; without this effort divisions will be inevitable. So then the family which makes this effort will manifest two virtues. First: magnanimity. In such a family there will be no worship of things, no idolatry. Second: universal and pure (i.e., Christian) love. But Christianity will be platonic love—idea-latry—if this striving for restoration remains only a striving and does not become a public action for the universal raising of the dead. Then in this great public action a third virtue will appear, or, rather, the first and only virtue, including all others: the process of becoming like the Triune Being.

Truly universal grief and so-called universal grief (suffering)

The son's grief over the death of his father is truly universal, because this death, like a law (or rather like an unavoidable accident) of blind nature, must bring about a response of severe pain in every being who has arrived at consciousness, in every being through whom there can and must be accomplished a transition from the world of blind force to the world where consciousness reigns and where, therefore, there can be no place for death. This truly universal suffering is objectively universal to the extent that death is common to all, and subjectively universal to the extent that sorrow for the death of fathers is common to all. Truly universal suffering is the bitter regret for lack of love for the fathers and for excessive love of self. It is a grief over the perversion of the world, over its fall, over the estrangement of the son from the father. But grief that does not spring from the fact that our fathers have died and we have outlived them, and therefore have not had sufficient love for them, grief simply over the fact that we will ourselves die, cannot be regarded as truly universal. It is only a pseudo-universal grief. In the same way the grief which appears within the circle of the intelligentsia cannot be called universal, for it is universal neither in scope nor in content. To demand happiness that is in no way deserved, to demand all goods without work, and to mourn over the unattainableness of the goal that all should belong to one, to do this is to wish to attribute to one that which can and must belong only to all. Grief over the inaccessibility of this goal is not only not universal, it is actually the most egoistical grief, concerned with nothing but one's own individual welfare.

In general, the bitter regret over the impossibility of happiness in isolation—even the impossibility of happiness for one whole generation—cannot be called universal suffering. In the same way so-called social grief cannot be called universal—such things as the bitter regret evoked by the failure of the French Revolution or the unrealized ideals of the epoch of the Renaissance (which were, after all, very limited). Christian universal suffering is the bitter regret over diversity (over enmity and hatred with all their consequences, i.e., suffering and death). This regret or sorrowing is a repentance, something active, containing hope, expectation, confidence; this penitence is the admission of one's guilt concerning diversity and of one's obligation in the task of reunification in universal love, in the elimination of all the consequences of diversity. Negative, passive Buddhism also grieves over evil, but it does not see the greatest evil in diversity, hatred, and enmity, just as it does not see the greatest good in reunification and universal love. On the contrary, Buddhism hopes to annihilate every evil by the renunciation of all love and attachment. It encourages life in isolation (diversity), life in the desert, life devoted to a constant contemplative inactivity, and then it grieves over the illusory nature of the world! As if not only thoughts and dreams but also the very manifestations of the ungoverned forces of nature could be anything but unrestrained, untamable, disappearing phenomena, difficult to distinguish from phantoms and mirages. Life itself seems either a light and pleasant, but deceptive dream . . . or a terrible nightmare! The phenomena of nature will be phantoms until they become the work of a corporate will, the action of all people working as the instruments of God. And thoughts will be illusory until they become the projects of corporate human and (by revelation) divine will.

Thus the feeling of suffering of the first Son of Man, the regret over the loss of the father, generated that universal suffering over the perishability of everything (over universal mortality) in which nature first attained an awareness of its imperfection. It marked the beginning of the renewal of the world, the beginning of the human epoch, in which the world must be re-created by the powers of man himself. And without this filial virtue, without family life, we would never be able to understand the lofty doctrine of the Triune God—an amazing doctrine, by reason of its grandeur scarcely accessible to the loftiest minds, and yet, because of the hearty, warm affection it suggests, accessible even to the mind of a child.

Profession of the Symbol of Faith
is both a repentance and a promise

That nation which could not be satisfied with the sonless God of Islam or with the gods which sanctioned the abandonment of fathers by sons and were indifferent to brotherhood, that nation which, after its acceptance of Christianity, hastened at once to canonize brotherly and filial love in the persons of St. Boris and St. Gleb, such a nation not only found the complete fulfillment of its highest ideal in faith in the Triune God, but at the same time saw that its actual position fell short of that required by faith in such a God. And so the examination of faiths became for it a self-judgment and repentance.

The confession of the Symbol of Faith in all its three main sections includes both repentance and a promise of amendment. In the first part of the Creed, while confessing God the Almighty and Creator of the world, we cannot avoid confessing also our depredation of what has been created by Him; we must also acknowledge ourselves as wreckers and destroyers who have not maintained but disrupted the order of nature. And we cannot see our destiny simply in the accumulation of things not created by our own labor—in the proprietorship of a world created by God —without denying our likeness to Him. Our destiny can consist only in becoming instruments for the fulfillment of God's will in the world, instruments for governing that force which, by virtue of its blindness, bears hunger, sickness, and death, and does not distribute its gifts and products according to need, but brings rain where it is not needed and scorches where it is only necessary to warm. Thus we are guilty not only for what we do (our rapacity) but also for the evil which comes as a result of our doing nothing. Nor can it be said that God created this blind force, since He created also rational force, and only through the inactivity of the latter does the former bring about evil. Therefore the precept contained in the first section of the Creed demands of all people without exception a knowledge both of nature and of the government of nature, that it may be converted from a death-dealing force into one that gives life.

All people are summoned by the doctrine of the Only-begotten Son of God (in the second part of the Creed) to an acknowledgment of themselves as sons of all the departed fathers and therefore as brothers of all the living. The doctrine of the Son of Man presupposes a daughter also, to the extent that daughters have anything in common with sons, not just when the son's birth is considered but also precisely when the son is referred to as the Word, i.e., as the knowledge with which the process of becoming a likeness of God begins. This means that the daughter also must participate not only in the knowledge of all the fathers (understood as one father) but also in the knowledge of nature as the means of converting blind death-dealing force into a force that vivifies. The daughter of man particularly is summoned by the doctrine of the Holy Spirit (the third part of the Creed) to repentance, to an acknowledgment of herself as the daughter of all departed parents, to an acknowledgment of herself as existing not in separation or diversity but within the corporate body of mankind; she is summoned to the office of an anointer (one who revivifies, brings to life). Nor does the parable of the prodigal son refer to sons only. In forgetting brotherhood and God (as the most perfect Being who reminds us of our imperfection and unworthiness) we are led to self-knowledge, which becomes consciousness of our own merits and of our own superiority over others. For this reason the sons of men should constantly have the Son of God before their eyes, and the daughters of men should contemplate the Holy Spirit; it is in this sense that we speak of the likeness of the sons to the Son of God, and of daughters to the Holy Spirit. But are we acting in accordance with the Gospel criterion when we take the Holy Spirit as the pattern for the daughter of man? Not to accept the one God worshiped in three Persons as the pattern for individuals and for society would be insincerity, indifference, dead faith. For under the figure of children (to whom the Kingdom of God belongs) there is assumed a love for the fathers, not the sons' love only, but also the daughters'. But if the Kingdom of God is a likeness of the Divinity, then Divinity itself is a Spirit-inspired Son and Daughter, nourishing an infinite love for the Father.

In the Apostolic Canons the bishop is compared with the Father, the deacon with the Son, and the deaconess with the Holy Spirit. If we put all living fathers in the place of the bishop, all sons in the place of the deacon, and all daughters in the place of the deaconess, then we have a truly catholic comparison, without any social stratification. And if in the fathers we understand all the departed, then the diaconate (the service of sons and daughters) acquires a definite meaning, the meaning of the raising of the dead. In a monastic Trinity (which is less Christian than it is Platonic) there is no room for a daughter, even though there is nothing sensual in an eternal daughter, for everything conjugal and maternal is excluded here and only that which pertains specifically to a daughter remains (i.e., duty to parents). No woman is forgotten in this doctrine, for though not all women are wives and mothers, all are daughters. If in the doctrine of the Trinity the Spirit is not taken as the pattern for the daughter, then the Trinity itself is turned into something lifeless, monastic, Platonic. If the daughter is not a likeness of the Holy Spirit, the spirit of love, then she will be imbued with the spirit of destruction and nothingness.

Knowledge: what it is and what it ought to be

If revelation on the part of God is the revelation of perfection and the indication of an obligation, of what ought to be, then consciousness of one's guilt is man's discovery of his unlikeness to God. The awareness that our birth is costing our fathers their lives, that we are pushing them aside, is the awareness of guilt. With us, there is no son as a single son (as an only-begotten son), and therefore if our sons still have a love for their fathers this love is without knowledge or power, and cannot preserve their fathers from death. A further revelation makes clear the nature of our shortcoming, of our unworthiness: it says that the Son is *the Word of God*, and so not a being born unconsciously. We cannot fail to be aware of our own unworthiness and impurity, for although we were not conceived by lust alone, yet it was not without it. While we know that there is within us the same Logos (reason, knowledge)—which tends to redeem the natural consequences of childbearing and to restore what this has thrust aside—we also realize that this restoration is taking place only in the realm of thought, and revelation, as if anticipating the enlikening of our word to the Divine Word, points out to us that the Son is the true God, a real Being and not just the mental image of the Father. An imaginary, mental, purely verbal restoration would not be a likeness of Him. In order that there be a

genuine likeness of Him the genealogical tree of mankind must
not be just a tree of knowledge, but also a tree of life, in which
inner kinship becomes clear, external, tangible, and not just a
vague feeling as it is now.

The content of the Logos changes with the changes in relations between people. If there were no divisions (if all sons were
a single son) then the Logos would also represent the corporateness of the individual images of all fathers as one father, i.e.,
would represent a genealogy, which was partly the case in the
family life of old. The primitive life of man was a family life;
the first word of man, the first knowledge of the race was
genealogy. One of the most ancient writings, the Book of Genesis, is just such a genealogy.

Action: what it is and what it ought to be

In the doctrine of the Divine Triunity, in the doctrine of the
birth of the Son of God, we see the law of vivification in the
Incarnate God-Man. We see in Him an example, a pattern of
action, and in this pattern there is revealed to us, first, the great
power of love, which enables us to heal, to vivify, to calm the
storms of elemental forces; and second, the still greater power
which enables us to remain silent before those who curse us and
to bless our persecutors. This is that active power, ruling over
the senseless, unbridled forces of nature, and cosuffering with
beings capable of suffering even as they compel Him to suffer too.

If we do not separate Christ's resurrection from our own
(from the universal raising of the dead) we must ascribe to ourselves guilt for the absence of vivification as well as guilt for
Christ's departure from the earth, for His ascension to heaven;
just as we may expect His gracious—or dreadful—return to earth
to come as a result of our own unification in the task of raising
the dead.

Arianism and paganism cannot disappear as long as civic,

economic, political relationships exist instead of family relationships. Family relationships will be established among people
only when the Son of God is the pattern for the sons of men and
the Holy Spirit for their daughters. Until we set this pattern as a
goal for ourselves it cannot be realized and cannot find application in society. But while it calls the Word of God a Son, Orthodoxy has not yet given the title of Daughter to the Holy Spirit. In
everyday life, the daughter stands incomparably lower than the
son, so that if such a name were used, public opinion would regard it more as a degradation of the Divinity than as an exaltation
of the daughter. And yet there is not only nothing pagan in this
admission of a Daughter-Spirit and a Son-Logos, no admission of
conjugality (unconscious childbearing) in the Divine Being, but
also nothing Arian, which would introduce the imperfections of
human life into the Divine Being. The agelong, gradual transition from subservience to the blind force of nature (from conjugality and childbearing) to a unification of all sons and
daughters in common love for all parents in the task of the
universal raising of the dead—this gradual transition is in fact
the assimilation of the doctrine of the Son and Holy Spirit in
their relations with the Father, the real assimilation of the
doctrine of the Trinity.

In comparing the Christian concept of God with that of Islam,
we cannot fail to say the same thing about the Spirit which was
said above about the Son. Islam itself proves the imperfection of
its concept of God by its polygamy, by its degradation of women.
It is precisely Islam which has not grasped the doctrine of the
Spirit as the pattern for the daughter of man, so that polygamy
might be abolished and woman raised to equality with man
(whereby the male sex also would be elevated). Our weakness
lies in the fact that we have what Mohammed calls a female
companion. The abandonment and forgetting of our parents
(and ancestors) is the consequence of just this weakness. To have
a female companion in the sense understood by Islam means to
have a sexual feeling. But when Christianity says that there is

nothing male or female in Christ it acknowledges woman as a
daughter and not just a wife, and man as a son and not just a
husband. As son and daughter the male and female sexes do not
appear as bodies endowed simply with sensations and lusts,
unconsciously and passively obeying the blind force of nature
which, when it unites them, produces in them a new creature
(having the same form, incidentally, which they themselves had
in their lowest stage of evolution, before the appearance of reason, will, and feeling). This new creature, as it grows, separates
itself from its parents, is alienated, and finally abandons them
altogether, making them rather like an eggshell from which a
bird has been hatched, or like the dried-up petals of a flower in
which the seed has matured. Thus do the male and female sexes
appear when they forget their worth as sons and daughters. They
will be altogether different when they preserve a memory of, and
attachment to their fathers. United in feeling, reason, and will
through participation in the task of the fathers, they will become
whole, and not just half (sexual) beings. Christian marriage
must also be understood in this sense; here the sexual feeling and
childbearing are only temporary, left over from the animal state.
They will be abolished when the task of the fathers becomes the
raising of the dead.

May we limit ourselves to faith alone?

To make a vow and not to fulfill it means to break faith, because faith is a vow, even a sacred vow, unrepeatable, made once
and for all. Faith was understood in this way as long as people
remained faithful, but when they betrayed the vow they turned
faith from a task into thought, in order not to appear as traitors.
What is a testament from the standpoint of the fathers is a vow
from the standpoint of the sons . . . hence the unity of action.
The accomplishment of the path indicated to us in the doctrine

of the Holy Trinity must be the future history of mankind, the work of God fulfilled through us, and the Creed (understood dynamically and borne out in action) will find expression in this accomplishment. Such an achievement will be a living proof of the Symbol of a living Faith which will, in this way, be converted into a symbol of action, into a task, a liturgy.

The demonstration of this Creed by the history of the future (in which we must necessarily participate) does not contradict the science of theology. Although theology acknowledges God as inaccessible, nevertheless it has turned into objects of knowledge both the doctrine of the internal life of the Divinity (the Immanent Trinity) and the image of Divine revelation vis-à-vis the world (the Redemptive Trinity). It has tried to make accessible to human understanding both the inner life of God and His relationship to the world. But knowledge alone does not exhaust or resolve the question; knowledge alone can only be a pointer toward the ideal. Just as the Immanent Trinity tells us what we must be like in our family corporateness, i.e., just as the doctrine of the Triunity leads into the question of our human multiunity or altogetherness (the doctrine of the Church), so, too, the doctrine of God's relationship to us (the doctrine of the Redemptive Trinity) includes also the doctrine of our relationship to God and how we must act in accordance with the divine plan of salvation. Theological knowledge has examined questions on the relationship of the Word to the creation of the world, on the immediate manifestation of Divinity through the forces of nature (Providence), on the manifestation of God in the visions of the prophets and in the work of redemption; but as far as we know it has not touched on the question of re-creation as the fulfillment of the prophetic sayings. It has not touched on the question of the manifestation of the divine will through us, as free and rational beings, in the task of the re-creation or universal raising of the dead. It has not raised the question of how to turn the pattern given to us in the Person of the Redeemer into a law of activity, not just for separate individuals, but for the whole of mankind, into the law of future history which will actualize the ideal revealed to us in the Immanent Trinity.

If the Word of God is not mere knowledge, but also action, then theology too, as the word about God, must, before all other sciences become a task. It cannot remain as knowledge only. The preparation of the whole human race as an instrument worthy of serving the divine will is the task of the theologians, who, working with all the other representatives of knowledge as educators of the people, have called them to the defense of the fatherland and to warfare with the blind force of nature, to its conversion from a death-dealing force into a vivifying one (which will also make unnecessary the defense of the people against others like themselves).

The common and generic obligation; a consciousness of the obligation is the natural consequence of self-condemnation and repentance[6]

All the obligations laid upon us by the doctrine of the Triune God are expressed in a single precept, in the commandment concerning the duty of raising the dead. In contrast to Mohammedanism we can say: "There is no God other than the Triune God, and the raising of the dead is His precept." The duty is the one duty common to all people, just as death is common to all. The definition of our duty as the raising of the dead is not an arbitrary one. The concept of duty already involves the demand for the raising of the dead, just as every debt inevitably involves the obligation of repayment; but with this difference, that in a strict sense this debt—as a universal Christian filial debt calling

[6]Fyodorov indulges in a kind of mystical play on words in this whole section, taking advantage of the various meanings of the Russian word *dolg* (debt, duty, obligation, office), and the similarity of the words *tyaga* (pull, gravitation, weight, draw) and *tyaglo* (a family tax or assessment in pre-Revolutionary Russia).

for complete repayment—requires an *identical* restoration and not a restoration of that which is only similar, since the filial debt is a product not just of abstract reason but also of filial feeling. Thus the fulfillment of the filial obligation is a taking upon oneself of the labor or tax of raising the dead, not just the generation of a likeness (and thus the expectation of condemnation and punishment). In the same way, marriage is not the abandonment of the parents, not simply a joining together in fleshly unity, but a union, in a taxable unit of labor, in the common task of the fathers, in the task of the whole human race, made up of many such taxable units. We have nothing which we have produced ourselves; everything is given or loaned to us. Our life certainly is not ours, it is removable, alienable, mortal. We have received life from our fathers, who stand in the same debt toward their own parents, and so on, and so on. Childbearing is therefore the transmission of the debt, not its repayment. From our parents then, or in general from our ancestors, we have received not only life but also the means of life, those modes of work which belong largely to our ancestors and only in a small way and in exceptional circumstances belong personally to us. "Why should we be concerned about a sin committed before our birth?" asks diversity in the figure of Cain (in Byron's well-known romance). But if we do not wish to accept the consequences of a sin which we have not personally committed, then we ought not to accept the good which we did not produce; and this would be to reject all the redemptive and other work accomplished not by one generation but by generations of generations.

If to lay down one's life for others (the death of the innocent for the guilty) is the highest virtue for people taken separately, then what will be the highest virtue for people taken all together? Not only does the obligation to parents have a moral character, it is also expressed in physical dependency, bondage, nonfreedom. Being born is nonfreedom. The land and all other circumstances of life are not our own property; we are not landholders, but serfs of the land, just as the earth is dependent on the sun (the sun is its center of gravity) and the sun, in turn, is in the same state of dependency on some other body, and so on. The regulation of this blind gravitation (which is not just an earthly gravitation but something universal, with death as its condition) must also be a tax upon the human race. It follows from this that the raising of the dead is a labor which converts what is received on loan into one's own property; it is a clearing of the debt.

But we live not simply at the expense of someone alien to us, not simply at the expense of blind nature, but also at the expense of those who are like us . . . even those closest to us, displacing them, pushing them aside; and such an existence makes us not only undeserving people, but also criminals. All moral as well as physical misfortunes are the natural consequence of submission to the blind force by which we live, since in obeying the impulses of blind, alien, dissimilar force (dissimilar to us, although very much alive in us) we become the enemies of those like ourselves. Thus present-day life makes us not only unworthy of happiness but also unhappy. And if the depth of self-condemnation makes the last judgment immanent instead of transcendental, then salvation also requires effort and labor on our part to convert what is not brought about by us into that which is. The obligation arises not only out of the fact that something has been borrowed but also out of sin and crime. By its bearing of children each generation brings death upon its parents, so that the debt is also a guilt. The realization that this debt has not been repaid is the realization of one's dependence, slavery, bondage, mortality, in a word: nonbrotherhood. In the unpaid debt there lies a punishment, by way of slavery and death. The payment of the debt is the restoration of life to one's parents; it is the restoration of the debt to one's creditors and of freedom to oneself. Unconscious, involuntary, original sin is the basic mortal sin, the sin against the Holy Spirit, against true enlightenment. Not to accept responsibility for this sin, i.e., not to trouble oneself about it, not to take part in the task of raising the dead, means to deprive mankind of a future, to doom it to a semianimal existence. The task of the human race is the conversion of everything unconscious, self-operative, self-generating into a conscious, enlightened, genuine, universal, and personal raising of the dead.

It should be noted in this connection that the content of the debt is always the same, there is a difference only in the repayment (in the way we reckon the repayment). An eye for an eye and a life for a life is a repayment in which values are equated to the point of cruelty. The indemnity or material compensation for man power paid, in the days of old, to the family of a murdered man was a repayment, but an extremely unequal one; the repayment was obviously unrealistic and arbitrary and did not diminish the debt; it actually doubled it. All crimes and offenses, from the least insult to murder, have the effect of destroying life; but the juridical remuneration for life does not restore it. The economic compensation for things and services is also unrealistic. It is true that we can make a repayment for things and services received from others by means of similar things and services; but we cannot restore that force, that part of life which was expended in their production. The exchange does not constitute a mutual restoration of the expended forces of life, but leads to further mutual disruption and death. All this proves that the content of the debt is always life, and so therefore only restoration of life, the raising of the dead, can be the liquidation of the debt.

What constitutes the fulfillment of the obligation?

The whole obligation is contained in the ten Old Testament commandments, understood in the light of Christianity and modified into a single precept: that of the universal raising of the dead. This is the pathway which ancient and modern Judaism can and must traverse on its way to Christianity. The obligation in its truly Christian sense requires that the commandment to serve the true God and not to make likenesses to oneself be under-

stood in the broadest positive sense, not in the Old Testament
or negative sense. The Old Testament did not attach a proper
meaning to the first two commandments, since (as understood
by Christianity) they are obviously contradicted by the third,
and especially by the fourth. Contrary to the first two commandments, which require an unconditional worship of the one true
God, the third permits the worship of false gods, forbidding
only the confusion of such worship with the worship of God; this
permission evidently has the same significance as that implied in
the fourth: Six days shall you do all that you have to do, but the
seventh day you shall devote solely to the worship of God. To
serve only your own private welfare and gain for six days (the
sanction of diversity); during those six days to make any kind of
likeness (to deify things, to become the instrument of nature's
blind power, and to forget about one's true likeness); and then
on the seventh day to worship God in idleness, simply in thought
—all this means really to worship the true God in thought only
for one day (the Sabbath is the negation of diversity, but it is
not a positive, genuine brotherhood) and for six days actually to
worship false gods. It means to create one's own artificial little
world in the likeness of the natural world, and not to re-create the
natural world according to the image of the Triune God. It
should be noted that by "likeness" we do not mean those harmless idols which the Hebrew people so zealously destroyed, but
that whole situation which serves as the cause or occasion for
the quarrels and disputes which lead to death. But in the event
of a re-creation or identical restoration to life such a bifurcation
could not occur. Then the work of God would be expressed in the
whole six days of man's work, and the voice of the Son of Man
would be heard in the voice of mankind itself: "The hour is
coming and now is, when the dead shall hear the voice of the
Son of God, and those who hear will live" (John 5:25). Will
live, of course, in a material way, visibly, tangibly. Christianity
elevates weekday work to the work of raising the dead, and it
turns holiday idleness into the task of revivification.

The contradiction between the first two commandments and the third and fourth will come to an end when the third commandment is understood as a prohibition of the worship of the manufactured commercial vanity of the city, and the fourth commandment is taken not as a permission to worship the blind death-dealing power of nature but as a command to turn it into a vivifying (Paschal) power, for the worship of the God not of the dead but of the living. Understood positively, the second commandment means that the fourth requires a conversion of daily and annual work into a liturgy outside the churches, a conversion of blind progress into a Paschal procession, a conversion of the six days of private business into a common task which will govern the daily and annual changes in nature. The fifth commandment will have a Christian meaning when the respect for parents in their lifetime becomes their revivification after death, and when length of days becomes immortality. The sixth and seventh commandments (all crimes can be considered as infractions of these two), even when understood from the Christian viewpoint, only serve as a preparation of the heart, cleansing it of thoughts of hatred, envy, and lust—they only pave the way to the one positive commandment of the universal raising of the dead, which releases us from the sin of the expulsion of the older generation by the younger. By forbidding hatred and unfriendliness the sixth commandment requires that we love, and in forbidding adultery the seventh commandment cautions against the perversion of love. Blind love is condemned by the seventh commandment, since like all evil, unconscious sensual love (the separation of feeling from knowledge) brings death. In its broadest sense, i.e., that one shall not take the life of a single living creature and shall not even entertain thoughts of evil, the sixth commandment is unrealizable. The same is true of the seventh commandment when understood in a strict sense; its fulfillment would cause the extinction of the race. The impracticability of the negative commands requires the fulfillment of the positive command: to raise the dead.

Thus all crimes can be considered as direct or indirect infractions of the sixth commandment, just as all virtues are subsumed directly or indirectly under one great virtue: *the Universal Raising of the Dead* . . . which is not just an imagined or inner repentance, but a real restoration of all that has been taken away or plundered, the full expiation for all infractions of the sixth commandment. Not only does every kind of affront come under the broad heading of crimes against this commandment, but also the stealing of things, infraction of the eighth. For in stealing we steal a certain part of life. By "stealing" we also mean the acquisition of things at too low a price, a custom which gives rise to the hazards of supply and demand and which economic science has turned into a law which rational beings are supposed to obey. By stealing a portion of life in another's work we free ourselves from work and at the same time manifest an unwillingness to restore life, for all true labor is already (at least in part) the work of raising the dead. The value of labor is determined only in its relation to raising the dead; to lay down one's life in labor means to hasten one's own and others' resurrection. The Old Testament "Do not kill" is converted into the New Testament "Give life," in the sense of a universal corporate task.

What is the essence, the task, of Christianity?

Even though they were a fulfillment of the law of God given on Mt. Sinai, Jubilees (cf. Leviticus 25:8–17) could find expression only in the action of the people themselves; they were therefore acts of human will in accordance with divine command. When later on they were turned into a mere expectation of restoration, this was a perversion of the law, and Christianity has once again turned man from a passive expectation to his forgotten task of salvation. In calling the Old Testament religion a shadow or figure of the New, Christianity is hereby unable to limit itself to the liturgy inside the churches; if it did, it would be nothing but a shadow or figure of the Resurrection. Originally all sacraments were united in the liturgy, it was itself the Sacrament of Sacraments, the work of salvation. It was not only a church service; it was bound up inseparably with life. The liturgy was a task which, in the early Church, embraced and absorbed the whole of life. The spread of Christianity (the catechizing of the pagan world, the addition of new members to the original nucleus, the spread of brotherhood) was the Liturgy of the Catechumens, and the whole liturgy was still only the work of gathering and uniting, since the question of regulation (the conversion of the blind, death-dealing force of nature into vivifying power) could not yet have arisen. The catechizing was often concluded then by public confession and baptism by fire and blood; this was how the liturgy entered the history of Christianity. Churches then did not remain aloof from one another but communicated by way of epistles which were read at the assemblies of the faithful, who were in those days not merely believers but also people bound together by love, i.e., men of faith. In the reading of these epistles, there was an expression of the oneness of those gathered in the image of heavenly harmony; this oneness or communality was supported and strengthened by the epistles. We would have preserved the tradition more faithfully if we had not limited ourselves to the rereading of the old writings. By turning the preaching of the Gospel into mere reading we are flagrant violators of the tradition. This can even be seen in the position of the reader of the Gospel in the churches today, who stands by the altar facing away from the people.

When Christianity became the dominant (as the saying goes) religion, then the extension of Christianity and the restoration of those fallen away was turned into coercion, and catechizing into a holy war; the baptizers and apostles themselves became swordbearers, and repentance took the form of inquisition; external incorporation into the Church became internal isolation, the

liturgy became just another church service, and all the sacraments were separated from it, losing their unity; instead of being
public acts they became private family affairs.

Briefly, the extremely close connection between the liturgy and
the other sacraments can be expressed as follows: the transition
from the *Liturgy of the Catechumens* (from the educating or
uniting of the living, including *marriage*, the relating of the unrelated) to the *Liturgy of the Faithful* (the *Holy Communion*,
and also *extreme unction*, as forms of raising the dead) is
accomplished through *baptism* (adoption) together with *chrismation* and *confession* (the return of prodigal sons).

The Liturgy of the Catechumens was either the conversion of
the pagan world (people who had lost brotherhood as a result of
forgetting their fathers as one father) to Christianity through
baptism alone, or the restoration, again through repentance, of
those who had fallen back into paganism after conversion. The
conversion itself was a catechizing or education which, however,
drew attention neither to the reasons for nonbrotherhood, nor to
the fact that Christianity had not become a genuine brotherhood
of sons, nor to why the Christian task (the Liturgy of the Faithful) was not a visible raising of the dead, but only a sacramental
raising, a figure, a shadow.

Outside the Greco-Roman world (and especially with us) the
conversion consisted in a general baptism without preliminary
catechism. We had no special, separate, national schoolhouse
apart from the church building, and no special schooling apart
from the church services. Participation in the general worship
in the churches, with the icons serving as a great picture book,
was the means of popular education. Participation in this worship could have had an influence on the formation of the nation,
of course. But was it used as a means of forming the nation? Has
the duty of Godfather been fulfilled?

Kievan Russia extended Christianity and, while baptizing
without catechizing, carried out its obligation as a Godfather by
introducing services with the old Greek chant and building the

churches with icons, doing all this as a means of education, choosing the type of worship which had the most powerful educational
effect upon the people. Muscovite Russia did not examine foreign
faiths and did not subject itself to self-examination, which meant
that it had faith but not knowledge, so that divine worship was
not used as a means of education. Muscovite Russia could not
accept the doctrine of the Trinity as the pattern for its corporate
life. The princes, and even more, the people, drawn directly or
indirectly into compulsory service and absorbed in the protection
and defense of their fatherland, could regard the services of the
Church as a sacramental means of salvation only. Church services
were not, for them, a means of education. Under the shadow of
war the Archangel Michael and the Most Holy Virgin Mother
of God came to be especially reverenced in Russia, for a while
virtually eclipsing the worship of the Holy Trinity. Victories
were expected from the Archangel and consolation in the midst
of the losses inevitable even in victory was sought from the
Mother of God. As long as there is guard duty and compulsory
military service in the struggle against other nations, just so long
will the cult of the heavenly vanquisher and the consolatrix dis-
place the veneration of the Trinity, who calls instead for a universal education in fulfillment of the office of Godfather. The
universal raising of the dead is the fulfillment of the office of
executor, and universal education is the fulfillment of the office
of Godfather . . . which Vladimir took upon himself, but which
has not yet been fulfilled by his descendants.

The present state of Christianity,
or the liturgy inside the churches

When baptism (adoption—the reception of new members as
sons) or repentance (the receiving again of fallen prodigal sons—
the immediate assimilation of all to the universal Church

through the education of all, as one beloved son and heir) are separated from the liturgy, when the liturgy no longer has in view the strengthening of mutuality and brotherhood, then it ceases to be effective and begins to die. The services are performed, but no advance is seen in communality, in the bringing together of near and far. (It should be noted, however, that the work of the liturgy must not be limited simply to the uniting of the living for the common task, since the liturgy itself is also this task, as has already been indicated, i.e., it is the general raising of the dead, but in the form of a sacrament and not of plain work). The Church today is in this position, while history and life flow along another course (yet still through us). Life is moving, not along the path of conjunction, but along the path of disjunction; and this disjunction is brought about by education, the academic sciences, art, delinquency, crimes, and in general by the whole of civic and political life; since life no longer has any common goal, it no longer constitutes a common task. The common task (the liturgy) has been abstracted from real life and has become simply a service inside the churches. But in the meantime, Christianity is in essence, not just a doctrine of redemption but precisely the work of redemption. Science, art, and the whole of modern secular life do not have this goal. Hence the bifurcation which is indeed at the heart of the problem of our era.

At present, worship inside the churches has lost the significance even of the Liturgy of the Catechumens, since it no longer leads either to a real addition of new members or to the increase of mutuality and brotherhood. As long as those who have fallen away (traitors) exist in the Church, and as long as there are people in the world not united to the Church (unbaptized, unadopted), just so long will it be impossible to have a full Liturgy of the Faithful (faithful to Christ and to one another, i.e., to all, to brotherhood). To call the Church Ecumenical while unbelievers (those who have not yet accepted the fraternal obligation, have not given their word to be faithful, or who have broken it) still exist in the world would be opposed to truth and

age; ancestors do not exist for it, it is world-wide in space, but
in time. Finally, it is only *citizenship*, not kinship, and its
mula might well be: "Where there is more to be gained, there
y fatherland." But it is better to be the lowest, the last of
an sons than to be the king of all the elect minds, like
o, or Aristotle, or all the philosophers from Thales down to
latest in time (who cannot understand that they too are
digal sons," i.e., brothers). The worldly god of the philoso-
s is the god of the living generation only, but not of the
g in the Christian sense.

hus, as a precept, signifying persons conceived not separately
s brought together for the common family task, the doctrine
e Triunity is the demand or obligation which must lead the
an family not only out of the power of natural selection, so
it exists, i.e., out of the power of strife and bondage, but
ut of the power of sexual selection. The doctrine of the
begotten Son explains the plan of that communion in
independence consists not in separateness but in a unity
ich there is no bondage, no oppression; and the doctrine of
oly Spirit explains the plan of that common activity in
the obligation of human sons and daughters to their uni-
fatherland finally takes precedence over their obligation to
mmunity of sexual selection.

mparing the present state of the human family with what
t to be, the question of the reasons for nonkinship arises.
iunity is the highest expression of kinship.

ite of all the difficulties, the universal raising of the dead
the return to the normal condition when mankind (in
trol of nature as well as of its own forces) will actualize the
thought in the unlimited riches of matter, not under
sion, but out of a superabundance of spiritual power, hav-
s pattern a Divine Being who is accessible to the con-
ion of the human family. Of course one must not bring
"life of the world to come" the conditions of reality in

reality. But if there is no Ecumenical Church, then there is no
Liturgy of the Faithful. Our Church does not wish to exalt
herself when she calls herself Orthodox. On the contrary, she
wishes in this way to express her sense of a lack of fullness since
the time of the breaking away of the Western Church, as a result
of which she no longer considers her councils Ecumenical, nor
does she regard the decisions of her territorial councils as
Ecumenical truths. The continued use of the name "Catholic"
by the Church of Rome (since the time when she was almost
such in fact) only testifies to the fact that she acknowledges the
necessity of the Ecumenical Church, which she prays for constantly in her prayer "For the Unity of the Church." Orthodoxy
is a bitter regret (remorse) for disunity and a desire for the fullness of unity in space (of all the living), in time (of all the
dead), and in power (revivification to a life without end). The
Liturgy of the Catechumens (the uniting of the living—the creation of fraternity), i.e., the visible earthly Church called to
fulfill the Liturgy of the Faithful, originates in regret for the disunity of the living. The common task (the Liturgy of the Faithful—the restoration of the dead in reality, so that the invisible
Church becomes visible) originates in regret for the departed
(the remembrance of the dead, their restoration in thought).

Pagan, false worship of fathers, and true, Christian worship—revivification

The mistake of both ancient and modern philosophers is that
they see in paganism only one fault: the exclusive worship of
private gods and the resulting limitation to family (community)
of duty, justice, and kindness; while for Christianity they acknowledge but one merit: the removal of this pagan exclusiveness—in other words, universality. In the meantime, they have
not noticed that the pagan worship of gods was at the same time

the self-denying worship of fathers. In the language of the philosophers this self-denying worship was called slavery to family, kin and community . . . the absence of personal freedom. On the other hand, the philosophers have not seen that Christianity rendered something more than merely negative service by its destruction of exclusiveness. They have not seen that Christianity established as its goal the replacement of a superstitious worship of fathers (thought of as still living) by a real and universal raising of the dead.

At first glance, past history presents two periods, two developments, which apparently have nothing in common; so that if the more recent one be acknowledged as true (as it is today), then the earlier development, the earlier period of history must be accepted as unconditionally false. But in fact both developments served the same function, although they were not conscious of this. The feeling of morality created an obligation toward the departed, toward the fathers, and out of this obligation there arose the family, the kin, the community. "The idea of a fatherland was born in the grave." But the form in which this obligation was expressed was not the true, genuine fulfillment of the obligation, was not the restoration of life to the fathers. Here is the first weak point in the earlier period. The second weak point is that worship was offered by each family and by each community exclusively to its own fathers and heroes. As a result of this mistaken view, each family could exalt its own fathers above the fathers or ancestors of other families, and completely deprive other people of a fatherland, i.e., consider them as un-families. And so there arose enmity, oppression; clients and hirelings appeared; then orphans, plebeians, and, in general, a host of children of unknown parentage. These same weak sides of the first period in ancient history also led to the breakdown of the ancient family and community. It was easy for philosophy to come along and prove that the dead need no food, that no prayers or curses whatever can change the fate of the departed. But philosophy won an empty victory. And if, as living men, the

people as a whole did not know how to sepa
life and even ascribed life to the dead, then t
class of people separated from living realit
journing in the realm of dead abstractions
the reality of death. So there was superstiti
losophy did have a certain amount of trut
ing out the invalidity of the worship of
period. But its error lay in the fact that
life of its sacred character, it killed love
replaced this by patriotism, i.e., pride in
rowed down the sphere of man's activity
pose of life simply profit, comfort. If
departed created the family and the co
phy destroyed the family in part, and
community, creating first the Macedon
Empires. Stoicism encouraged the spre
to all; it expressed the idea of a world-
a world-wide god, but not the God of
the dead, since, of course, under the te
munity" they included only the livin
cism has anything at all in common
because stoicism is its perversion; nc
completely perverted than in stoicism
the idea of a world-wide civic comm
process of which the first and mos
complished by the common people
who shifted from the gods of the
fraternity, and the civic community
cestors, on which the undying flar
pritanei) represented the invisible
ders of the state. If the idea of ma
grasped, then the family hearth n
forefathers. But there is a treme
people's idea of the human fam
citizenship. The latter attaches

life as it is now, of reality as it is now, characterized by failings and sufferings, by the transition from worse to better. Another way is possible: the transition from one good thing to another no less excellent, without the destruction of the first, which is still retained. To remain forever in an all but resurrected state is a luxury we can do without!

Why the universal raising of the dead did not immediately follow the Resurrection of Christ

How is one to understand, how is one to imagine why the resurrection of all did not follow the Resurrection of Christ? Christianity would not be Christianity (i.e., world-wide love), Christ would not be the Son of Man (the son of the departed fathers), He would not be heart and soul in the grave of the fathers (in hell), He would be completely incomprehensible, if the connection between His Resurrection and the universal resurrection were broken. But according to Christian teaching, as expressed not only in word but also in the whole celebration of the Bright Feast,[7] the Resurrection of Christ is inseparably bound up with universal resurrection. We must see the raising of the dead as a not yet completed action. But then it is not an action to be completed only in the future, as the Mohammedans believe. It is neither altogether in the past nor exclusively in the future, but a public action in process of completion. "The hour is coming, and now is" (John 5:25). Christ is its initiator and through us it has been continued and is continuing even now. The raising of the dead is not a thought only, but also not an accomplished fact; it is a project. As a word, a precept, a divine command, it is an accomplished fact. But as a task or fulfillment of the command, it is an action not yet completed. As a work

[7] Easter.

of God it is already finished; as a work of man it is not yet finished.

The Protestant, academic, or Western understanding of Christ's exploit on the Cross

If Christ's exploit on the Cross is regarded from an abstract, academic, snobbish point of view, from the learned point of view, then the work of Christ is justification and nothing more; not a work, but simply a thought. Catholicism's perversion of Christianity consists in its replacement of revivification by works of justification—of course it is incomprehensible how revivification could ever be the consequence of such works, since "justice" alone cannot be the cause of restoration of life, and can even be the cause of its destruction. Protestantism, on the other hand, having rejected works of justification, has become simply the thought of justification (instead of the one task, the task of raising of the dead). If Christ's exploit is seen as justification and nothing more, then it must be admitted that only the sufferings of the Innocent One can propitiate the One who is Omniscient and All Powerful. But if it is admitted that His exploit involves a joining together of knowledge and the power which restores life, then the exploit will be seen as the demand on God's part for man to become a likeness of Himself, and not as a mere propitiation of His wrath. There is only an imagined immortality in the system of justification, no real vivification. Justification, redemption, regeneration, sanctification, reconciliation—all these are but abstract expressions for the raising of the dead. If justification is the enlikening of man to Christ as the pattern of perfect virtue, then virtue must be understood not as abstract goodness but as revivification, as the full expression of love for the fathers and of the brotherhood of sons, since Christ is the one Who raises from the dead—as Saviour—and His whole significance lies in this, just as the whole significance and last word of morality lies in the raising of the dead.

What, then, is history?

In trying to explain to ourselves why the universal raising of the dead did not follow the Resurrection of Christ, we are not trying to excuse the alleged contradictions in Christianity, as those do who believe more in the might of civilization than they do in the power of Christianity. Rather, we are trying to save history itself from becoming a disgrace, trying to lead it to an actualization of the "Good News." We are accusing the learned people who justify their labors of making a false evaluation, of a reduction in the worth of their labors, of disgracing their task by regarding it as aimless. If history is seen as an actualization of the "Good News," it will become apparent that—since a general revivification did not come about immediately after Christ's Resurrection—His Resurrection was the beginning of universal revivification, with subsequent history its continuation. Universal revivification could not have been brought about at the same time as the Resurrection of Christ, since it involves the conscious labor of the whole human race joined together over the face of the whole earth and even extending beyond the limits of this earthly planet. By converting the influences of Earth into conscious work, the whole united human race will place the blind forces of other heavenly bodies under the control of earthly forces which will themselves be governed by both reason and feeling (and thus be vivifying). The human race has not yet consciously addressed itself to such a task, although the work of raising the dead (the unification of the human race) has indeed gone on in perverted ways. The great common task (which alone contains the whole essence of Christianity) has been replaced by competition in the production of trinkets, and by marching into battle and war. The investigation of the reasons for the perver-

sion (the question of nonkinship) is a return to a direct, conscious unification in the task of revivification, since, of course, this
investigation has in view something more than mere knowledge.
Its goal is to reveal the task of all (not just one, or a few) mortals. For learned people, history is a judgment or verdict which
they, the learned ones, pronounce. But for the unlearned, i.e.,
for people as a whole (among whom the learned are as a drop
in the ocean), history is a remembrance of the dead. And if the
remembrance of the dead is sincere, it cannot forever remain
simply a remembrance, simply a regret over that which is lost,
"never to return."

The unlearned definition of history

The question is: Can present-day knowledge devote itself to
this great task? Is the learned class capable of becoming a ministry of unification in this common task? Is that class which
maintains itself with prejudices and whose religion is the acceptance of a dead, lifeless god and a lifeless immortality, whose
ethic consists not even in egoism but in solipsism (which, when
combined with the claim to an absurd "altruism," makes this
class the worst of all pharisees), is such a class capable of such
a transformation? Is that class capable of action which, even as
it turns every thought and word into coveted private property,
asserts that its renunciation of a future life is a laudable kind of
disinterestedness; that class which, as it renounces belief in the
future, pharisaically melts with emotion over its own cheap sacrifice? The learned class, freed as it is from compulsory military
service, considers itself peace-loving; it even mourns the fact that
people are unable to live in peace, and becomes indignant when
they take up arms. This class preaches peace in words, but does
not notice that in whatever work it is doing, whether it be pure
or applied science, it is itself promoting the business of war, ei-

ther directly (if the application of its knowledge is related to the perfection of weapons) or indirectly (when the application of its knowledge is related to industry and commerce, which in themselves promote enmity and therefore serve to stimulate war). But if the learned class occupies itself with pure science and is not concerned about application (which, incidentally, others will be concerned about, for no pure science will remain long without application to war or industry), it will be digressing from true knowledge, which is not just knowledge of general causes but the knowledge of the causes of nonkinship, enmity, and war. And these will be eliminated, not by preaching (no matter how persuasive), not by indignation (no matter how vigorous), not by banishing descriptions of war from the history books, but only by the elimination of the very causes of diversity, nonkinship, enmity, and war.

So then for learned people history is just a story. But for the unlearned history is a project, a participation in the universal raising of the dead, inseparable from knowledge when knowledge stands at the pinnacle of morality and religion. The pinnacle of morality is the point where one does not separate oneself from others, does not separate "one's own" from what is common, where there is no contradiction between thought and action. And the pinnacle of religion is Christianity, which does not separate the Resurrection of Christ from the resurrection of all.

Translated by Asheleigh E. Moorhouse
April, 1964

Vasily Vasilyevich Rozanov

1856 - 1918

In his *History of Russian Literature*, D. S. Mirsky wrote: "Dostoevsky . . . for the profundity, complexity, and significance of his spiritual experience, has only two possible rivals in the whole range of Russian literature—Rozanov and of course Tolstoy. . . ." Yet Rozanov is still very little known and those who know him are deeply divided on the significance of his message. The man was indeed a living contradiction. He combined an almost physical attachment to the Church, its clergy, its liturgy and customs, with the most violent criticism of Christianity; a love for the Old Testament with vulgar anti-Semitism; a unique literary gift with journalistic cynicism. And in everything —in religion, politics, literature —he was unique, disclaiming adherence to any school or movement, defending his loneliness and independence.

Born in a very poor family, he spent the first half of his life as a rather unsuccessful teacher of geography in provincial schools, where pupils hated him. He went through the influences of Dostoevsky, the Slavophiles, Konstantin Leontiev: it was a long way to originality, to "his own" words in "his own" way. He idolized Dostoevsky so much that at the age of twenty he married the writer's former mistress, Polina Suslova, who was forty! Later in life he married a humble, poor, and ill-educated daughter of a provincial deacon and was happy with her and with their five children. His first writings attracted attention, and in 1893 he settled in St. Petersburg where he began his brilliant journalistic career with the conservative paper *Novoye Vremya* (New Times), which was unanimously hated by the "progressive" intelligentsia. Although a free lance by nature, Rozanov took part in the activities of the Religious Philosophical Society, founded by Merezhkovsky in 1901. There, at the beginning of the century, "a new encounter took place—the encounter of the intelligentsia with the Church after the stormy experience of nihilism, denial, and forgetfulness" (G. Florovsky).

Rozanov left no system and it is almost impossible to detach his ideas from the highly personal and original language and style in which he expressed them. He wrote on many subjects— culture, history, sex, literature—

but there can be no doubt that the heart of all his suffering and intuition was a tremendously real experience of God—but an experience radically opposed to an equally real experience of the world. He could not reconcile the truth of God, whom he personally loved, with the truth of the world. Hence the complexity of his writings, which are deeply religious even when fighting religion. And it is the unique way in which he communicates and describes this experience that makes him one of the "strongest Russian religious philosophers" (Zenkovsky). Rozanov died at peace with the Church in 1918.

Bibliography

Rozanov's writings have not been collected even in Russian. His most important books are:

Religia i Kultura ("Religion and Culture"). 1899.
V mire neyasnago i nereshennago ("In the World of Things Obscure"). St. Petersburg: Merkushev, 1899.
Temny Lik ("The Dark Image"). 1911.
Okolo tserkovnykh sten ("At the Walls of the Church"). St. Petersburg: Weisberg and Gershunin, 1906.

Uyedinennoe ("The Intimate"). St. Petersburg, 1916.
Opavshie listia ("Fallen Leaves"). St. Petersburg: Suvorin, 1913.

In English:

Solitaria, intro. by James Stephens. London: Wishart, 1927.
There is an excellent analysis in Zenkovsky, *A History of Russian Philosophy*, Vol. I, Ch. XII. New York: Columbia University Press, 1953.

Sweet Jesus and the Sour Fruits of the World[1]

THOSE SAME THEMES which disturbed the "Religious-Philosophical Meetings" of 1902–1903 are being raised in meetings today. Those questions about the spirit and the flesh, "Christian community," and society in the broad sense; about the relationship of the Church and art; marriage and virginity; the Gospel and paganism; and so on and so on. In his brilliant paper, "Gogol and Father Matvey," D. S. Merezhkovsky has urgently raised the question of the relationship of Christianity to art, especially the relationship, for example, of Orthodoxy to the character of Gogol's work. In contrast with Father Matvey, Gogol's famous spiritual counselor, he thinks that the Gospel is compatible with sweet devotion to the muses, that it is possible both to listen to the preaching of Father Matvey and to read and reread *The Inspector General* and *Dead Souls*, heartily laughing at the characters there. The pathos of Dmitry Sergeyevich, at least at that moment, was in the idea of the *compatibility* of the Gospel with all that man has loved so much in the thousands of years of his culture. The reverend fathers, even the higher clergy, and all the secular theologians backed him up, nodding in agreement that "of course the Gospel is in harmony with everything high

[1] From *Temny Lik*, reprinted in V. V. *Rozanov Izbrannoe* (New York, Chekhov Publishing House, 1956), pp. 95–108.

and noble"; that it is "cultural"; and therefore culture and the Church, clergy and writers, can sit down "harmoniously" at one table, carry on nice conversations with one another, and sip out of the same pot of tasty tea. All this was extraordinarily nice, and in the highest degree tranquilizing. Servetus in Geneva and Savonarola in Florence, both burned at the stake, could not raise their voices in our disputes. On the other hand, the "Union of the Russian People" had not yet started its activities. We were debating this in 1902, forgetting the past and not forseeing the future, surrendering ourselves to the sweet moment.

It seems to me that the question is resolved with the help of mental inlays. If one were to put into the Gospel a piece of Gogol's prose, the most well-intended piece, directed, so to speak, toward the best possible goal, then we would get a murderously unbearable cacophony, stemming not just from the dissimilarity of the human and the divine, of the weak and the strong, but from the fact that there are two categories here. Not only is it impossible to put a piece of Gogol into the Gospels, but also into any of the apostolic epistles. Saul was not gradually brought up to be Paul, he was *converted* into Paul; he did not add a new kernel to his older rabbinical wisdom—not even a whole new ear—in the form of faith in Christ. No, he vomited up his rabbinic tradition. The relationship within him was Saul vs. Paul: each "I" devouring the other. And this happens with anyone who has turned to Christ; the old devours the new. The apostle Paul certainly did not propose to the Athenians that they "believe in Christ and *at the same time* go to the Olympic games." In moments of rest—any kind of rest, for a day, for an hour—he did not enter the Greek theater to see a tragedy. We know for sure, by a subtle feeling for psychological nuances, that this is not only not mentioned in "Acts," but simply *could not have been.* Paul in the theater—an impossible scene! Acclaiming the play of the actors—cacophony! the destruction of all Christianity! And yet this would only be the same "reconciliation" and "harmony" for which D. S. Merezhkovsky is pleading.

Yes, Paul labored, ate, smelled, walked about, lived in the material conditions of life; but he had made a profound break with them, since he no longer *loved* or *admired* anything in them. He took matter only as something *necessary* and *utilitarian*, he knew and felt the need of only what was prose to the flesh. Christ was the one flower of the flesh, a mono-flower, if it's all right to put it that way. "I walk, eat, sleep, taste; but I am satisfied only by Christ" is something every real Christian can say about himself.

Christ never *laughed*. Isn't it obvious that all Gogol's laughing was culpable in him insofar as he was a Christian? I don't remember if Christ *smiled* or not. But the imprint of sorrow, of consuming sorrow, is obvious in the Gospel. There are joys in it too, but completely different, schematic, heavenly joys; joys coming from an immeasurable height above the earth and mankind. Let's not be deceived by the "lilies of the field." In any case, this is not botany, or gardening, or science, or poetry, but only a design, a scheme, a smile at the earth. The point is that the Gospel really isn't an *earthy* book, and everything earthy is extremely hard to connect or is simply not connected with it; or if connected, then artificially and temporarily. I shall permit myself a little parallel. Words buzz past our ears: "Christian marriage," "the Christian family," "Christian children." What an illusion! Of course there never was such a thing and there never will be before the end of time! I suggested that you make an inlay of Gogol in the Gospel, and you got a cacophony. I now propose that you imagine one of the young wives of the Gospel, or any of the apostles (excuse my temerity) as being in love. I ask to be excused, and indeed you feel that I *ought* to ask to be excused. Why? Because of the *complete incompatibility* of physical love and the Gospel. I have not read Renan's *Life of Jesus*, but I have repeatedly heard, in words of profound indignation, that the temerity of this French freethinker went so far that he depicted one of the Gospel's figures as being in love. The *taste* of the whole world, of all the throngs of readers of the

Gospel, sensed in this the deepest sacrilege against divine nature. This is the same question as the one about Father Matvey and Gogol. It is only another instance. But the apostles, including Peter and Paul, were *married*. Yes, but then in a kind of special, gospel marriage. The example I have indicated is not an empty one even in a practical matter. The Church permits its priests to marry, but to marry *anyone* and right now, *without courtship or the attraction of love*; i.e., everything is arranged in their marriage so that the groom cannot and must not be in love with his bride, any more than an officer is with a soldier. The relations of officer and soldier are preserved, but there's no love. The relations of husband and wife are preserved in Christianity, but love—out of which one would have thought that marriage is born—is passed over in sepulchral, even *intentional, fatal, darkling* silence. There is no laughing or physical love in the Gospel, and one drop of either would reduce all the pages of this wondrous book to ashes, would "tear asunder the curtains" of Christianity.

Yes, the "dead" were restored when Christ died; but on the other hand the mysterious "curtain of Solomon's temple" was "torn asunder" . . . and didn't the "law" of this "temple"[2] state, in the meantime, that it was forbidden to use, either as an instrument in its making or as a part of it, the smallest scrap of iron, since "weapons come from iron, and weapons shorten life."[3] Consequently the mysterious meaning of the temple is the "lengthening of life." But let us leave these and a host of other observations. Let us turn to our special theme.

Neither Gogol nor literature in general, as a game, as a frolic, a smile, a graciousness, as the flower of human everyday life, is

[2] In Ezekiel's vision of the mysterious temple such terms are used as: "it is necessary to know the *law* of the temple that is being built," "to know the *law* of the sacrificial altar within it," i.e., the *principle*, the *essence*, the *hidden idea* both of the temple and the altar. (V. V. R.)

[3] Thus a certain passage of the Talmud explains the complete and careful elimination of iron from the materials of its construction, and from the tools and instruments with which it was built. (V. V. R.)

in any way compatible with the *mono*-flower, "sweetest Jesus."
What about the *world* then? I cry out with Merezhkovsky.
What about us, in the *flower* and *joy* of our life?

Everything that the religious people said then, on the occasion
of D. S. Merezhkovsky's paper, for instance that they "would go
to the theater, if the theater were *better*," was evasive and
really stemmed from the need to say something when they
obviously could not say *nothing*. Yes, of course, if actors were to
come out on the theater's boards and begin to bellow about
their godlessness, then the gentlemen bishops would have gone
to such a spectacle with pleasure. But suggest that the rather
innocent song "In the Meadows" be played for them on the
flute, and they will refuse. It is not *sinful* pleasures that are forbidden to them, but pleasures as such. All that is not sorrowful
is not permitted for them. Wine, tea, fine fish, jam, fine apart-
ments, and furniture—are really smuggled in to them like contraband. But officially, under the law, under the "Church's
regulations," it is definitely impossible to say: "A bishop can in-
dulge himself with a fine table of fish." He must eat only dried
mushrooms—this is what can be said officially. In saying this I
am distinguishing the legal merchandise from the contraband
within Christianity. The arts, the muses, Gogol, a fine table, and
jam are all smuggled into the Christian world as contraband.
"This is permissible"; but nobody adds "this is convenient" (the
formula of the apostle Paul), and yet this addition contains the
whole point, all of poetry, the little flower—which the *mono*-
flower, Jesus, definitely does not allow.

Christianity and the Gospel have really extended their embrace—I was about to say their clutch—endlessly. Christianity
has let down the broad mouth of its net on eternity, but
this is only something "permissible," it is really just the expression of its own goodness, condescension, and forgiveness. It
even "forgives" Gogol, you see, and Pushkin, and jam . . . even
the adulteress and adultery; without which, incidentally, all
the saints—beginning with blessed Augustine, who experienced

such a stormy youth—would not have fallen into the net. But a *forgiveness* is not at all the same as a summons. Christians are summoned to one thing only—to love Christ. Of course Gogol and all his work (without any interruption whatever) could be "saved." But there are different kinds of salvation: there are *heroes* of salvation, there are *great ones* in Christianity, there is a poetry of Christian salvation, in its own way a kind of *spiritual romance*. Only martyrs have passed as heroes, and Gogol became, and had to become, a martyr in order to enter into the romance and poetry of Christianity.

The point is that an *action*, an *effort*, a *jump*, a *game*—either in the sphere of art or of literature—or laughter, or pride, etc., is impossible from the Christian point of view. In general, jam is permitted; but not too tasty . . . better if it be spoiled, or still better—that there be no jam at all. But if there is jam, and tasty jam at that, well then it's forgiven . . . the possibility of Christian *breadth* is based on this. By means of the net of "forgiveness," of goodness, of condescension, Christianity has embraced a whole abyss of quite unnecessary, and in its own eyes, worthless articles. It has seized the "prince of this world" and dragged him off to a *diminution*. Christianity is the religion of a descending progression, eternally striving toward, but never attaining, the quantity "Christ plus something," "Christ plus wealth," "Christ plus glory," "Christ plus the comforts of life." This "something" added to Christianity has always been simply condescended to, and diminished in our souls in proportion to the ascendancy of Christ. The "prince of this world" has melted away near the Christ-sun like a snowball, like a snowman in spring. Really what has been left for Christians is an outline of the "prince of this world," of family, literature, and art. The *nerve* has been drawn out of it all—a doll remains, not a living being. As soon as you try to enliven the family, art, and literature, as soon as you surrender yourself to anything "heart and soul," you immediately begin the fatal exit from Christianity. Hence Father Matvey's yelling at Gogol. It wasn't that Gogol was working in the field of literature. Let him work. But the jam had to be sour. Gogol was working *passionately* in the field of literature, and this was forbidden! A monk may commit adultery with a young lady; a monk may have a child; but the child must be thrown into the river. The minute the monk clings to the child and says "I won't let him go"; the minute he clings to the young lady and says "I love her and will not stop loving her"— Christianity is ended. As soon as the family becomes *serious*, Christianity suddenly turns into a joke; as soon as Christianity becomes serious, the family, literature, and art turn into a joke. They all exist, but not in their true form. They all exist, but without an ideal.

What about it? Where is there a place for *all this?* D. S. Merezhkovsky is indignant over the grey or variegated aspect of Christianity, its striation; a black strip, a white strip; affliction— but not eternal; monasteries and fasts—but set in the midst of a lovely landscape. One can write an ode—"Reflections on the Majesty of God While Viewing the Northern Lights"—but it's a sin to write "The Bronze Horseman." But what is the *pure black color?* It is *death*, the *grave*, about which I have spoken in one of my previous papers and which can definitely not be torn away from Christianity. This is its backbone and four legs. It goes forward by way of the "grave," it is created on the grave. What is the *pure white color?* The Hellene and the Jew revivified, Egypt revivified. All three in a resplendent new embodiment, with various modern nuances, but in essence the same. The dancer before the Ark of the Covenant; "Sing praises to the Lord upon the harp," as Judith said. The Hellene is the tranquil, undisturbed Jew; the Jew without depth. The Jew is the yolk of that Easter egg whose shell and white are Hellenism; a decorated literary shell, with the inscription "Christ has risen," with figures, painting, the arts, the whole of Hellenistic civilization. But while the shell with all its inscriptions is strong, the white is poorly nourished and has not grown. The most important thing is the yolk hidden within and the embryonic spot on that yolk . . .

I return to the details of D. S. Merezhkovsky's paper. God does not have just one child—Jesus—but two: the world and Jesus. The world is the child of God because it was created by Him. Like a fragment in proportion to its existence, Gogol too exists in the world, and poetry, plays, games, graciousness, the family, the Hellene, the Jew, and all of paganism. All this is the kingdom of God the Father and the product of His generative power. It was not all at once, not in the Apostolic Age, but later, two or three hundred years after Christ, that the Church began to wonder "What about the *world?*" and clarified, was compelled to clarify the fact that the "Son of God" is Jesus, "Who stands in the shadow and likeness of the Father." But the Church only *named* the Father, not being in any position to imagine Him; if she depicted Him in the form of an old man she fell into obvious anthropomorphism. "No one has ever seen God" are the words of the New Testament; "It is impossible to see Me and not die" God said about Himself to Moses. Christian teachers see, and always have seen, part of the Scriptures; never, it seems, have they taken the whole into consideration. And in general all the Church's concepts are constructed as if in a dream: here you'll find rabid spiritualism, the coarsest anthropomorphism, and even fetishism. Everything has found a place in her eclectic, "variegated" building. Into this *Fatherly* Hypostasis (defined only numerically), the world enters with its radiancy, its ideals, comedies, tragedies, with its common everyday life; the world is by its physical nature holy, holy not, however, in the physical nature of the Son, but by its *procession* out of the physical nature of the Father. Thus in the realm of Jesus-ism, Merezhkovsky's question has found no response whatever —or receives a sharply negative response—while in the realm of the trihypostatic confession of the Church the question finds a full and satisfactory resolution. But the Church herself has done nothing about the Father, other than her anthropomorphic and sinfully artistic representations, other than her issuing of a kind of "license of residence." It is true that she says "Creator of the world" and "Providence." But these are abstract predicates. The Jews also have prayed to the Creator of the world and to Providence, calling Him by their own never actually pronounced name—as have the Egyptians and Babylonians. Generally speaking, every people has always known the Creator of the world and Providence, and in acknowledging the "Fatherly Hypostasis," the Church's teachers unconsciously acknowledged, in fact, the whole pagan world. If this had happened three centuries earlier the apostle Paul would have had nothing to fight against. His struggle, from the loftiest points of view of the Church herself, is foolishness. There were no real reasons for his conversion from Saul into Paul, for the shaking of Sinai, for his becoming a despised blot on Olympus and the Capitoline, where the true being of God was being worshiped under lesser, incorrect names; where they were glorifying the holy Creator in His holy creations. But the historical enigma consists precisely in the fact that there was a *Saul* and later a *Paul*, and not just a Paul who added the knowledge of Christ to his rabbinical wisdom. It will always be a mystery: Why did Nicodemus not accept Christ? Why did Gamaliel not accept Him, and in general all those kind Jews who were really wholly Christian in heart, in character, and in everyday life? They have said nothing about this and have hidden the greatest mystery of the world in silence. If they had spoken about it there would have been no clash between Father Matvey and Gogol. There would have been no Inquisition, there would have been no destruction by the Inquisition of the Incas and Peruvians. The Jesuit order with its "secrets" would never have arisen, an order fanatical to the point of madness and given to lying like "forty thousand brothers," to use Shakespeare's expression.[4]

The point is, are the children of God—the World-Child and

----

[4] A curious reference, since the passage, in Act V, Scene 1 of *Hamlet*, does not suggest or deal with the idea of deceit. (Trans.)

the Jesus-Child—in harmony? This is the question to which
Merezhkovsky's paper leads us. I do not know how to answer
this question, and it cannot be answered without detailed re-
search, examination, and comparison.

The world had fallen apart—and the Gospel fell into it. The
world *accepted it, accepted it with love*. The Gospel was inlayed
into the world.

But Gogol does not enter the Gospel as an inlay; love, physical
love, is not to be inlayed in the Gospel. And in general the Gospel
does not *open itself up for the world*, does not accept it into
itself. The world stands *beyond the binding* of the heavenly
book. The world's ruddy glow departs, it pales as soon as it comes
close to this binding. Here I recall the Pale Horseman[5] of the
Apocalypse, but right now I'm unable to remember exactly what
he signifies. We cannot resolve Merezhkovsky's question but
can only lay the groundwork for its resolution.

As far as I can tell, listening here to the religious gentlemen,
they do not have *any* metaphysics of Christianity, let alone a
true one. Christianity simply appears to them as something good.
"We are good people and do not understand what you want of
us"; this is the sense of all their replies to the world's perplexity.
When reproaches sound, they say, "We are humble people and
we admit our errors," and a smile of satisfaction almost spreads
across their faces. It is impossible to shake their position of
virtue. "We firmly confess the most virtuous faith and are ourselves virtuous to the point of humility and the admission of our
sins, the most exquisite state which man can attain." In the
meantime, secular perplexity rolls round inside the hoop of
metaphysics. Religion simply as virtue, as *summa virtutum*,
seems impossible to us as people of the world. Religion is a
mystery, a mysterious design of steely hardness, with not a bit
of flexibility in it. We would prefer that the religious people
would thunder with indignation and anathemas, then we'd see

[5] Actually a pale horse, not horseman (cf. Revelation 6:8)—but the point
is made: the rider's name is Death. (Trans.)

the *borderline* between ourselves and them, something we definitely do not see now. "What the devil, we're good people too
. . . I, Merezhkovsky, and the others." In the indignation of the
religious people we would see what they love—and we'd rush to
analyze, inspect, and perhaps even love this thing beloved by
them. "Christianity is the grave and death," we say to them.
"What are you talking about? Absolutely not!" they answer.
"Why, we sympathize with every joy!" Well then, go to the
theater, if only to *Boris Godunov*—a patriotic work, or to *Life
with the Tsar*, even more so. Passing over Godunov and Glinka
in silence, they say "The theater is insufficiently serious." Yes, but
what about the fact that the Alexander Nevsky Monastery has
granaries, while trading was forbidden by the Saviour? They let
this one go by, or say instead, "But look here, Christ did not
estrange Himself from the land, He ate with the publicans and
sinners." "Then go to the opera." "We can't, it's vulgar." But
it isn't that it's vulgar, it's because it's *fun*. It's just that their
"regulations" don't permit them anything that is *fun*, or *happy*.
Fun and happiness are the negation of death, a forgetting of
the coffin. The family and art are the decorations of life. Even
the coffin is sometimes decorated with trimmings, with little
silver handles. These lovely landscapes around the monasteries
are just like the little silver handles around the coffin. Merezhkovsky's paper, coming after my paper on death as the main
ideal of Christianity, raises the question a second time: "What is
Christianity?" And it is definitely impossible to answer this by
saying, "We are good people." It is necessary instead to answer
metaphysically and with demonstrations. It seems to me that
we should set aside one meeting to hear the clergy's answers to
this question, not their eloquent and well-turned, nor their
moral and evasive answers, but just indignant and even anathe-
matizing answers, which reply directly to the question. For our
ignorance is painful. It hurts.

As an aid to future discussions I shall allow myself a little
personal conjecture, by no means dogmatic. Jesus is certainly

more beautiful than anything in the world or even the world itself. When He appeared, then, like the sun, He dimmed the stars. Stars are needed at night. The stars are science, family, art. It cannot be denied that the Face of Christ depicted in the Gospel—at least as we have read about Him and as we have understood Him—is "sweeter" and more attractive than family, or kingdoms, or power, or wealth. Gogol is a straw before the chief of the evangelists. So if there is a death in Christ, then it is a sweet death, a death-weariness. Hermits, of course, have their delights too. They die from weariness, renouncing every world. Let us pass on to the phenomena of the world. Since the birth of Christ, since the shining forth of the Gospel, all the fruits of the earth have suddenly become sour. The world has become sour in Christ, precisely as a result of His sweetness. As soon as you have tasted the sweetest, most unheard-of, genuinely heavenly bread—you lose the taste for ordinary bread. Who wants a potato after eating a pineapple? This is the essence of idealism in general, of the ideal, of the greatest thing. Great beauty makes us immune to ordinary beauty. Everything is "ordinary" in comparison with Christ. Not just Gogol but also literature in general, science in general. Still further, the whole world and everything, be it ever so mysterious, ever so interesting, yields to Christ precisely in the area of *sweetness*. When His extraordinary beauty enlightened the world, then the most sensitive being in the world, man, lost his taste for the world that surrounded him. The world simply became sour, flat, boring. This is the main consequence proceeding from the coming of Christ. Let us draw a little parallel. We would study all the princes of the Middle Ages if it hadn't been for Charlemagne. If it had not been for the El Ladhi we perhaps might have studied, in the most careful way, the history of the various Mongol tribes. We would be attentive to the small and the ugly. But when there is something great at hand, what interest can there be in something small? Thus the world began to *sink* around Jesus. A general inundation of former ideal things began. This inundation is also called Christianity. The gods, Jehovahs, and Dianas sank; the relative ideals of man sank before the universal ideal of heaven. You must see that you can surrender yourself to the arts, family, politics, and science *only by not looking attentively at Jesus*. Gogol looked *attentively* at Christ—and threw down his pen and died. And to the extent that it looks attentively at Jesus the whole world throws down its work, whatever it is, and dies. "It is impossible for you to see Me and not die," God said to Moses. The young man from Saïs looked at the "being of God" and died. In general, death and knowledge of God are somehow mutually inclusive. God is not the world. And as soon as you glance at God you have begun to "pass out of the world," have begun to "die." I have observed that the tone of the Gospel is sorrowful, melancholy, "funereal." But sorrow is loftier than joy, more ideal. Tragedy is loftier than comedy. We are all good people now; but we'll become excellent people in the world of sadness, when we have lost our wives, our children. A beggar is more beautiful than a millionaire; and poets bring beggars into their descriptions. But who ever described a millionaire? He's a subject of satire. So one of the great enigmas of the world is the fact that suffering is more ideal, more aesthetic, than happiness—more sorrowful, more majestic. We are incredibly attracted to the sorrowful. Doesn't the secret of the religious sacrifice of children to God lie here? the never-explained secret of Moloch? People survived heavenly sorrow and sought to experience it; they sacrificed all for it, *even the chief thing*. A "death before death" . . . Moloch!

Let us turn to our particular question. Isn't the universal burial of the world in Christ the most aesthetic event, the high point of worldly beauty? Gogol cannot be inlayed into the Gospel; he cannot, therefore, be introduced into Christianity; he must simply be tossed out. Not from the earthly point of view, but precisely from the monastic viewpoint, as a sweet reconciliation with Christ. This is what is delaying the end of the world. All history in general, everyday life, songs, literature, the family, are impediments (but already weak impediments) to the burning up of all things in a Christ-death. Death: here is the loftiest affliction and the loftiest sweetness. However, nobody has discovered the secret of death. It crowns afflictions, but there is the weariness of a mysterious aesthetic in these afflictions. The tragedy of tragedies. From this point of view, Christ is a Tragic Person, as He has always revealed Himself to man. We don't know what the whole of Divinity is, and don't know it precisely to the extent that we are still alive, since life is the "other," the "reverse" side of God. People are trying to identify death with birth. It's possible. But why, for instance, is birth not identical with death? When a man is born, in reality he dies; his mother's belly is a tomb; his very conception is a move into death. But the point is that "here" and "there" are divided by a chasm, like "down" and "up," "external" and "internal." And however much you make them the same, whatever term, whatever sign you use, one term must exclude the other. "The world," "existence," "our life," are not divine. Or vice versa, "the world," "existence," "our life," are divine; and then "the grave," "the afterlife," "the world to come," are demonic.

But obviously Jesus is that "world to come" which is vanquishing "this world," our world, and has already vanquished it. And out of either series of equally possible predicates for this world you make a choice according to your own best judgment. The Church has always considered Christ as God, and *eo ipso* has been compelled to consider the whole world, our life, birth itself (not to mention the sciences and arts), as demonic, "lying in sin." And this is the way she has behaved toward them. Not that anything has to be improved, but simply that everything must be done away with.

Translated by Asheleigh E. Moorhouse
August, 1963

Nikolai Aleksandrovich Berdyaev

1874 - 1948

Of all modern Russian thinkers, Berdyaev is undoubtedly the one who is best known outside Russia. Many even in the West simply identify him with Russian Orthodoxy and make him a spokesman for the Church. But Berdyaev himself, it must be stressed, consistently and emphatically rejected all such identifications and, although a member of the Church till his death, was often at odds with many official doctrines. He was, in his own definition, a free religious philosopher, a nonconformist by nature and vocation who valued freedom above everything else. Yet for all his freedom and nonconformity, Berdyaev certainly belongs to the mainstream of the Russian religious revival as it was shaped by the contradictory, yet at the same time complementary influences of Khomyakov and Solovyov, Dostoevsky and Rozanov.

He was born in an aristocratic family and his first training was in a military school. But he preferred the University where, almost immediately, he joined the Social-Democratic party, was caught in its illegal activity and exiled for two years to Vologda. After a stay in Germany, he returned to Russia and became an active participant in the movement "from Marxism to idealism," and then from idealism to religion. During the revolutionary years Berdyaev was one of the moving spirits of the Free Religious Philosophical Academy, but in 1922 he was deported and spent his most creative years in Clamart, near Paris. From 1925 to 1940 he edited the remarkable quarterly *Put* ("The Way"), wrote more than twenty books, and won universal recognition and fame.

Bibliography

For a complete list of major works, see D. I. Lowrie, *Rebellious Prophet*, 1960.

Available in English:

The Meaning of the Creative Act. New York: Harper & Row, 1955.
Dostoevsky. London: Sheed & Ward, Ltd., 1934.
The Meaning of History. New York: Scribner, 1936.

The End of Our Time. London: Sheed & Ward, Ltd., 1932.

Leontiev. London: Bles, 1940.

Freedom and the Spirit, 11 vols. New York: Scribner, 1935.

Christianity and the Class War. London: Sheed & Ward, Ltd., 1933.

The Destiny of Man. New York: Harper & Row, 1935.

Solitude and Society. London: Bles, 1938.

The Fate of Man in the Modern World. New York: Morehouse–Barlow Co., 1935.

Spirit and Reality. London: Bles, 1937.

The Origin of Russian Communism. London: Bles, 1937.

Slavery and Freedom. New York: Scribner, 1939.

The Russian Idea. New York: Macmillan, 1946.

The Beginning and the End. New York: Harper & Row, 1952.

The Divine and the Human. London: Bles, 1947.

Dream and Reality. London: Bles, 1950.

The Realm of Spirit and the Realm of Caesar. New York: Harper & Row, 1953.

Truth and Revelation. New York: Harper & Row, 1954.

Books about Berdyaev:

Clarke, O. F., *Introduction to Berdyaev*. London: Bles, 1950.

Seaver, G., *Nicolas Berdyaev*. London: Clarke, Irwin & Company, 1950.

Spinka, M., *Nicolas Berdyaev: Captive of Freedom*. Philadelphia: Westminster, 1950.

Lowrie, D. I., *Rebellious Prophet*. New York: Harper & Row, 1960.

The Ethics of Creativity

1   The Nature of Creativeness

THE GOSPEL constantly speaks of the fruit which the seed must
bring forth if it falls on good soil, and of talents given to man
which must be returned with profit. Under cover of parable,
Christ refers in these words to man's creative activity, to his
creative vocation. Burying one's talents in the ground, i.e., absence of creativeness, is condemned by Christ. The whole of
St. Paul's teaching about various gifts is concerned with man's
creative vocation. The gifts are from God and they indicate that
man is intended to do creative work. These gifts are various, and
everyone is called to creative service in accordance with the special gift bestowed upon him. It is therefore a mistake to assert, as
people often do, that Holy Writ contains no reference to
creativeness. It does—but we must be able to read it, we must
guess what it is God wants and expects of man.

Creativeness is always a growth, an addition, the making of
something new that had not existed in the world before. The
problem of creativeness is the problem of whether something
completely new is really possible.[1] Creativeness, from its very
meaning, is bringing forth out of nothing. Nothing becomes
something, nonbeing becomes being. Creativeness presupposes

[1] See my books *Smysl Tvorchestva* (*The Meaning of the Creative Act*)
and *Freedom and the Spirit*.

nonbeing, just as Hegel's "becoming" does. Like Plato's Eros, creativeness is the child of poverty and plenty, of want and abundance of power. Creativeness is connected with sin and at the same time it is sacrificial. True creativeness always involves catharsis, purification, liberation of the spirit from psychophysical elements and victory over them. Creation is different in principle from generation and emanation. In emanation, particles of matter radiate from a center and are separated out. Nor is creation a redistribution of force and energy, as evolution is. So far from being identical with evolution, creation is the very opposite of it. In evolution, nothing new is made, but the old is redistributed. Evolution is necessity, creation is freedom. Creation is the greatest mystery of life, the mystery of the appearance of something new that had never existed before and is not deduced from, or generated by, anything. Creativeness presupposes nonbeing, Μὴ ὄν (and not οὐκ ὄν), which is the source of the primeval, precosmic, pre-existent freedom in man. The mystery of creativeness is the mystery of freedom. Creativeness can only spring from fathomless freedom, for such freedom alone can give rise to the new, to what had never existed before. Out of being, out of something that exists, it is impossible to create that which is completely new; there can only be emanation, generation, redistribution. But creativeness means breaking through from nonbeing, from freedom, to the world of being. The mystery of creativeness is revealed in the biblical myth of the Creation. God created the world out of nothing, i.e., freely and out of freedom. The world was not an emanation from God, it was not evolved or born from Him, but created, i.e., it was absolutely new, it was something that had never been before. Creativeness is only possible because the world is created, because there is a Creator. Man, made by God in His own image and likeness, is also a creator and is called to creative work.

Creativeness is a complex fact. It presupposes, first, man's primary, meonic, uncreated freedom; secondly, the gifts bestowed upon man the creator by God the Creator; and, thirdly, the world as the field for his activity. Thus three elements are involved in human creativeness: the element of freedom, owing to which alone creation of new and hitherto nonexistent realities is possible; gifts and vocations connected with them; and the already created world from which man can borrow his materials. Man is not the source of his gifts and his genius. He has received them from God and therefore feels that he is in God's hands and is an instrument of God's work in the world. Nothing can be more pitiful and absurd than to pride oneself on one's genius. There would be more excuse for being proud of one's holiness. The genius feels that he acts not of himself, but is possessed by God and is the means by which God works His own ends and designs. The "demon" of Socrates was not his self but a being that dwelt in him. A creator constantly feels himself possessed by a demon or a genius. His work is a manifestation through freedom of gifts bestowed upon him from above.

Man cannot produce the material for creation out of himself, out of nothing, out of the depths of his own being. The creative act is of the nature of marriage, it always implies a meeting between different elements. The material for human creativeness is borrowed from the world created by God. We find this in all art and in all inventions and discoveries. We find this in the creativeness of knowledge and in philosophy which presupposes the existence of the world created by God—objective realities without which thought would be left in a void. God has granted man the creative gift, the talent, the genius, and also the world in and through which the creative activity is to be carried out. God calls man to perform the creative act and realize his vocation, and He is expecting an answer to His call. Man's answer to God's call cannot consist entirely of elements that are given by and proceed from God. Something must come from man also, and that something is the very essence of creativeness, which brings forth new realities. It is, indeed, not "something" but "nothing" —in other words, it is freedom, without which there can be no creative activity. Freedom not determined by anything answers

God's call to creative work, but in doing so it makes use of the gift or genius received from God and of materials present in the created world. When man is said to create out of nothing it means that he creates out of freedom. In every creative conception there is an element of primeval freedom, fathomless, undetermined by anything, not proceeding from God but ascending toward God. God's call is addressed to that abyss of freedom, and the answer must come from it. Fathomless freedom is present in all creativeness, but the creative process is so complex that it is not easy to detect this primary element in it. It is a process of interaction between grace and freedom, between forces going from God to man and from man to God. In describing it, emphasis may be laid either on the element of freedom or on the element of grace, of gracious possession and inspiration. But there can be no inspiration without freedom. Platonic philosophy is unfavorable to the interpretation of creativeness as the making of new realities.

Creativeness has two different aspects, and we describe it differently according to whether we dwell upon one or the other. It has an inner and an outer aspect. There is the primary creative act in which man stands, as it were, face to face with God, and there is the secondary creative act in which he faces other men and the world. There is the creative conception, the primary creative intuition, in which a man hears the symphony, perceives the pictorial or poetic image, or is aware of a discovery or invention as yet unexpressed; there is such a thing as an inner creative act of love for a person, still unexpressed in any way. In that primary act, man stands before God and is not concerned with realization. If knowledge is given me, that knowledge is not a book written by me or a scientific discovery formulated for other people's benefit and forming part of human culture. In the first instance, it is my own inner knowledge, as yet unexpressed, unknown to the world and hidden from it. This alone is real firsthand knowledge, my real philosophy in which I am face to face with the mystery of existence. Then comes the secondary creative act, connected with man's social nature—the realization of the creative intuition. A book comes to be written. At this stage there arises the question of art and technique. The primary creative fire is not art at all. Art is secondary and in it the creative fire cools down. Art is subject to law and is not an interaction of freedom and grace, as the primary creative act is. In realizing his creative intuition, man is limited by the world, by his material, by other people; all this weighs on him and damps the fire of inspiration. There is always a tragic discrepancy between the burning heat of the creative fire in which the artistic image is conceived and the cold of its formal realization. Every book, picture, statue, good work, social institution, is an instance of this cooling down of the original flame. Probably some creators never find expression; they have the inner fire and inspiration, but fail to give it form. And yet, people generally think that creativeness consists in producing concrete, definite things. Classic art requires the greatest possible adherence to the cold, formal laws of technique.

The aim of creative inspiration is to bring forth new forms of life, but the results are the cold products of civilization: cultural values, books, pictures, institutions, good works. Good works mean the cooling down of the creative fire of love in the human heart just as a philosophical work means the cooling down of the creative fire of knowledge in the human spirit. This is the tragedy of human creativeness and its limitation. Its results are a terrible condemnation. The inner creative act, in its fiery impetus, ought to leave the heaviness of the world behind, to "overcome the world." But in its external realization, the creative act is subject to the power of "the world" and is fettered by it. Creativeness, which is a fiery stream flowing out of fathomless freedom, has not only to ascend but also to descend. It has to interpret to the world its creative vision and, in so doing, submit to the laws of art and technique.

Creativeness by its very nature implies genius. In his creative aspect man is endowed with genius; it is the image of God the

Creator in him. This does not mean that every man has an outstanding talent for painting pictures, writing poems, novels, or philosophical books, ruling the state, or making inventions and discoveries. The presence of genius in man has to do with his inner creativeness and not with its external realization. It is a characteristic of human personality as a whole and not a specific gift; it indicates that man is capable of breaking through to the primary source of life and that his spiritual activity is truly original and not determined by social influences. A man's genius may, however, be out of keeping with his powers of realization. The presence of genius and originality together with a great talent for realizing the products of creative activity, makes a man a genius in the usual sense of the term. But there may be something of genius in a man's love for a woman, in a mother's love for her child, in a person's concern for other people's welfare, in inner intuitions which find no outer expression, in the pursuit of righteousness and the suffering of trying to discover the meaning of life. A saint may be a genius in his work of making himself into a perfect and transfigured creature, though he may have nothing to show for it. It is wrong to draw comparisons between different men's genius and talent, for it means ignoring their individuality. Creativeness brings with it much sorrow and bitterness. It is a great failure, even in its finest achievements, for they always fall short of the creative conception.

There is a tragic conflict between creativeness and personal perfection. The greatness of creative genius is not correlative with moral perfection. A great artist may be an idle pleasure seeker, "of the world's worthless children, the most worthless he may be." This problem has been stated in all its poignancy by Pushkin, who said the most remarkable things that have ever been said about artistic creation. Creative genius is bestowed on man for nothing and is not connected with his moral or religious efforts to attain perfection and become a new creature. It stands, as it were, outside the ethics of law and the ethics of redemption and presupposes a different kind of morality. The creator is justified by his creative achievement. We come here upon a curious paradox. Creative genius is not concerned with salvation or perdition. In his creative work the artist forgets about himself, about his own personality, and renounces himself. Creative work is intensely personal and at the same time it means forgetfulness of self. Creative activity always involves sacrifice. It means self-transcendence, exceeding the confines of one's own limited personal being. A creator forgets about salvation; he is concerned with values that are above man. There is nothing selfish about creativeness. In so far as a man is self-centered, he cannot create anything, he cannot abandon himself to inspiration or imagine a better world.

It is paradoxical that ascetic experience absorbs a man in himself, makes him concentrate upon his own improvement and salvation, while creative experience makes him forget himself and brings him into a higher world. Creativeness involves a renunciation and asceticism of its own, but it is of a different kind. The Christians who suggest that one should first practice asceticism and attain perfection, and then take up creative work have no idea of what creativeness means. The asceticism required by creativeness is different from that which is concerned with personal perfection and salvation. No amount of ascetic practice will give one talent or ability, to say nothing of genius. Genius cannot be earned, it is given from above, like grace. What is required of the artist is intensity of creative effort and not an ascetic struggle for self-improvement. If Pushkin had practiced asceticism and sought the salvation of his soul, he would probably have ceased to be a great poet. Creativeness is bound up with imperfection, and perfection may be unfavorable to it. This is the moral paradox with regard to creativeness.

When a man begins to seek moral perfection—whether he follows the Catholic, the Orthodox, the Tolstoyan, the Theosophical, the Yoga, or any other path—he may be lost to creative work. Creativeness requires that a man should forget about his own moral progress and sacrifice his personality. It is a path that demands heroism, but it is different from the path of personal improvement and salvation. Creativeness is necessary for the Kingdom of God—for God's work in the world—but it is not at all necessary for saving one's soul. Or, if it is, it is only necessary in so far as a creator is justified by his creative achievement. If a man feels nothing but humility and a perpetual sense of sin, he can do no creative work. Creativeness means that one's mind passes on to another plane of being. The soul may live simultaneously on different planes, in the heights and in the lowest depths; it may boldly create and be humbly penitent. But creativeness in all its aspects, including the moral—for there is such a thing as moral creativeness—testifies to the presence in man of a certain principle which may be the source of a system of morality different from the ethics of law and the ethics of redemption. Creativeness, more than anything else, is reminiscent of man's vocation before the Fall and is, in a sense, "beyond good and evil." But since human nature is sinful, creativeness is distorted and perverted by sin, and may be evil.

Man's creative activity alone bears witness to his vocation and shows what he has been destined for in the world. The law says nothing about vocation, nor does the ethics of redemption, as such. The Gospel and St. Paul's Epistles speak of man's gifts and vocation only because they go beyond the mystery of redemption. True creativeness is always in the Holy Spirit, for only in the Spirit can there be that union of grace and freedom which we find in creativeness. Its meaning for ethics is twofold. To begin with, ethics must inquire into the moral significance of all creative work, even if it has no direct relation to the moral life. Art and knowledge have a moral significance, like all activities which create higher values. Secondly, ethics must inquire into the creative significance of moral activity. Moral life itself, moral actions and valuations, have a creative character. The ethics of law and norm does not as yet recognize this, and it is therefore inevitable that we should pass to the ethics of creativeness, which deals with man's true vocation and destiny.

Creativeness, a creative attitude to life as a whole, is not man's right, it is his duty. It is a moral imperative that applies in every department of life. Creative effort in artistic and cognitive activity has a moral value. Realization of truth and goodness is a moral good. There may, however, be a conflict between the creation of perfect cultural values and the creation of a perfect human personality. The path of creativeness is also a path to moral and religious perfection, a way of realizing the fullness of life. The frequently quoted words of Goethe, "All theory is grey but the tree of life is eternally green," may be turned the other way round: "All life is grey but the tree of theory is eternally green." "Theory" will then mean creativeness, the thought of a Plato or a Hegel, while "life" will stand for a mere struggle for existence, dull and commonplace, for family dissensions, for disappointments, and so on. In this sense, "theory" means rising to a higher moral level.

2 The Creatively Individual Character of Moral Acts

The ethics of creativeness differs from the ethics of law, first of all, because every moral task is for it absolutely individual and creative.[2] The moral problems of life cannot be solved by an automatic application of universally binding rules. It is impossible to say that in the same circumstances one ought always and everywhere to act in the same way. It is impossible if only because circumstances never are quite the same. Indeed, the very opposite rule might be formulated. One ought always to act individually and solve every moral problem for oneself, showing creativeness in one's moral activity, and not for a single moment become a moral automaton. A man ought to make moral inventions with regard to the problems that life sets him. Hence, for

[2] See M. Scheler, *Der Formalismus in der Ethik und die materielle Werte-thik*. In my book *Smysl Tvorchestva* (*The Meaning of the Creative Act*), I said long ago that moral acts are creative and individual in character.

the ethics of creativeness, freedom means something very different from what it means for the ethics of law. For the latter, so-called freedom of will has no creative character and means merely acceptance or rejection of the law or the good and responsibility for doing one or the other. For the ethics of creativeness, freedom means not the acceptance of the law but individual creation of values. Freedom is creative energy, the possibility of building up new realities. The ethics of law knows nothing of that freedom. It does not know that the good is being created, that in every individual and unrepeatable moral act new good that had never existed before is brought into being by the moral agent whose invention it is. There exists no fixed, static, moral order, subordinated to a single universally binding moral law. Man is not a passive executor of the laws of the world order. Man is a creator and an inventor. His moral conscience must, at every moment of his life, be creative and inventive. The ethics of creativeness is an ethics of dynamics and energy. Life is based upon energy and not upon law. It may be said, indeed, that energy is the source of law. The ethics of creativeness takes a very different view of the struggle against evil than does the ethics of law. For the ethics of creativeness, that struggle consists in the creative realization of the good and the transformation of evil into good, rather than in the mere destruction of evil. The ethics of law is concerned with the finite: the world is a self-contained system and there is no way out of it. The ethics of creativeness is concerned with the infinite: the world is open and plastic, with boundless horizons and possibilities of breaking through to other worlds. It overcomes the nightmare of the finite from which there is no escape.

The ethics of creativeness is different from the ethics of redemption: it is concerned, in the first place, with values and not with salvation. For it, the moral end of life is not the salvation of one's soul but creative realization of righteousness and of values which need not belong to the moral order. The ethics of creativeness springs from the personality but is concerned with

the world, while the ethics of law springs from the world and
society but is concerned with the personality. The ethics of
creativeness alone overcomes the negative fixation of the spirit
upon struggle with sin and evil and replaces it by something
positive, i.e., by the creation of the valuable content of life. It
overcomes not only the earthly but the heavenly, transcendental
selfishness with which even the ethics of redemption is infected.
Fear of punishment and of eternal torments in hell can play no
part in the ethics of creativeness. It opens a way to a pure, disinterested morality, since every kind of fear distorts moral experience and activity. It may indeed be said that nothing which is
done out of fear, whether it be fear of temporal or of eternal
torments, has any moral value. The truly moral motive is not
fear of punishment and of hell, but selfless and disinterested
love of God and of the divine in life, of truth and perfection and
all positive values. This is the basis of the ethics of creativeness.

The ethics of creativeness affirms the value of the unique and
the individual.[3] This is a new phenomenon in the moral world.
It is with the greatest difficulty, and only as late as the nineteenth century, that ethics has recognized the value of the
individual. An enormous part was played in this by such men as
Dostoevsky, Nietzsche, Ibsen, Kierkegaard. Christian ethics was
for a long time blind to the significance of individuality and
conceived of moral life as subordinated to a universally binding
law. The unique, the individual, has a twofold significance for
ethics. In the first place, moral valuations and actions must proceed from the concrete personality and be unique and individual
in character. Each individual man must act as himself and not as
another would have acted in his place; his moral activity must
spring from the depths of his own conscience. Secondly, the
individual and individuality must be recognized as moral values
of the highest hierarchical order. The unique, concrete personality is the highest value; it is not a means to the triumph of the
universal, even if that universal be a generally binding moral law.

[3] See G. Gurvitch, *Fichtes System der konkreten Ethik.*

To be a personality to the end, not to betray oneself, to be individual in all one's actions, is an absolute moral imperative, paradoxical as it sounds. It means "be thyself, to thine own self be
true." Sacrifice of self is a way of being true to one's self. Ibsen's
Peer Gynt wanted to be original, he affirmed individualism. But
individualism always destroys personality and individuality. Peer
Gynt never was himself, he lost his personality and dissolved in
the melting pot. The figure of the button moulder is one of the
most striking images in the world's literature.

The ethics of creativeness is by no means identical with individualism. The difference between personalism and individualism has already been explained. To be oneself means to realize
God's idea of one's self. This is the essence of personality as the
highest value. Personality is realized spiritually and not biologi-
cally. Ethics is based upon personality and cannot exist apart
from it. Human personality, as God's idea and God's image, is
the center of moral consciousness, a supreme value. It is a value,
not because it is the bearer of a universally binding moral law,
as with Kant, but just because it is God's image and idea, the
bearer of the divine principle in life. It is therefore impossible to
use the moral good in order to humiliate and destroy man. A
person's moral activity has not only a personal but a social and
even a cosmic significance. A personality emits, so to speak,
moral rays which are diffused throughout the world. Human
personality always remains a fiery center of the world. In the
moral life of society the fire is cooled down: it is the life of customs, manners, public opinion. Personality is the only truly
creative and prophetic element in moral life; it coins new values.
But it suffers for doing so. Creative personality defends the firsthand, pure, virginal character of moral thought and conscience
against the constant resistance of hard-set collective thought and
conscience, the spirit of the times, public opinion. In doing so,
the creative personality may feel itself a part of a spiritual whole
and be neither solitary nor self-assertive; this, however, is another
question. A person is connected with a communal spiritual

whole through his own free conscience and not through social compulsion and authority. The ethics of creativeness is always prophetic, directed toward the future; it originates in the individual and not in a collective unit, but it is social in import.[4]

Within the Christian world there are two conflicting moral tendencies: humility and creativeness, the morality of personal salvation and fear of perdition, and the creative morality of values, of devoting oneself to the transformation and transfiguration of the world. Both humility and creativeness are based upon sacrifice, but the nature of sacrifice is different in the two cases. Humility may require that a man give up personal creativeness but go on perpetually thinking of his own personality and of the way to make it perfect; creativeness may require that, while preserving personal creative inspiration, a man forget about himself and think only of values and perfect works for the world. The sacrifice is connected with two different kinds of perfection. But the religious ideal of humility, which has, as we have seen, a profound ontological meaning, easily becomes distorted. In the name of the abstract idea of personal perfection and obedience to God, man may be required to renounce every kind of creative inspiration, even if it be the inspiration of love for his fellow creatures. Like everything else, humility is paradoxical and may lead to the denial of perfection. There is a lack of humility in being too perfect, good, and loving. This kind of attitude is inspired by a false conception of God as a Being who requires of man, first and foremost, sacrifice and suffering, submission and obedience. Humility may become hostile not only to creativeness but to moral life as a whole. It may become a superstition. Our religious life is still full of idolatry, and to get rid of it is a great moral task. Creativeness is, by its very nature, opposed to idolatry, and therein lies its great significance. The ethics of creativeness is concerned with revealing human values and the value of human personality as such; in doing so it frees man from unendurable fear for himself and his future—fear which

[4] See my book, *Freedom and the Spirit*.

gives rise to idolatry and superstition. A man whose spirit is occupied with the creation of objective values ceases to be "a trembling creature." Creative inspiration is a way to victory over fear which, owing to original sin, is the ruling emotion of life. At moments of creative elation an artist or a man of science becomes free from fear; afterwards, when he descends to everyday life, he feels it again. He may indeed feel fear in connection with his creative work if he longs for fame and success, if he is complacent and worships his own work. But these feelings have nothing to do with pure creativeness.

The ethics of creativeness strives for the victory of eternity over time. Creative work takes place in time, but the creative act is directed upon the eternal—eternal values, truth, beauty, righteousness, God and divine heights. All the products of man's genius may be temporal and corruptible, but the creative fire itself is eternal, and everything temporal ought to be consumed by it. It is the tragedy of creativeness that it wants eternity and the eternal but produces the temporal and builds up a culture which is in time and a part of history. The creative act is an escape from the power of time and an ascent to the divine. An inventor, in his creative inspiration, is transported beyond the earth and time, but he creates a machine which may prove to be a weapon in the struggle against eternity. It is another instance of the contradictory character of creativeness in our sinful world. Creativeness is the struggle against the consequences of sin, the expression of man's true vocation; but creativeness is distorted and debased by sin. Hence the ethics of creativeness deals with the agonizing struggle of the human spirit. Creativeness needs purification, needs the purifying fire. In the civilized world, creativeness becomes so degenerate that it calls forth a moral reaction against it and a desire for ascetic renunciation and escape from the world. We find such degeneration in many of the tendencies of modern art and literature, in which the spirit of eternity is finally surrendered to the polluted spirit of the time. We find it in the unendurable complacency of scientists and in the new religion of science. We find it in social and political life, where the struggle for gain and power destroys the creative desire for social justice. In every sphere the lust for life damps the creative burning of the spirit. It is the direct opposite of creativeness. Creativeness is victory over the lust for life. That lust is overcome through humility and through creativeness.

The soul is afraid of emptiness. When there is no positive, valuable, divine content in the soul, it is filled with negative, false, diabolical content. When the soul feels empty it experiences boredom, which is a truly terrible and diabolical state. Evil lust and evil passions are, to a great extent, generated by boredom and emptiness. It is difficult to struggle against that boredom by means of abstract goodness and virtue. The dreadful thing is that virtue at times seems deadly dull, and then there is no salvation in it. Cold, hard-set virtue, devoid of creative fire, is always dull and never saves. The heart must be set aglow if the dullness is to be dispelled. Dull virtue is a poor remedy against the boredom of emptiness. Dullness is the absence of creativeness. All that is not creative is dull. Goodness is deadly dull if it is not creative. No rule or norm can save us from dullness and from the lust engendered by it. Lust is a means of escape from boredom when goodness provides no such escape. This is why it is very difficult—almost impossible—to conquer evil passions negatively, through negative asceticism and prohibitions. They can only be conquered positively, through awakening the positive and creative spiritual force opposed to them. Creative fire, divine Eros, overcomes lust and evil passions. It burns up evil and boredom and the false strivings they engender. The will to evil is at bottom objectless and can only be overcome by a will directed toward an object, toward the valuable and divine content of life. Purely negative asceticism, preoccupied with evil and sinful desires and strivings, so far from enlightening the soul, intensifies its darkness. We must preach, therefore, a morality based not upon the annihilation of will but upon its enlightenment, not upon the humiliation of man and his external submission to God but upon the creative realization by man of the divine in life—of the values of truth, goodness, and beauty. The ethics of creativeness alone can save the human soul from being warped by arid abstract virtue and abstract ideals transformed into rules and norms. The ideas of truth, goodness, and beauty must cease to be norms and rules and become vital forces, an inner creative fire.

Christian teachers of spiritual life constantly speak of sinful passions and the struggle against them. They are right, of course, in saying that sinful passions torture man and distort his life. But passions are the material which may be transformed into the higher qualitative content of life. Without passions, without the unconscious element in life, and without creativeness, human virtue is dry and deadly dull. The fathers of the Church themselves sometimes say that passions may become virtues. This shows that, in the struggle with passions, it is wrong to adopt an exclusively negative point of view and practice solely a negative asceticism. It is necessary to attain positive qualitative states into which passions will enter in an enlightened, transfigured, sublimated form instead of being uprooted and destroyed. This applies, in the first instance, to the most fatal of fallen man's passions—that of sex. It is impossible simply to destroy it, and it is useless and even dangerous to concentrate upon a negative struggle with it. Modern psychology and psychopathology talk about its sublimation. And it appears that there are many ways in which man can struggle with sinful sexual passion. Every form of creative inspiration and deep spiritual feeling overcomes and transfigures it. The experience of intense erotic love may weaken passion and make a man forget physiological sexual craving. This is a well-known paradox verified by experience. An intense feeling of pity and compassion may also paralyze sexual passion and make a man forget about it. The energy of sex transfigured and sublimated may become a source of creativeness and inspiration. Creativeness is unquestionably connected with the energy of sex, the first source of creative energy, which may assume other forms just as motion may pass into heat. Creativeness is bound up with the ultimate basis of life and indicates a certain spiritual direction assumed by the primary vital energy. The whole problem is to give that energy a spiritual, instead of an unspiritual, direction, and thus save spiritual forces from being wasted upon sexual passion. No purely negative asceticism, no effort of will aimed at suppressing sexual, or any other sinful passion, instead of replacing it by something positive, can be successful; it is defeated by what modern psychology calls *la loi de l'effort converti*.[5] The only thing that can help is a change of spiritual direction, the sublimation of passion and its transformation into a source of creative energy. Love may overcome the sexual passion that tortures man; but the sacrifice of love, its suppression for the sake of creative work, may be a source of creative energy. I have already referred to this in the case of Ibsen, as well as in that of Kierkegaard, who renounced the woman he loved and intended to marry.[6] Sexlessness is as bad for creative activity as the waste of vital energy in sexual passion.

Most of the so-called sinful passions can be sublimated and transformed into a source of positive creativeness. The ethics of law, with its formal virtues, refuses to recognize this, but not the ethics of creativeness, with its creative and dynamic virtues. The Greeks succeeded in converting even hatred, one of the most evil and sinful of human passions, into noble rivalry. Anger, ambition, jealousy, and love of gambling may undergo a similar transformation. Love is, as it were, the universal vital energy capable of converting evil passions into creative forces. Thus the thirst for knowledge is love directed in a certain way; and the same is true of philosophy, which means love of truth; and there may be love of beauty and love of justice. Evil passions become creative through Eros. Hence the ethics of creativeness, in contradistinction to the ethics of law, is erotic.

But love can only transform evil passions into creative ones if

---

[5] See Baudouin, *Suggestion et Autosuggestion*.
[6] See the interesting book by Przywara, *Das Geheimnis Kierkegaards*.

it is regarded as a value in itself and not as a means of salvation. Love in the sense of good works useful for the salvation of the soul cannot give rise to a creative attitude to life and be a source of life-giving energy. Love is not merely a fount of creativeness but is itself creativeness, radiation of creative energy. Love is like radium in the spiritual world. The ethics of creativeness calls for actual, concrete realization of truth, goodness, spirituality; for a real transfiguration of life and not for a symbolic and conventional realization of the good through ascetic practices, good works, and so on. It demands that we should love every man in his creative aspect, which is the image and likeness of God in him, i.e., that we should love that which is good, true, superhuman, and divine in him. We do not know why we love a person; we love for no reason. One cannot love a man for his merits; and in this respect love is like grace which is given freely, not for merits but for nothing. Love is a gracious radiating energy. To interpret love for one's neighbor as a means of saving one's soul is a complete misinterpretation of love and an utter failure to understand its nature. It is a legalistic perversion of Christianity. Love is taken to be a law, for the fulfillment of which man is rewarded.

Equally false is the position of the idealist who knows love for an idea but does not know personal love and is always ready to turn man into a means for carrying out the idea. This attitude gives rise to religious formalism and pharisaism, which is always a denial of love. The religion of law condemns the man who disobeys the will of God. Ethical idealism condemns the man who disobeys the moral law. The religion of redemption and the ethics of creativeness have no such condemnation. The Christian religion has placed man above the Sabbath, and the ethics of creativeness accepts this truth absolutely. Man is a value in himself, independently of the idea of which he is the bearer; our task in life is to radiate creative energy, which brings with it light and strength and transfiguration. Hence the ethics of creativeness does not pass judgment but gives life, receives life, heightens the quality and the value of life's content. Its tragedy is connected with the conflict among values recognized as equally deserving of creative effort. Hence the ethics of creativeness inevitably presupposes sacrifice.

There are two different types of enjoyment—one reminds us of original sin and always contains poison; the other reminds us of Paradise. When a man is enjoying the gratification of sexual passion or the pleasure of eating he ought to feel the presence of poison and be reminded of original sin. This is the nature of every enjoyment connected with lust. It always testifies to the poverty, and not to the richness, of our nature. But when we experience the delight of breathing the sea or mountain air or the fragrance of woods and fields, we recall Paradise. There is no lust in this. Here we are comparing pleasures that have a physiological character. But the same comparison may be made in the spiritual realm. When a man is enjoying the satisfaction of his greed or vanity he ought to feel the poison and be reminded of original sin. But when he is enjoying a creative act, which reveals truth or creates beauty or radiates love upon a fellow creature, he recalls Paradise. Every delight connected with lust is poisoned and reminiscent of original sin. Every delight free from lust and connected with love of objective values is a remembrance or a foretaste of Paradise and frees us from the bonds of sin. The sublimation or transfiguration of passions means that a passion is purified of lust and that a free creative element enters into it. This is a point of fundamental importance for ethics. Man must strive, first and foremost, to free himself from slavery. Every state incompatible with spiritual freedom and hostile to it is evil. But every lust (*concupiscentia*) is hostile to the freedom of the spirit and enslaves man. Lust is both insatiable and bound to pall. It cannot be satisfied, for it is the bad[7] infinity of craving. There exists a different kind of craving which also

[7] The word "bad" encompasses several meanings in Berdyaev's writings. Usually the Russian original is *durnoï*, which means primarily "defective," "vitiated," "incomplete."

extends into infinity, e.g., the hunger for absolute righteousness; those who hunger and thirst after righteousness are blessed because they are concerned with eternity and not with bad infinity. The divine reality which fills our life is the contrary of the boredom and emptiness born of the evil lust for life. Lust, by its very nature, is uncreative and opposed to creativeness. Creativeness is generous and sacrificial, it means giving one's powers, while lust wants everything for itself, is greedy, insatiable, and vampirish. True love gives strength to the loved one, while love-lust vampirically absorbs another person's strength. Hence there is opposition both between lust and freedom and between lust and creativeness. Lust is a perverted and inwardly weakened passion. Power is a creative force, but there is such a thing as the lust for power; love is a sacrificial force, but there is also the lust of love.

The moral life of our sinful world is made up of paradoxes and contradictions. A man is tormented by pride and ambition when he is lower than others; inaccessible heights lure him on and rouse a lustful desire in him. But when he is higher than others, when he has attained the longed-for pre-eminence, he is tormented by a sense of emptiness and futility. The same thing happens in sexual erotic life. A man suffers because he cannot possess the object of his sexual love, but when he gains possession, he tires of it and life becomes dull and empty. All this indicates an uncreative and lustful direction of the will, not giving but taking, absorbing energy instead of radiating it. It is the greatest mystery of life that satisfaction is felt not by those who take, and make demands, but by those who give, and make sacrifices. In them alone the energy of life does not fail, and this is precisely what is meant by creativeness. The positive mystery of life is therefore to be found in love, in sacrificial, giving, creative love. As has been said already, all creativeness is love and all love is creative. If you want to receive, give; if you want to obtain satisfaction, do not seek it, never think of it, and forget the very word; if you want to acquire strength, manifest it, give it to others. The presence of strength and energy does not by any means presuppose a belief in freedom of the will. It is paradoxical that movements characterized by remarkable strength and energy, such as Calvinism or Marxism, for instance, altogether reject the doctrine of free will. It is a rationalistic doctrine, concerned with judgment and reckoning. It is a product of reflection and dividedness. But true freedom is gracious energy.

The ethics of creativeness is the highest and most mature form of moral consciousness, and at the same time it is the morality of eternal youth. Creativeness is the youth of the soul and its power is bound up with the soul's virginity. The relation between spiritual youth and old age must not be interpreted chronologically. The morality of law is the morality of old age—and yet it is the earliest human morality. The ever-youthful nature of creative activity raises the question of the relation between creativeness and development. Is creativeness a developed, an unfolded state? It may be said, paradoxical as it seems at first sight, that development and unfolding is the deadly enemy of creativeness and leads to its cooling down and drying up at the source. The highest point reached by creativeness is not the unfolding of results but the first flight of inspiration; its birth and virginal youth, not its final achievement. Development, unfolding, improvement, completion mean deterioration of creativeness, the cooling down of the creative fire, decay and old age. This can be seen in the fate of men of genius and of creative spiritual movements in history, in the fate of prophecy and holiness in the world, and of all inspirations, intuitions, and original ideas. Early Christianity cannot be compared with developed Christianity as far as the creative flame of the spirit is concerned. It is impossible to compare the prophets with those who were guided by prophecies; the Franciscan order with the fire of love in St. Francis; the developed Protestantism—influenced by Melanchthon—of the seventeenth, eighteenth, and nineteenth centuries with the fiery spirit of Luther. It is impossible to compare the cooled-down results of all the revolutions in the world with the burning enthusiasm in which they began. It is impossible to compare Marxists with Marx or Tolstoyans with Tolstoy, or any established system of thought with the fiery, prophetic genius of its founders. It is impossible to compare the tepid love of middle age with the ecstasy of its early beginnings.

The essence of development and evolution is that it conceals firsthand intuitions and first origins of human feelings and ideas. It envelops and stifles them with secondary emotions and social constructions, making access to them almost impossible. This has happened to Christianity also, and herein lies its historical tragedy. This happens to every human feeling and idea. Development destroys creative youth, virginity, and originality. That which was born in the free creative act is unrecognizable in its developed form. True life is creativeness and not development, freedom and not necessity, creative fire and not the gradual cooling down and fixation involved in the process of unfolding and perfecting. This truth has particular importance for moral life. Moral life must be eternal creativeness, free and fiery, i.e., perpetual youth and virginity of spirit. It must rest on primary intuitions, free from the suggestions of man's social environment which paralyze the freedom of his moral judgments. But in actual life it is difficult to break through to this youth of the spirit. Most of our moral actions and judgments do not come from that primary source. The ethics of creativeness is not the ethics of development but of the youth and virginity of the human spirit; it springs from the fiery first source of life—freedom. Therefore, true morality is not the social morality of the herd.

3   The Part of Imagination in the Moral Life

The Ethics of Energy

The ethics of creativeness presupposes that the task which confronts man is infinite and that the world is not completed. But the tragedy is that the realization of every infinite task is finite. Creative imagination is of fundamental importance to the ethics of creativeness. Without imagination there can be no creative activity. Creativeness means, in the first instance, imagining something different, better, and higher. Imagination calls up before us something better than the reality around us. Creativeness always rises above reality. Imagination plays this part not only in art and in myth making but also in scientific discoveries, technical inventions, and moral life, creating a better type of relation between human beings. There is such a thing as moral imagination, which creates the image of a better life; it is absent only from legalistic ethics.[8] No imagination is needed for automatically carrying out a law or norm. In moral life the power of creative imagination plays the part of talent. By the side of the self-contained moral world of laws and rules, to which nothing can be added, man builds, in imagination, a higher world, a free and beautiful world, lying beyond ordinary good and evil. And this is what gives beauty to life. As a matter of fact, life can never be determined solely by law; men always imagine for themselves a different and better life, freer and more beautiful, and they realize those images. The Kingdom of God is the image of a full, perfect, beautiful, free, and divine life. Only law has nothing to do with imagination, or rather, it is limited to imagining compliance with, or violation of, its behests. But the most perfect fulfillment of the law is not the same as the perfect life.

Imagination may also be a source of evil; there may be bad imagination and phantasms. Evil thoughts are an instance of bad imagination. Crimes are conceived in imagination. But imagination also brings about a better life. A man devoid of imagination is incapable of creative moral activity and of building a better life. The very conception of a better life, towards which we ought to strive, is the result of creative imagination. Those who have no imagination think that there is no better life and that there ought not to be. All that exists for them is the

[8] See B. Vysheslavtsev's articles in Put: "Suggestion and Religion" and "The Ethics of Sublimation as the Victory over Moralism" (in Russian).

unalterable order of existence in which unalterable law ought to
be realized. Jacob Boehme ascribed enormous importance to
imagination.[9] The world is created by God through imagination, through images which arise in God in eternity and are both
ideal and real. Modern psychologists also ascribe great importance to imagination, both good and bad. They have discovered
that imagination plays an infinitely greater part in people's lives
than has been hitherto thought. Diseases and psychoses arise
through imagination and can also be cured by it. The ethics of
law forbids man to imagine a better world and a better life, it
fetters him to the world as given and to the socially organized
herd life, laying down taboos and prohibitions everywhere. But
the ethics of creativeness breaks with the herd existence and
refuses to recognize legalistic prohibitions. To the "law" of the
present life it opposes "the image" of a higher one.

The ethics of creativeness is the ethics of energy. Quantitative
and qualitative increase in life's intensity and creative energy is
one of the criteria of moral valuation. The good is like radium in
spiritual life and its essential quality is radioactivity, inexhausti-
ble radiation. The conceptions of energy and of norm come
into conflict in ethics. The morality of law and the morality of
creative energy are perpetually at war. If the good is understood
as a real force, it cannot be conceived as the purpose of life. A
perfect and absolute realization of the good would make it unnecessary and lead us completely to forget moral distinctions and
valuations. The nature of the good and of moral life presuppose dualism and struggle, i.e., a painful and difficult path.
Complete victory over the dualism and the struggle leads to the
disappearance of what, on the way, we had called good and
moral. To realize the good is to cancel it out. The good is not at
all the final end of life and of being. It is only a way, only a
struggle on the way. The good must be conceived in terms of

9 See his *Mysterium magnum* and *De signatura Rerum*. A. Koyré empha-
sizes the part played by imagination in Boehme's philosophy. See his book,
La Philosophie de Jacob Boehme.

energy and not of purpose. The thing that matters most is the realization of creative energy, not the ideal normative end. Man realizes the good, not because he has set himself the purpose of doing so, but because he is good or virtuous, i.e., because he has in himself the creative energy of goodness. The source is important, not the goal. A man fights for a good cause, not because it is his conscious purpose to do so, but because he has combative energy and the energy of goodness. Goodness and moral life are a path on which the starting point and the goal coincide: the emanation of creative energy.

But from the ontological and cosmological point of view, the final end of being must be thought of as beauty and not as goodness. Plato defined beauty as the magnificence of the good. Complete, perfect, and harmonious being is beauty. Teleological ethics is normative and legalistic. It regards the good as the purpose of life, i.e., as a norm or a law which must be fulfilled. Teleological ethics always implies absence of moral imagination, for it conceives the end as a norm and not as an image, not as a product of the creative energy of life. Moral life must be determined not by a purpose or a norm but by imagery and the exercise of creative activity. Beauty is the image of creative energy radiating over the whole world and transforming it. Teleological ethics based upon the idea of the good as an absolute purpose is hostile to freedom, but creative ethics is based upon freedom. Beauty means a transfigured creation, the good means creation fettered by the law which denounces sin. The paradox is that the law fetters the energy of the good; it does not want the good to be interpreted as a force, for in that case the world would escape from the power of law. To transcend the morality of law means to put infinite creative energy in the place of commands, prohibitions, and taboos.

Instinct plays a twofold part in man's moral life: it dates back to ancient, primitive times, and ancient terror, slavishness, superstition, animalism, and cruelty find expression in it; but at the same time it is reminiscent of Paradise, of primitive freedom and power, of man's ancient bond with the cosmos and the primeval force of life. Hence the attitude of the ethics of creativeness toward instincts is complex: it liberates instincts repressed by the moral law and at the same time struggles with them for the sake of a higher life. Instincts are repressed by the moral law, but since they have their origin in the social life of primitive clans, they themselves tend to become a law and to fetter the creative energy of life. Thus, for instance, the instinct of vengeance is, as has already been said, a heritage of the social life of antiquity, and is connected with law. The ethics of creativeness liberates not all instincts but only creative ones, i.e., man's creative energy hampered by the prohibitions of the law. It also struggles against instincts and strives to sublimate them.

Teleological ethics, which is identical with the ethics of law, metaphysically presupposes the power of time in the bad sense of the word. Time is determined either by the idea of purpose which has to be realized in the future or by the idea of creativeness which is to be carried on in the future. In the first case, man is in the power of the purpose and of the time created by it; in the second, he is the master of time, for he realizes in it his creative energy. The problem of time is bound up with the ethics of creativeness. Time and freedom are the fundamental, and the most painful, of metaphysical problems. Heidegger, in his *Sein und Zeit*, formulates it in a new way, but he connects time with care and not with creativeness. There can be no doubt, however, that creativeness is connected with time. It is usually said that creativeness needs the perspective of the future and presupposes changes that take place in time. In truth, it would be more correct to say that movement, change, creativeness, give rise to time. Thus we see that time has a double nature. It is the source both of hope and of pain and torture. The charm of the future is connected with the fact that the future may be changed and to some extent depends upon ourselves. But to the past we can do nothing, we can only remember it—with reverence and gratitude, or with remorse and indignation. The future may bring with it the realization of our desires, hopes, and dreams. But it also inspires us with terror. We are tortured with anxiety about the unknown future. Thus the part of time which we call the future and regard as dependent upon our own activity may be determined in two ways. It may be determined by duty, by painful anxiety and a command to realize a set purpose, or by our creative energy, by a constructive vital impulse through which new values are created. In the first case, time oppresses us, we are in its power. The loftiest purpose projected into the future enslaves us, becomes external to us, and makes us anxious. Anxiety is called forth not only by the lower material needs but also by the higher ideal ends. In the second case, when we are determined by free creative energy, by our free vital force, we regard the future as immanent in us and are its masters. In time everything appears as already determined and necessary, and in our feeling of the future we anticipate this determinateness; events to come sometimes appear to us as an impending fate. But a free creative act is not dominated by time, for it is not determined in any way: it springs from the depths of being, which are not subject to time, and belongs to a different order of existence. It is only later that everything comes to appear as determined in time. The task of the ethics of creativeness is to make the perspective of life independent of the fatal march of time, of the future which terrifies and torments us. The creative act is an escape from time; it is performed in the realm of freedom, not of necessity. It is, by its very nature, opposed to anxiety, which makes time so terrible. And if the whole of human life could be one continuous creative act, there would be no more time; there would be no future as a part of time; there would be movement out of time, in nontemporal reality. There would be no determination, no necessity, no binding laws. There would be the life of the spirit. In Heidegger, reality subject to time is a fallen reality, though he does not make clear what was its state before the Fall. It is the realm of the "herd man." It is connected with care for the future and anxiety. But Christ teaches us not to care about the future. "Enough for the day is the evil thereof." This is an escape from the power of time, from the nightmare of the future born of anxiety.

The future may or may not bring with it disappointment, suffering, and misfortune. But certainly, and to everyone, it brings death. And fear of the future, natural to everyone, is, in the first place, fear of impending death. Death is determined for everyone in this world; it is our fate. But man's free and creative spirit rises against this slavery to death and fate. It has another view of life, springing from freedom and creativeness. In and through Christ, the fate of death is canceled, although empirically every man dies. Our attitude to the future, which ends for us in death, is false because, being divided in ourselves, we analyze it and think of it as determined. But the future is unknowable and cannot be subjected to analysis. Only prophecy is possible with regard to it, and the mystery of prophecy lies precisely in the fact that it has nothing to do with determinations and is not knowledge within the categories of necessity. For a free creative act there exist no fate and no predetermined future. At the moment when a free creative act takes place there is no thought of the future, of the inevitable death, of future suffering; it is an escape from time and from all determinateness. In creative imagination the future is not determined. The creative image is outside the process of time, it is in eternity. Time is the child of sin, of sinful slavery, of sinful anxiety. It will stop and disappear when the world is transfigured. But the transfiguration of the world is taking place already in all true creativeness. We possess a force by means of which we escape from them. That creative force is full of grace and saves us from the power of the law. The greatest moral task is to build a life free from determinateness and anxiety about the future and out of the perspective of time. The moral freedom to do so is given us, but we make poor use of it.

Freedom requires struggle and resistance. We are therefore confronted with the necessarily determined everyday world in which processes are taking place in time and the future appears as fated. Man is fettered and weighed down. He both longs for freedom and fears it. The paradox of liberation is that in order to preserve freedom and to struggle for it one must, in a sense, be already free, have freedom within oneself. Those who are slaves to the very core of their being do not know the name of freedom and cannot struggle for it. Ancient taboos surround man on all sides and fetter his moral life. In order to free himself from their power man must first be conscious of himself as inwardly free; only then can he struggle for freedom outwardly. The inner conquest of slavery is the fundamental task of moral life. Every kind of slavery is meant here—slavery to the power of the past and of the future; slavery to the external world and to oneself, to one's lower self. The awakening of creative energy is inner liberation and is accompanied by a sense of freedom.[10] Creativeness is the way of liberation. Liberation cannot result in inner emptiness—it is not merely liberation *from* something but also liberation *for the sake of* something. And this "for the sake of" is creativeness. Creativeness cannot be aimless and objectless. It is an ascent and therefore presupposes heights, and that means that creativeness rises from the world to God. It does not move along a flat surface in endless time but ascends toward eternity. The products of creativeness remain in time, but the creative act itself, the creative flight, communes with eternity. Every creative act which we perform in relation to other people—an act of love, of pity, of help, of peacemaking—not only has a future but is eternal.

Victory over the categories of master and slave[11] in moral life is a great achievement. A man must not be the slave of other men, nor must he be their master, for then other people will be slaves. To achieve this is one of the tasks of the ethics of creativeness, which knows nothing of mastery and slavery. A creator is neither a slave nor a master, he is one who gives, and gives

[10] Maine de Biran justly connects freedom with inner effort.
[11] Hegel has some striking things to say about this category.

abundantly. All dependence of one man upon another is morally degrading. It is incomprehensible how the slavish doctrine that a free and independent mind is forsaken by divine grace could ever have arisen. Where the Spirit of God is, there is liberty. Where there is liberty, there is the Spirit of God, and grace. Grace acts upon liberty and cannot act upon anything else. A slavish mind cannot receive grace and grace cannot affect it. But slavish theories which distort Christianity build their conception of it not upon grace and liberty but upon mastery and slavery, upon the tyranny of society, of the family, and of the state. They generally recognize free will, but only for the sake of urging it to obedience. Free will cannot, however, be called in merely to be threatened. The "freedom of will" which has frequently led to man's enslavement must itself be liberated, i.e., imbued with gracious force. Creativeness is the gracious force which makes free will really free, free from fear, from the law, from inner dividedness.

The paradox of good and evil—the fundamental paradox of ethics—is that the good presupposes the existence of evil and requires that it should be tolerated. This is what the Creator does in allowing the existence of evil. Hence absolute perfection, absolute order and rationality, may prove to be an evil, a greater evil than the imperfect, unorganized, irrational life which admits of a certain freedom of evil. Absolute good which is incompatible with the existence of evil is possible only in the Kingdom of God, when there will be a new heaven and a new earth, and God will be all in all. But outside the Divine Kingdom of grace, freedom, and love, absolute good which does not allow the existence of evil is always a tyranny, the kingdom of the Grand Inquisitor and the Antichrist. Ethics must recognize this once and for all. So long as there exists a distinction between good and evil, there must inevitably be a struggle, a conflict between opposing principles, and resistance, i.e., exercise of human freedom. Absolute good and perfection outside the Kingdom of God turns man into an automaton of virtue, i.e., really abolishes moral life, since moral life is impossible without spiritual freedom.

Hence our attitude to evil must be twofold: we must be tolerant of it as the Creator is tolerant, and we must mercilessly struggle against it. There is no escaping from this paradox, for it is rooted in freedom and in the very fact of a distinction between good and evil. Ethics is bound to be paradoxical because it has its source in the Fall. The good must be realized, but it has a bad origin. The only thing that is really fine about it is the recollection of the beauty of Paradise. Is the struggle waged in the name of the good in this world an expression of the true life, the "first life"? And how can "first life," life in itself, be attained? We may say with certainty that *love* is life in itself, and so is *creativeness*, and so is the *contemplation* of the spiritual world. But this life in itself is absent from a considerable part of our legalistic morality, from physiological processes, from politics, and from civilization. "First life," or life in itself, is to be found only in firsthand, free moral acts and judgments. It is absent from moral acts which are determined by social environment, heredity, public opinion, party doctrines—i.e., it is absent from a great part of our moral life. True life is only to be found in moral acts in so far as they are creative. Automatic fulfillment of the moral law is not life. Life is always an expansion, a gain. It is present in firsthand aesthetic perceptions and judgments and in a creatively artistic attitude to the world, but not in aesthetic snobbishness.

Nietzsche thought that morality was dangerous because it hindered the realization of the higher type of man. This is true of legalistic morality, which does not allow the human personality to express itself as a whole. In Christianity itself, legalistic elements are unfavorable to the creative manifestation of the higher type of man. The morality of chivalry, of knightly honor and loyalty, was creative and could not be subsumed under the ethics of law or the ethics of redemption. And in spite of the relative, transitory, and even bad characteristics which chivalry has had as a matter of historical fact, it contained elements of permanent value and was a manifestation of the eternal principles of the human personality. Chivalry would have been impossible without Christianity.

Nietzsche opposes to the distinction between good and evil, which he regards as a sign of decadence, the distinction between the noble and the low. The noble, the fine, is a higher type of life—aristocratic, strong, beautiful, well-bred. The conception of "fineness" is ontological, while that of goodness is moralistic. This leads not to amoralism, which is a misleading conception, but to the subordination of moral categories to the ontological. It means that the important thing is not to fulfill the moral law but to perfect one's nature, i.e., to attain transfiguration and enlightenment. From this point of view, the saint must be described as "fine," not as "good," for he has a lofty, beautiful nature penetrated by the divine light through and through. But all Nietzsche knew of Christianity was the moral law, and he rebelled against it. He had quite a mistaken idea about the spirit and spiritual life. He thought that a bad conscience was born of the conflict between the instincts and the behests of society—just as Freud, Adler, and Jung suppose. The instinct turns inward and becomes spirit. Spirit is the repressed, inward-driven instinct, and therefore really an epiphenomenon. For Nietzsche, the true, rich, unrepressed life is not spirit, and indeed is opposed to it. Nietzsche is clearly the victim of reaction against degenerate legalistic Christianity and against the bad spirituality which, in truth, has always meant suppression of the spirit. Nietzsche mistook it for the true spirituality. He rejected God because he thought God was incompatible with creativeness and the creative heroism to which his philosophy was a call. God was, for him, the symbol not of man's ascent to the heights but of his remaining on a flat surface below. Nietzsche was fighting not against God but against a false conception of God, which certainly ought to be combated. The idea, so widespread in theology, that the existence of God is incompatible with man's creativeness, is a source of atheism. And Nietzsche waged an agonizing struggle against God. He went further, and asserted that spirit is incompatible with creativeness, while in truth spirit is the only source of creativeness. In this connection, too, Nietzsche's attitude was inspired by a feeling of protest. Theology systematically demanded that man should bury his talents in the ground. It failed to see that the Gospel required creativeness of man and confined its attention to commands and laws; it failed to grasp the meaning of parables and of the call to freedom; it sought to know only the revealed and not the hidden. Theologians have not sufficiently understood that freedom should not be forced, repressed, and burdened with commands and prohibitions. Rather, it ought to be enlightened, transfigured, and strengthened through the power of grace. A curious paradox is exemplified in the teaching of the Jesuits.[12] Jesuitism is, in a sense, an apotheosis of the human will: a man may increase the power of God. Jesuitism teaches a new form of asceticism: asceticism of the will and not of the body. It takes heaven by storm and gains power over the world. And at the same time, Jesuitism means slavery of the will and a denial of man's creativeness. The real problem of creativeness, so far from being formulated and solved by Christianity, has not even been faced in all its religious implications. It has been considered only as the problem of justifying culture, i.e., on a secondary plane, and not as the question of the relation between God and man. The result is rebellion and rejection of the dominant theological theories.

Human nature may contract or expand. Or, rather, human nature is rooted in infinity and has access to boundless energy. But man's consciousness may be narrowed down and repressed. Just as the atom contains enormous and terrible force which can be released by splitting (the secret has not yet been discovered),

12 See the interesting book by Fülöp-Miller, *Macht und Geheimnis der Jesuiten.* The author is not a Catholic, but his book is a curious apology for the Jesuits and contains instances of subtle psychological analysis.

so the human monad contains enormous and terrible force which can be released by melting down consciousness and removing its limits. In so far as human nature is narrowed down by consciousness it becomes shallow and unreceptive. It feels cut off from the sources of creative energy. What makes man interesting and significant is that his mind has, so to speak, an opening onto infinity. But average, normal consciousness tries to close this opening, and then man finds it difficult to manifest all his gifts and resources of creative energy. The principle of *laisser faire*, so false in economics, contains a certain amount of truth in regard to moral and spiritual life. Man must be given a chance to manifest his gifts and creative energy, he must not be overwhelmed with external commands and have his life encumbered with an endless number of norms and prohibitions.

It is a mistake to think that a cult of creativeness means a cult of the future and of the new. True creativeness is concerned neither with the old nor with the new but with the eternal. A creative act directed upon the eternal may, however, have as its product and result something new, i.e., something projected in time. Newness in time is merely the projection or symbolization of the creative process which takes place in the depths of eternity.[13] Creativeness may give one bliss and happiness, but that is merely one of its consequences. Bliss and happiness are never the aim of creativeness, which brings with it its own pain and suffering. The human spirit moves in two directions: toward struggle and toward contemplation. Creativeness takes place both in struggle and in contemplation. There is a restless element in it, but contemplation is the moment of rest. It is impossible to separate and to oppose the two elements. Man is called to struggle and to manifest his creative power, to win a regal place in nature and in the cosmos. And he is also called to the mystic contemplation of God and the spiritual world. By comparison with active struggle, contemplation seems to us passive and inactive. But contemplation of God is creative

[13] See my book, *Freedom and the Spirit*.

activity. God cannot be won through active struggle similar to the struggle we wage with cosmic elements. He can only be contemplated, by creatively directing our spirit upwards. The contemplation of God, Who is love, is man's creative answer to God's call. Contemplation can only be interpreted as love, as the ecstasy of love—and love is always creative. This contemplation, this ecstasy of love, is possible not only in relation to God and the higher world but also in relation to nature and to other people. I contemplate, in love, the human faces I love and the face of nature, its beauty. There is something morally repulsive about modern activistic theories which deny contemplation and recognize nothing but struggle. For them, not a single moment has value in itself; each moment is only a means to what follows. The ethics of creativeness is an ethics of struggle and contemplation, and of love, both in the struggle and in the contemplation. By reconciling the opposition between love and contemplation it reconciles the opposition between aristocratic and democratic morality. It is an ethics both of ascent and of descent. The human soul rises upwards, ascends to God, wins for itself the gifts of the Holy Spirit and strives for spiritual aristocratism. But it also descends into the sinful world, shares the fate of the world and of other men, strives to help its brothers, and gives them the spiritual energy acquired in the upward movement of the soul. One is inseparable from the other. To forsake the world and men for the lofty heights of the spirit and to refuse to share one's spiritual wealth with others is unchristian, and implies not only a lack of love but also a lack of creativeness, for creativeness is generous and ready to give. This was the limitation of pre-Christian spirituality. Plato's Eros is ascent without descent, i.e., an abstraction. The same is true of the Indian mystics. But it is equally unchristian and uncreative completely to merge one's soul in the world and humanity and to renounce spiritual ascent and acquisition of spiritual force. And when the soul takes up a tyrannical attitude toward nature and mankind, when it wants to dominate and not to be a source of sacrificial help and regeneration, it falls prey to one of the darkest instincts of the subconscious and inevitably undermines its own creative powers, for creativeness presupposes sacrifice. Victory over the subconscious instinct of tyranny is one of the most fundamental moral tasks. People ought to be brought up from childhood in a spirit completely opposed to the instincts of tyranny which exhaust and destroy creative energy. Tyranny finds expression in personal relations, in family life, in social and political organizations, and in spiritual and religious life.

Three new factors have appeared in the moral life of man and are acquiring an unprecedented significance. Ethics must take account of three new objects of human striving. Man has come to love *freedom* more than he has ever loved it before, and he demands freedom with extraordinary persistence. He no longer can or wants to accept anything unless he can accept it freely. Man has grown more *compassionate* than before. He cannot endure the cruelty of the old days. He is pitiful in a new way to every creature—not only to the least of men but also to animals and to everything that lives. A moral consciousness opposed to pity and compassion is no longer tolerable. And, finally, man is more eager than ever before *to create*. He wants to find a religious justification and meaning for his creativeness. He can no longer endure having his creative instinct repressed, either from without or from within. At the same time, other instincts are at work in him, instincts of slavery and cruelty, and he shows a lack of creativeness which leads him to thwart creativeness itself and deny its very existence. And yet the striving for freedom, compassion, and creativeness is both new and eternal. Therefore the new ethics is bound to be an ethics of *freedom, compassion,* and *creativeness.*

Georgy Petrovich Fedotov

1886 - 1951

Born in Saratov in 1886, Fedotov followed a familiar path: while a student at St. Petersburg he took part in underground Marxist circles and was expelled from Russia in 1906. For two years he studied at the Universities of Berlin and Jena and, upon his return to Russia, graduated from the Faculty of Philosophy and History in 1908. In 1914 he began teaching mediaeval European history at the University. After the Communist Revolution, Fedotov joined the "Christian Underground"—a group of intellectuals fighting for spiritual freedom. In 1920 he was elected Professor of Mediaeval History at the University of Saratov but in 1922 resigned his post in protest against political pressure. In 1925 Fedotov left Russia and settled in Paris. Here, in exile, he led what to many of his friends and enemies was a "split" life. He became a professor at St. Sergius Theological Institute and, for many years, taught hagiology—the history and the content of holiness in the Church. Several outstanding monographs on the Russian saints, including *Sv. Philip, Mitropolit Moskovskii* ("St. Philip of Moscow"), 1929, and *Sviatye drevnei Rusi* ("Saints of Ancient Russia"), 1931, were the outcome of this activity. At the same time, Fedotov continued to be very active in left-wing *émigré* political circles, contributing articles of political commentary to their magazines. In 1931, with some friends, he founded a review, *Novy grad* ("The New City"), devoted to the search for a Christian solution to the political and social problems of our time. This political activity provoked conflicts and accusations, but Fedotov never yielded to any pressure. In 1940 he left France for New York where, in 1943, he joined the faculty of St. Vladimir's Orthodox Seminary and was instrumental in its reorganization as a graduate school. The two books he published in English, *The Russian Religious Mind* (1946) and *A Treasury of Russian Spirituality* (1948), were widely acclaimed.

Bibliography

A complete bibliography of Fedotov's writing was compiled and published by his widow under the title, *G. Fedotov, Bibliography* (1886–1951). Paris: Beresniak, 1956.

His most important works in English are:

The Russian Religious Mind. Cambridge, Mass., 1946.

A Treasury of Russian Spirituality. New York, 1948.

The Russian Church Since the Revolution. London, 1928.

"Orthodoxy and Historical Criticism," in *The Church of God.* London: SPCK, 1934.

The Christian Origins of Freedom[1]

> "Shadow has embraced half the sky.
> Only there, in the west, is there
> a glow on the horizon . . ."

"MAN IS BORN FREE, but dies in chains." There is nothing more false than this remarkable assertion.

Rousseau wanted to say that freedom is the natural, innate state of man, which he loses with civilization. In reality the conditions of natural organic life provide no basis whatever for freedom.

Iron laws hold sway in the biological world: the laws of instincts, of the struggle of species and races, of the cyclic, repetitious nature of the processes of life. Where everything is ultimately determined by necessity, it is impossible to find a chink or crevice through which freedom can burst in. Where organic life acquires a social character, it is totalitarian through and through. Bees have their communism, ants are in bondage, in the herd of wild beasts there is the absolute power of the lead buck (the "leader").

In the eighteenth century nature was looked upon romantically—or, more precisely, theologically. The Church's doctrine

[1] Translated from G. P. Fedotov, *Khristianin v revolyutsii* (Paris, 1957), pp. 173–187.

of the first-formed nature of man was shifted to nature itself and
the lost Paradise of the Bible was placed in Polynesia. It is no
accident that biology is the basis of all modern ideologies of
slavery. Racism has its roots in the biological world and, as an
utterly bad philosophy of culture, it is closer to natural or animal
reality than Rousseau's thought.

Rousseau really wanted to say: Man must be free; or: Man is
created to be free; and the eternal truth of Rousseau lies here.
But this is not at all the same thing as saying that man is born
free.

Freedom is the late, refined flower of culture. This does not
diminish its value in any way; nor is it so simply because the most
precious thing is always rare and fragile. Man becomes fully man
only in the process of culture, and only in culture, at its summits,
do his loftiest aspirations and potentialities find their expression.
The nature and significance of man can be judged only in the
light of these attainments.

Even within the world of culture, freedom appears as a rare
and tardy guest. In reviewing the ten or a dozen high civilizations known to us which, according to a modern historian (Toyn-
bee), comprise a historical process that once seemed unique, we
find freedom in our sense of the word in only one of them—and
then only in the last phase of its existence. Of course I have in
mind our civilization and our time, leaving undefined for the
time being the limits of our space and time.

Other cultures may impress us with their grandeur, may cap-
tivate us with their refinement, may amaze us with the complexity and well-ordered nature of their social institutions, even
with the depth of their religion and thought, but we will not
find freedom anywhere as the basis of social life. Individuality is
everywhere subjected to the collective, which itself defines the
forms and boundaries of its own power.

The Greeks fought and died for freedom; but they understood
freedom either as the independence of their city-state or as its

democratic self-government. This was freedom for the state, a freedom to which neither the individual person nor the minority group could lay claim. We are often deceived by the liberty and ease of life in the classic period of the Athenian democracy—in those brief hundred and fifty years which divide the Greco-Persian War from the Macedonian conquest. But this liberty was the result of a decomposition, was more a licentiousness than a law of life. The new merchant-industrial classes had undermined the solidity of the rural patriarchal mores, the teaching of the sophists had shattered the ancient faith; it became easier to live in the void that had formed, that is, it became easier to enjoy life without being hindered by obsolete norms.

But just at the time of Athens' greatest freedom there occurred the trial and execution of Socrates, the persecution of Anaxagoras and Protagoras and—what is much more terrible—the social utopia of Plato. The greatest of the Greek philosophers was the theoretician of the absolute, totalitarian state. Perhaps only in Sophocles' *Antigone* does the glow of our freedom begin to shine: the prediction, the anticipation of a completely different spiritual era.

The exceptional nature, the uniqueness of freedom must not disturb us. Only coarse biological or sociological thinking, operating with numerical quantities, repetitions, and average magnitudes, can see a vice in uniqueness. Yes, freedom is an exception in the series of great cultures. But culture itself is an exception in natural life. Man himself, with his spiritual life, is a strange exception among living beings. But then life too, as an organic manifestation, is also an exception in the material world. Of course we enter here into the area of the unknown, but there are many foundations for those theories which hold that favorable conditions for the appearance of organic life could be created only on the planet Earth. But what is the significance of Earth in the solar system, what is the significance of the sun in our Milky Way, what is the significance of our "galaxy" in the whole universe?

One of two things: either we remain with an externally impressive "natural science" point of view and then arrive at the conclusion of pessimism. Earth, life, man, culture, freedom—all are such insignificant things that they aren't worth talking about. Arising out of the accidental play of forces on one of the particles of world creation, they are destined to disappear without a trace in the cosmic night.

Or we must turn all our scales of value upside down and proceed not from numerical quanitities but from qualities. Then man, with his spirit and his culture, will become the crown and goal of the creation of the world. All the countless galaxies exist only to produce this miracle—a free and rational corporeal being destined to exercise a kingly rule over the universe.

What are we speaking about? What kind of freedom? It is time to define our terms. But this should be done briefly, without needless complexities. In these days it is above all the enemies of freedom who are demanding definitions of freedom. They have lost the ability to understand it; the simplest things begin to seem to them monstrously difficult. Blowing up these difficulties to absurd proportions, they turn freedom into philosophical nonsense. However (along with every reader), they have the right to a clear and precise answer. What is understood by freedom here on these pages?

We are not speaking about freedom in the philosophical or religious sense; our freedom is not the freedom of the will—that is, of choice—which nothing, no blindness of sin or prejudice, can ever completely take away from man. The members of both the Young Communist League and the *Hitler-Jugend* possess this freedom.

Nor is this the freedom from passions or from the demands of our lower nature toward which the Stoic philosopher and the ascetic are striving; Epictetus achieved this freedom in slavery; the saints found it in the voluntary prison of the monastic cell.

Nor is it the dynamic freedom of social destruction and construction in which fascist youth are caught up, as they place their personal wills in complete subjection to their leaders for the sake of the feeling of collective might and power.

Our freedom is simultaneously social and individual. It is the freedom of the individual from society—more precisely, from the state and from all such compelling social bonds. Our freedom is negative—freedom from something—and at the same time it is relative, since absolute freedom from the state is an absurdity.

Freedom in this sense is simply a setting of limits to the power of the state in terms of the inalienable rights of the individual. While it is relative in its forms and measure, while it is defined in different ways in the different countries of modern democracy, this freedom is, however, founded on certain absolute premises which we must establish. The loss of these premises, a complete relativization, would be fatal for freedom; and in our opinion this is indeed the main reason for its present eclipse.

Looking over the long list of freedoms by which modern democracy lives—freedom of conscience, of thought, of speech, of assembly, etc.—we see that they can all be reduced to two basic principles—to two, mind you, and not to one, much to the sorrow of logical aesthetics. This dualism bears witness to the difference in the historical roots of our freedom.

Its chief and most valuable element consists in freedom of conviction—religious, moral, scientific, political—and of the public expression of this conviction—in speech, in print, in organized social activity. Historically this whole group of freedoms develops out of the freedom of faith.

On the other hand, another whole group of freedoms defends the individual from the arbitrary will of the state (which is independent of questions of conscience and thought)—freedom from arbitrary arrest and punishment, from insult, plundering and coercion on the part of the organs of power; such freedoms define the content of constitutional guarantees for which an agelong struggle has been waged against the monarchies. They found expression in the characteristic English statute known as habeas corpus. Using this symbol, we could call this group of freedoms the freedoms of the body, as distinct from the other group—the freedom of the spirit.

The unrelated nature of these two freedoms is explained by one simple consideration. The ideal Christian, the saint, can, without a murmur, give up his body, his property, and his life to a tyrant; he can even regard this nonresistance as his duty, as the imitation of Christ. But he will not worship idols, he will not deny Christ on the command of the emperor. The greatest conflicts between the state and the Church proceed mainly from this freedom—the freedom of the spirit; while conflicts between the state and secular society proceed mainly from questions of the freedom of the body.

Of course we are using the word "body" in a very broad sense; it includes the property of the person as well as his honor—that is, not only his physical but also his social individuality, with the exception of his spiritual properties, or, putting it another way, everything that belongs to the person and is not manifested by the person. Faith and conviction do not belong to personality, rather personality itself belongs to them; in a sense its actual existence coincides with them.

Perhaps the majority of democratic people in our time are convinced that these freedoms are the triumph of the modern period: of the English Revolution of the seventeenth century, or even of the French Revolution of the eighteenth. For many people the Puritans and Jacobites seem to be fathers of our freedom, and revolution generally the place of its birth. Hence the optimistic view of the outcome of modern revolutions. They are represented as leading inevitably to freedom and as actualizations of freedom after severe trials.

We shall have more to say about the kind of role the great historical revolutions have played in the development of our freedom. But first it is necessary to emphasize and insistently repeat that freedom was born in the Middle Ages, even though it attained its full development in the nineteenth century. That same Christian mediaeval period which is the mother country of our whole culture, as distinct from the culture of the classic world, is also the mother country of our freedom. Magna Charta is dated A.D. 1215.

But long before the revolt of the barons against John the Landless, Europe had seen wars and revolutions which had been waged for freedom. The end of the eleventh century was full of the thunder of popular movements and international wars. Freedom was the very slogan of battle in those years—but freedom in a special sense: *libertas Ecclesiae*. And this brings us back to the origins of the first freedom—the freedom of faith.

The Western Church survived the crisis of the Roman Empire and of the Hellenistic culture which it had preserved. She victoriously met the waves of barbarian invasions and subjected them to the Cross and to Rome. She did not become dissolved in the German kingdoms and did not merge with them into a "symphony," like the Byzantine Church, but preserved her independence from the state and, even more, preserved her magisterial and disciplinary power over it. However, this did not reach the point of becoming a theocracy. The barbarian element rebelled against Roman tutelage. A dual authority, a double citizenship, was established. A double justice—spiritual and secular —was its external expression. But still more important, each person was the subject of two kingdoms: the City of God and the earthly city. Both sovereignties came together and frequently collided in the heart of the individual, but one—and only one— laid claim to absolute significance. The Church took a man's soul, the king his body. It was difficult to set boundaries, for life was more complex than this dualism. The complexity of life evoked a constant conflict, essentially unresolvable. And in this conflict the first dim consciousness of freedom was created and affirmed.

Man was obliged to choose; by the will of fate, every Christian became a judge in the dispute of the two supreme authorities: pope and emperor. In the huge conflicts of the eleventh, twelfth, and thirteenth centuries the whole of society was split in two in this dispute. No matter what the social foundations of society might be, under these conditions there could be no talk about the absolute nature of secular power. Even in its divergence from the very content of spiritual sovereignty, even in the absurd proposition that any non-Christian religion could have such sovereignty, the very fact of a Church-State dualism limited the power of the state created a sphere of personal freedom. But of course, on consideration one realizes that no other known religion could fulfill the role of spiritual sovereignty; for this purpose it had to be a religion of the absolutely eternal and at the same time of that which is connected with, and related to, the corporeal and the earthly. Neither a this-worldly paganism nor an otherworldly spiritualism (Buddhism, Platonism) could create a sphere of religion above the state yet occupying a separate domain beside it. Islam does not enter into this question, since (like Byzantium) the supreme spiritual power there coincides with the state.

In Catholic Europe the Church had one important piece of good fortune in its struggle for freedom: the feudal character of the state. Of course, violent and warlike knighthood was the occasion for much evil and trouble in the Church. The Church found more obedience among the city guilds, among the workers of the first industrial cities of Italy and the Netherlands. But even if they were plunderers, the barons also weakened royal power and smashed secular sovereignty. The menace of Leviathan did not rise before the Church.

In turning to the feudal world itself, we find in it the genesis of another freedom, less exalted but perhaps more highly valued by contemporary democracy: the genesis of what we are accustomed to call the freedom of the body. In the feudal state the barons were not subjects, or rather not only subjects but also vassals. Their relations to the suzerain were defined by treaty and custom, not by the will of the monarch. On the territory of the stronger seigneurs, if not of all, the seigneur himself carried out the laws of the sovereign among his serfs and even among the free population.

The formula, "sovereign landlord," even though not free of exaggeration, catches a basic feature of feudal society. There were, in this case, not one but thousands of sovereigns, and the person of each one of them—his "body"—was defended from arbitrary action. He must not be insulted. He paid off an insult with blood; he had the right to wage war against the king. The baron's revolt in England in 1214 and Magna Charta were not revolutionary outbursts, the beginning of a new era, but normal episodes in the political struggle of the time.

At the coronation of English kings, at the most solemn moment, when the monarch places the crown on his head, all the peers and peeresses present in Westminster Abbey put on their own crowns. They too are sovereigns, the hereditary princes of England. Right now this is a symbol of almost nonexistent conventional privilege. But I would like to see in it also a symbol of contemporary democratic freedom. What was formerly the privilege of hundreds of families has, in the course of the centuries, been spread among thousands and millions, until it has become the inalienable right of every citizen.

It is not so much that the nobility has been abolished in Western democracy as that the whole people have inherited its privileges. This is an equality of nobility and not of the loss of rights as in the East. The "peasant" began to call his neighbor Sir and Monsieur, i.e., "my sovereign," and then in return demanded the plural "you" as a form of respect.

We are speaking here not of trifles, not of etiquette, but of what stands behind them. And behind all this, habeas corpus was gradually extended from the baron-sovereigns to the bourgeoisie of the city guilds and to the whole people. In Magna Charta the citizens of London shared some of the privileges of the barons. From the eleventh to the thirteenth century there existed everywhere in Europe free city guilds, collective seigniories, which shared the privileges of social and individual freedom. Enfranchized cities drew the villages after them. Serfdom was softened and died out under the influence of the free atmosphere of the cities.

We certainly do not wish to idealize the middle ages. The freedom-loving barons were for the most part cruel masters to their subjects. It is difficult for us to recognize the father of our freedom in a despoiler, a plunderer, and a tyrant, just as it is difficult to believe that the Catholic Church was struggling for spiritual freedom in burning heretics at the stake. Of course the princes of the mediaeval Church did not even dream of freedom of conscience. They needed freedom not for the individual believer but for the "Church," that is, for her hierarchy. Besides, the pope had to share this freedom with the universities, just as the barons shared theirs with the merchants. In fact, the delusion of a totalitarian state has been sown over many centuries in the West as a result of the struggle for freedom. But in spite of all the reactions of the Renaissance, a limit was also set to absolute monarchy and to the omnipotence of the state. And this limit was indicated by the two principles apparently always necessary for the existence of freedom: pluralism of power and the absolute character of spiritual (religious) norms.

The transition from the middle ages to the modern period brought not a broadening but a reduction of freedom. The brilliant cultural Renaissance signified the appearance of tyranny in the political sphere in Italy and of royal absolutism in Europe beyond the Alps. The centralized national or territorial state was created on the ruins of mediaeval class liberty. Parliaments lost their authority, *Etats Généraux* ceased to be convened, standing armies and an embryonic bureaucracy dislodged the feudal *aide et conseil*. Pluralism of power, one of the conditions of freedom, was limited—if it did not disappear altogether. The other, spiritual, condition was also shaken, with the decline or eclipse of religion.

The Church retreated from her universal positions and locked herself up within the walls of the church building. Her opposition to infringements upon the spiritual sphere of life became rare and weak. Caesar began to have power not just over the bodies but also partly over the souls of his subjects. Thomas More, humanist and martyr for the freedom of the Church, was a rare exception.

Perhaps a recollection of this fading away of freedom at the dawn of the splendid era of our culture can bring some comfort now, in the days of its second eclipse. It is still too soon to bury freedom. The socialistic revolution today, like the national state of the past, feeds on the blood of freedom. Now too, as in the time of the Renaissance, there is the threat of the final death of freedom, that is, of the conclusion of our culture in a totalitarian state. But if this danger was forestalled once before it is possible to win a victory over it again. It is important, however, to remember what the conditions were which made the victory possible.

The culture of the Renaissance, with its triumphant growth of despotism, found its limit in the Reformation. Every attempt to construct a genealogy of contemporary freedom which by-passes the Reformation is doomed to failure. The line which connects the Renaissance directly with the Enlightenment, or which connects Leonardo da Vinci directly with Newton, is suitable for a history of science, but not for a history of freedom. Of course the assertion of reactionary Catholics that all contemporary "individualistic" freedom was generated by Luther's fall into sin is a tremendous exaggeration. But it does contain a kernel of truth. After the Catholic struggle for the freedom of the Church (eleventh and twelfth centuries), the religious wars of the epoch of the Reformation (sixteenth and seventeenth centuries) mark the second stage in the development of freedom.

But the matter should not simply be presented as if Luther's principle of free interpretation of the Bible played this revolutionary role. In actual fact, the authority of the Catholic Church was at once replaced by the authority of the new prophets; and after the prophets there followed the scholastics, who created the Protestant catechisms. The Augsburg or Westminster Confessions are themselves no more free than the Tridentine catechism. The fanaticism of the new sects was no less vigorous than the intolerance of the old Church. The Protestants burned or hung heretics with no less zeal than the Catholics. Moreover, where the Reformation yielded power over the Church to princes—in England, in Germany, in the Scandinavian countries—state absolutism received a new reinforcement at the expense of the Catholic Church. The Tudors became the "administrators" of the Church and, by virtue of this, rulers of conscience. But the fact that in England—precisely in England—the dominant "Anglican" confession could not become the religion of the whole people had tremendous significance for the destiny of freedom. The religious storm raised at the beginning of the seventeenth century led not to the unity of the newly reformed Church but to the formation of many sects fighting passionately but unsuccessfully for supremacy. After Cromwell's tyranny, England returned to its point of departure, to the restoration of the Stuarts and the former themes of struggle: Church vs. sects, King vs. parliament. Freedom came, together with tolerance—limited tolerance of course—only at the end of the century, when the impossibility of the religious unification of England had become clearly apparent. The second "glorious" revolution brought with it a genuine habeas corpus and freedom for the major sects of Protestantism; Catholics and Jews had to wait until the nineteenth century.

We see almost the same thing in America. Here it was not the Anglican Church but the Congregationalists or Presbyterians who tried to establish a regime of confessional unity in various colonies. The suffocating atmosphere of intolerance in New England was no better than that of old England: in Connecticut they hung Quakers. However, the dividedness of the sects and their occupation of separate but contiguous domains forced them to create islands of freedom where people of different faiths could live side by side—like the State of Rhode Island.

Thus freedom, or oases of freedom, were gradually created in a world of intolerance; freedom was accepted—not on principle and not joyfully, but by necessity—as an unavoidable evil. But now a "virtue was made of a necessity." On the crossroads of spiritual highways you met people—and their number was growing—who affirmed freedom as a principle, who confessed the religion of freedom. For these chosen minds, for Milton, George Fox, Roger Williams, freedom was inseparable from Christianity. And the thesis of these utopians who strayed into the cruel age of religious wars has triumphed. Freedom has turned out to be more practical than coercion. Compulsory unity threatened to bring endless war and the destruction of culture: freedom has saved it.

A forced tolerance brings little gladness. If the future of freedom depended on the loss of spiritual unity, on the presence of heresies and schisms, then this would not hold out any promise for good or happier times to come, for a Europe which would again have found the wholeness of its cultural life. Fortunately, Christian freedom has deeper roots than practical despair. Ages have passed, and the convictions of a few utopians of the period of the Reformation have entered into the flesh and blood of the majority of Christians. In these days there are few who would dare to defend the idea of salvation by force. The most authoritarian churches stand today on the soil of freedom—not perhaps wholeheartedly, not altogether sincerely, but that is another question. The important thing is simply that they dare not sanction force for the sake of salvation, for the sake of love, as our ancestors have done through the course of the ages. Christianity has matured in many ways, has become wiser, more scrupulous in recent centuries. Midst the grievous failures and defeats, and even persecutions, which it has managed to survive, it has been able to go back into its origins, to perceive more clearly what its spirit is. Beyond doubt Christianity is closer now to the experience of the early Church, closer to Christ, than in the period of His illusory dominion over the world.

Perhaps no one has declared the meaning of freedom for the Christian Church with such force as Dostoevsky in his "Legend of the Grand Inquisitor." Dostoevsky, of course, was not a member of the clergy, not even a theologian. But it is striking that none of the reactionary elements of Pobedonostsev's Russia dared to rise openly against this "false prophet." No one said: This is heresy. They only pretended that "this doesn't concern us . . . he is talking about papism."

In the Gospel of John, and in Paul's Epistles, there are many inspired words on freedom. But they speak of that profound, ultimate freedom which can be approached even through a negation of freedom. At least such has been the thousand year dialectic of theology. The freedom about which we are speaking here—social freedom—is affirmed on the basis of two Christian truths. First—the absolute integrity of the individual ("soul"), which cannot be sacrificed for the sake of any collective, nation, state, or even Church ("the ninety and nine just persons"; cf. Luke 15:7). Second—the freedom of choosing the way between truth and falsehood, between good and evil. It was precisely this second terrible freedom which was so difficult for the ancient Christian conscience, just as it is difficult now for the conscience of the irreligious. To acknowledge it means to place freedom above love; it means to acknowledge the tragic significance of history, the possibility of hell. All the social instincts of man protest against such "cruelty." If it is possible to pull a drowning man out of the water by the hair, why, then, is it not possible to pull a man "by the hair" out of hell? But in the parable of the tares and the wheat it is said: "let them grow together until the harvest" (Matthew 13:30). And in the ancient myth of the Fall, which forms the basis of Christian theodicy, God creates man free, knowing that by this terrible freedom man will subvert God's beautiful world. And God wishes to save the fallen world, not by the word of power ("let there be"), but by the sacrifice of His own Son. How, then, can this sacrifice abrogate the freedom for the sake of which it was offered? In the light of this revelation, we acknowledge that it is Christian mankind which has erred and sinned for half a millennium, not that God erred in creating man free, or that Christ erred in ascending the Cross to save man in freedom.

Translated by Asheleigh E. Moorhouse
August, 1963

Sergei Nikolaevich Bulgakov

1871 - 1944

Son of a humble priest, Bulgakov followed a complex, yet not uncommon, spiritual itinerary. His childhood was entirely shaped by the Church, its worship, its customs, and its atmosphere, and everything seemed to foreordain him for priesthood. But in 1888, one year before graduation, he left the seminary of Orel and entered the secular school. His faith—or rather, the Christian expression of it—was gone. For, as Bulgakov repeatedly affirmed in his writings, his long wanderings through atheism, materialism, and Marxism were always religious in their deep motivations. In 1894 he graduated from the Law School of Moscow University and began preparation for an academic career in the field of political economics. His first book—a Marxist analysis of *Markets Under Capitalistic Production* —appeared in 1896. In Germany, where he spent two studious years, he was in close contact with the leaders of German social democracy. Returning to Russia in 1900, he taught first in Kiev, then, from 1906, in Moscow. It is during these years that he began his return to the "Father's house." He published

Ot Marksisma K Idealizmy ("From Marxism to Idealism") in St. Petersburg in 1904, and in 1909 he was one of the contributors to the famous symposium, *Vekhi* (Signposts), in which the former radical leaders of the Russian intelligentsia, according to S. Frank, "jointly criticized the predominant radicalism of the intelligentsia which was based on materialism and positivism. They asserted the necessity of a religious foundation to any consistent philosophy of life, and at the same time sharply criticized the revolutionary and maximalist tendencies of the radical-minded Russian intelligentsia. . . ."

Bulgakov, however, went further than any of his friends. In 1918 he was ordained a priest and gave himself entirely to theology. Deported from Russia in 1923, he joined the faculty of the newly founded St. Sergius Theological Institute in Paris, where he taught dogmatics until his death in 1944. During these twenty years he published no less than nine major books related to his theological system, known as Sophiology. He took a very active part in the Ecumenical Movement and in the work of the Student Christian Movement. His theological teaching, however, raised violent objections, both inside and outside the Institute. Some of his doctrines were condemned as heretical by synods of bishops in Moscow and in Yugoslavia, and his theological system as such has scarcely had any followers among Orthodox theologians. But no one would deny the importance of the problems Bulgakov raised nor that he tried to solve them with admirable integrity, depth, and conviction. Whatever the ultimate fate of his Sophiology, he himself will remain as a great and creative thinker who has contributed more than many others toward shaping the direction and the ethos of modern Orthodox theology.

Although none of his major works has been translated into English, Bulgakov summarized the main points of his Sophiology for his English readers (cf. following). But he was also a wonderful priest and a powerful preacher, and this side of his personality is almost ignored in the West. For this reason, we close this anthology with his Easter Sermons, which reflect so well the paschal joy of his theological inspiration.

Bibliography

For a complete bibliography, see L. A. Zander, ed., *Pamiati Otsa Sergeya Bulgakova* ("In Memoriam: Father Sergei Bulgakov"). Paris, 1945.

The Orthodox Church. London, 1935.
The Wisdom of God, a Brief Summary of Sophiology. London: Williams and Norgate, 1937.
"By Jacob's Well (John 4:23)" in *Journal of the Fellowship of St. Alban and St. Sergius.* London, 1933, W22, pp. 7–17.
"Religion and Art" in *The Church of God*, an Anglo-Russian Symposium by members of the Fellowship of St. Alban and St. Sergius, ed. by E. L. Mascall. London: SPCK, 1934.
"Revelation" in *Revelation.* 1937.
"Ways to Church Reunion" in *Sobornost*, Fellowship of St. Alban and St. Sergius, 1935, W2, pp. 7–15.

Meditations on the Joy
of the Resurrection[1]

Let Us Rejoice in the Lord!

> "That my joy will be in you, and that
> your joy will be full."
>
> John 15:11

> "O come let us receive the Divine
> gladness of the Kingdom of Christ."
>
> Paschal Canon

Christ is risen!

ON EASTER NIGHT when the Paschal procession going round the
Church comes to the closed doors and stops, our souls are
touched by an almost imperceptible and yet spiritually significant instant of uncomprehending, questioning silence: "Who
will roll away the stone for us from the door of the tomb?"
(Mark 16:3) And will the tomb be empty, with Christ risen?
When the doors are opened, before the Sign of the Cross, and
during the singing of the exultant Paschal hymn, we enter into

[1] Sergei Bulgakov, *Radost tserkovnaya, slova i poucheniya* ("The Joy of
the Church, Sermons and Instructions"), (Paris, 1938), pp. 67–73.

the Church all gleaming with lights, and our hearts are flooded
with joy, for Christ is risen from the dead. And then the Paschal
miracle is performed in our souls. For we "see the Resurrection
of Christ." "Having purified our senses," we see "Christ shining,"
and "as He comes out of the tomb we go to meet Christ, the
Bridegroom." Then we forget where we are, we pass out of ourselves, time stops, and we enter the "Sabbath rest of the People
of God" (Hebrews 4:9–10). In the radiance of the white light
of Easter, earthly colors are dimmed, and the soul sees only the
"unapproachable light of the Resurrection"; "now all things are
filled with light, heaven and earth and hell." On Easter night
it is given to man to experience in advance the life of the age to
come, to enter into the Kingdom of Glory, the Kingdom of God.
The language of our world has no words to express the revelation
of Easter night, for it is a mystery of the age to come, which has
a "silent language" of its own. The perfect joy given to us on this
night, according to the Lord's promise, is indeed the Holy Spirit,
who by the Father's will reveals to us the risen Christ. The Holy
Spirit is the joy which exists within the Holy Trinity, the Father's
joy in the Son and the Son's in the Father; He is also the joy
that is within us because of the Resurrection of Christ. Through
Him we see the risen Christ; He is, within us, the light of Christ's
Resurrection. Easter is, for us, not just one of the feasts, but "the
Feast of Feasts and the solemn Celebration of all Celebrations."
All the twelve great Feasts make known to us the Kingdom of
God in the works of God within events of this world. But Easter
is not the commemoration of such an event; it is directed rather
to the age to come. Easter is the forecourt on earth of the manifestation of glory for which Christ prayed to the Father in His
high-priestly prayer, the forecourt of the heavenly Jerusalem
which at the end of time will come down from heaven to earth,
according to the vision of the prophet: "Rise, shine, O thou new
Jerusalem, for the glory of the Lord has shone upon you." Easter
is indeed eternal life, the knowledge of God and communion
with God. It is the truth, peace, and joy of the Holy Spirit. The

first word of the risen Christ in His appearance to the myrrh-
bearing women was: "Rejoice" (Matthew 28:9); and His word
in the appearance to the apostles was: "Peace be with you"
(Luke 21:36; John 20:19–29).

The life of the age to come is not a simple negation of this age,
not its annihilation, but the making eternal of everything in it
worthy of such a transformation, just as eternity is not the forgetting or abolition of time, but the establishing of its un-
changing course. The glorification of creation in the Resurrection
is accomplished by the power of God, and yet actually in this
life by an exploit of self-denial. For the Resurrection of Christ
came about by virtue of His voluntary suffering and death on the
Cross: "having trampled on death by death." The victory over
death is accomplished from within, by death itself. The life of
this world is lived to the full in the wasting away of Christ's
death, just as death, known and experienced by Him to the full,
is already powerless to hold Him (Acts 2:29), for in Him death
itself is wasted away: "O death, where is thy sting?" (1 Corinthians 15:55) "Death is swallowed up in victory" (1 Corinthians
15:54). The Resurrection is not the creation of a new life, but a
victory over death in death itself, it is eternal life shining out of
death, shining in Christ the Bridegroom as He comes out of the
tomb. The Resurrection of Christ is therefore the making eternal
of His saving death, the death that crowned His redemptive
passion and the whole pathway of His Incarnation. The Resurrection of Christ is cruciform, since it was accomplished by the
Cross, by virtue of a sacrificial exploit of love and obedience.
"We bow down before thy Cross, O Lord, and we praise and
glorify thy Holy Resurrection." In the trampling down of death,
in the victory of the Resurrection, the Cross is the basis for, and
the power behind, our Easter joy. The felicity of Paradise retains
the idea of transfigured and victorious suffering, just as light is a
victory over "the darkness above the abyss," and as God's world
invests the "empty and formless land" with color and order.
While maintaining its own nature, this age passes into the next,

is transformed in it, as the earthly body of our Lord Jesus Christ was transformed in the Resurrection. The body of the risen Christ still has the holes of the nails and pierced side as proof of its identity; herein lies the unity between this life and that of the age to come; here, too, the power of Christ's Resurrection is revealed.

The image of the Resurrection is traced out *in nature*, and its mark can be seen in the resurrection of nature in spring. After the winter's slumber spring brings living shoots up out of the ground, new sprigs come up out of the ground with their sharp prickles, and they all soak up the juices of life. Spring is clothed with the multicolored vesture of resurrection under the sun's enlivening rays. And every spring in nature is a prophecy of the future spring of the whole world. The death of nature is conquered by the warmth of life, and the Easter of nature is naturally overcome and replaced by the Easter of Christianity. Just as winter, in its harsh way, leads to spring, so too in the Christian life the days of Lent and Holy Week bring us to Easter. Sometimes people want to avoid this path, they do not want to know and live through Holy Week. But their senses remain sealed, and the candle that will kindle the Paschal light is not in their souls. For "yesterday I buried you whom today I shall raise up, and I shall resurrect you whom yesterday I crucified." Blessed is he who can repeat these words of the Easter canticle in his heart. Joy is the crown of affliction, a great light gleams forth in the darkness and shadow of death, death is conquered by death, and our Paschal celebration is the spiritual fruit of sorrow and the discipline of fasting. After the sorrow of winter the Bridegroom calls to the Bride (to the soul): "Arise, my love, my fair one, and come away" (Song of Solomon 2:10).

The rays of the light of Christ's Resurrection penetrate *the whole of creation*. For us, the departed too are alive in this world, and we send our Easter greetings to them, the news of the Resurrection which, each one in his own way, they already know. It is not only animate and rational creation which receives the power of resurrection, rather, the whole of creation rises in Christ's Body, crying out exultantly with the joy of Easter. "Let the heavens rejoice worthily, let the earth rejoice, let the whole world visible and invisible celebrate the Feast." The unbridled joy of Easter is plain in nature even to the naked eye: the sun is "playing," the air, the water, and growing things are bathed in the rays of divine gladness. The human spirit—as it rises to life —can find no part of nature that is dead and not rising to life with it, and it summons all of nature to the Resurrection of Christ.

Easter is also a *Eucharistic* joy. The Lord did not withdraw Himself from us at His Ascension, but left us a bond with Himself in Holy Communion. By tasting the heavenly Bread and the Cup of life we touch Christ as He reveals Himself, and glorify Him then with the hymn of Resurrection: "O Great and most Holy Easter of Christ, O wisdom and word and power of God! Grant that we may truly partake of thee in the unending day of thy Kingdom." The Easter Feast is in fact the beginning of this unending day, and the joy of Easter is related to the joy of Communion. Believers are filled with Christ, the Lord is near to us, He *manifests Himself* to us as He showed Himself to the apostles before His Ascension. Easter is a kind of sacrament given to the Church by the Holy Spirit, that it may know the risen Lord: "Having seen the Resurrection of Christ, let us worship our Lord Jesus."

Easter is also joy in *the Church*. By virtue of Easter we find ourselves in the Church, within the one life of the one Body, the Body of Christ. That which is usually only a call and a promise appears now as the highest reality. The joy of the Church helps us to see one another in God, and in this knowledge to rejoice in those who are near us as a lover delights in his beloved. Easter fills us with the Holy Spirit, who is the joy of love. This gift is given to spiritual men as the reward for their self-denial. Easter was always glowing in the soul of St. Seraphim of Sarov, and he would greet those who came to him with the Easter greeting:

"Christ is risen, my joy!" In us too, so dark and sullen and sparing of kindness, our hearts are opened on this night to the joy of love, in the Paschal kiss and the welcoming cry: "Christ is risen!" Personal affronts are extinguished in this light, and mean feelings disappear. How can the lover not forgive, and is not forgiveness the highest joy of love? This is what likens us to God, who forgives the prodigal son and crowns him at the wedding feast. Easter is indeed a general forgiveness in the joy of love. In the love of Easter we attain to the love of God which passes all understanding. There is no place for darkness and shadow in this light. Within its fire all are brought together and united. "It is the day of the Resurrection, let us be enlightened by the Feast, and embrace one another. Let us kiss one another, brothers, and by the Resurrection forgive those who hate us for all things." The heart burns with the same joy of love which burned in the hearts of those two disciples when they saw Him and listened to Him, as He walked with them on the road. Even now He is among us, invisible and yet seen. Amen.

Having Trampled on Death by Death

A diptych

1

> "Love is strong as death"
> Song of Solomon 8:6

"God so loved the world that He gave His Son, that through Him the world might be saved" (John 3:16–17). The Son set aside the glory of His Godhood, "came down from heaven," was made man, and bore the whole weight of the life of a sinful world. He remained obedient to the will of the Father in word and deed—in suffering and in patience. "The Lord laid on Him the sins of us all" (Isaiah 53:6). Fainting under the weight of these sins, the Sinless One cried out: "My soul is afflicted even to death." "If it be possible, let this cup pass from me." But the cup did not pass. "It pleased God to bruise him, and He gave Him up to torment" (Isaiah 53:10). And this was the cup of death. The Father sent the Only-begotten to death for the sake of His people, and the Son went to meet this death. The God-Man died "for each and every one."

God's death cannot be contained in our thoughts; instead, it tears them apart. For God is Life, and Christ called Himself Life, and yet . . . there is Life in the tomb. "O Life, how can it be that you have died?" In Christ's death we bow down before the ultimate mystery of the Incarnation, of the sacrificial self-emptying of Godhood; this is indeed the power of God's love for man. This death is an ultimate fullness and therefore also the *limit* of love's sacrifice, the limit and end of its suffering. Otherwise this suffering would be an "eternal" torment. The sacrifice of Christ knows no limits. The Son gave up His *whole* self, His *whole* life, in sacrificial obedience; the unlimited continuation of His suffering would contradict its completedness, since then He would not have given up all. Yet the Son had to give up all. The sacrifice of divine love is subject to no limitations: *God so loved the world.* . . . Only His death could contain this fullness of sacrifice; it included all things within itself, even the One making the sacrifice.

But was not death contrary to the nature of the Sinless One, since God did not create death, rather death entered into the world by sin? Death had no power over the Sinless One, but it could be accepted *voluntarily*; it could be permitted, as a power exercised by the prince of this world. All the more mortal, then, was this death. Its mortal affliction—"my soul is afflicted even to death"—was the affliction of all afflictions and the sickness of all sicknesses. In order to accept death, God had to set aside His

Godhood and, as it were, cease to be God. "My God, My God, why has thou forsaken me!" Such was the cry of God dying on the Cross—the cry of God forsaken by God. It is as if the Holy Spirit Himself, the Giver of Life, had to "abandon" Him, so that this death might be "completed."

The sin of Adam brought death to the whole world, of which he was the center. The death of the God-Man, who gave up the Spirit on the Cross, was a new death of the whole world, and a judgment upon this world. It was the whole *fullness* of death: the sun darkened, the earth shook, and darkness covered the land during the hour of His dying on the Cross. This was, in a way, the mortal convulsion of the whole world. The death of the old Adam came as the fruit of his egocentricity, of that which separated him from God; he could no longer retain life within himself by his own strength, and death became for him a bitter necessity. But the Son of God had power over life, having—within His human nature—conquered this fatal egocentricity. "No one takes my life from me, but I myself give it up, I alone have power to give it up" (John 10:18). The God-Man Himself voluntarily accepts death in sacrificial self-immolation. In Him it is "finished," everything is given up in love for the world, there is nothing more to give up and nothing more to complete. This voluntary death is the love which conquered egocentricity.

The solemn rest of the Blessed Sabbath is at hand. The first Sabbath of God crowns the finishing of creation; the second Sabbath of God in the tomb crowns His sacrificial suffering. The parting of the soul from the body in death is contrary to the nature of man. It is the denial, the loss of life, not only in the anguish of dying but also in the affliction of the repose of death. Life in death is "hell," and the death of the God-Man is thus also a "descent into hell." For the One over whom death had no power, and by whom death was only permitted or accepted voluntarily—for Him the descent into hell was a continuation of His ministry. The Sun rose in a midnight land, in the darkness and shadow of death. "When thou went down to death,

O Life Everlasting, then hell was put to death by the radiance of Divinity." The word of Life resounds through hell, the disembodied shades hear the Good News of Christ. The Sun finishes its course in the land of the setting sun.

During His three-day sojourn in the tomb, the Lord tastes death along with the whole of mankind, and shares it with mankind. Nor is this death a lifeless slumber; rather, it is a continuing ministry, an uninterrupted obedience to the will of the Father. *This death is love.* Egocentricity is put to death in Christ's tomb, the sting of death is done away with, death itself dies. This death of the Immortal One is the victory over death, since the power of death is egocentricity, while the death of Christ is love. Love is as strong as death; but it is also more powerful than death.

2

"Life abides . . ."
St. John Chrysostom

How is death possible, if God did not create it? There is no death, since only life exists, the abiding life which comes from the Giver of Life. Death belongs to nonexistence, "out of" which, or "above" which, God created this world. Nonexistence is vanquished in creation by the creative power of God. And yet, having acquired a place in creation, it reared its head and became conditional existence in the egocentricity of a creature which had willfully fallen away from God. And this power of nonexistence, its life within creation, is death. The creature hid itself from the fullness of the gifts of the Life Giver, and in this way fell into mortality. Death became the cruel fate of all mankind, which could not protect itself from death by its own resisting force, its own self-affirmation. Death became for it a bitter *necessity*. But Christ's death was not a necessity, and was not the fruit of self-affirmation. On the contrary, it was a *voluntary* death, accepted out of love in order to save mankind. Such a death involves an inner contradiction, it loses its power and its rights: the ground is cut out from under it, since its ground is self-affirmation; the egocentricity of the creature is overcome by love. And so therefore "death could not hold Him" (Acts 2:24).

Voluntary death already conceals within itself the power of resurrection. It is the final victory of the spirit over the inertia of matter. The spiritual man is free and therefore all-powerful, since God Himself restores to him the power of life, and he is worthy and capable of receiving it. For this reason "God raised up His Son Jesus" (Acts 3:15). In the face of impending death, a death voluntarily accepted, a death nonetheless real and not illusory in its fatal power, He was abandoned by the power of God, by the power of the Holy Spirit. But this was a redemptive abandonment, since it opened the way for the redemptive exploit of death. For that One who accomplished the ultimate victory of love toward God and man, who manifested the ultimate obedience to the Father's will, this abandonment was the ultimate trial, as it was also the ultimate victory—a victory by death over death. He who accepted this voluntary death after abandonment by God will receive the power of the Holy Spirit from the Father in His Resurrection (Romans 10:9; 6:4). This sending down of the Holy Spirit after the abandonment, and as if in its place, is indeed the new creative action of God in the world, a new creation which could not take place one-sidedly, by the power of God's omnipotence working upon man. It required the participation of man himself, which in fact was accomplished in the person of the God-Man. It was necessary that the One who was raised from the dead be—and the One raising Him from the dead be revealed as—able to experience resurrection, by the power of His spiritual victory over death through the acceptance of death. The Resurrection of Christ was a Divine-

Human action—God in man and man with God. The Resurrection is the figure of the Pentecost of Christ, the descent of the Giver of Life, of the Holy Spirit, on the divine corpse. In the original sin of the old Adam, the Spirit of God left man, and death overtook him. The new Adam took this abandonment upon Himself, and in His death the Spirit of God returned to man; and so the life of the Resurrection becomes man's inheritance. In Christ all mankind after the old Adam coexpires, so that with Christ it may be coresurrected and receive new life. It receives this new life at Pentecost, which, along with other gifts, contains within itself the power of the general resurrection to come. Pentecost is the power of Christ's Resurrection, it is indeed the eternal life given to us by Christ. "As in Adam all die, so also in Christ shall all be made alive" (1 Corinthians 15:22). *Christ is risen from the dead, having trampled down death by death.*

Translated by Asheleigh E. Moorhouse
April, 1964

General Bibliography

WITH THE exception of the original editions or collected works of authors represented in this anthology, bibliographical indications are limited to works in English.

ANDERSON, P., *People, Church and State in Modern Russia*. New York: Macmillan, 1944.

BERDYAEV, N., *The Russian Idea*. New York: Macmillan, 1946.

FEDOTOV, G., *A Treasury of Russian Spirituality*. New York: Harper Torchbooks, 1961.

HARE, R., *Pioneers of Russian Social Thought*. London: Oxford, 1951.

LOSSKY, V., *History of Russian Philosophy*. New York: International Universities Press, 1951.

MASARYK, T., *The Spirit of Russia*. 2 vols. New York: Macmillan; 2nd ed., 1955.

MILYUKOV, P., *Outline of Russian Culture*, edited by H. Karpovich. 3 vols. Philadelphia: University of Pennsylvania Press, 1943.

MIRSKY, D. S., *History of Russian Literature*. New York: Vintage Books, 1958.

STEPUN, F., *The Russian Soul and Revolution*. New York: Scribner, 1935.

WEIDLÉ, V., *Russia Absent and Present*. New York: Vintage Books, 1961.

ZENKOVSKY, V., *History of Russian Philosophy*. 2 vols. New York: Columbia University Press, 1953.

ZERNOV, N., *The Russian Religious Renaissance of the Twentieth Century*. New York: Harper & Row, 1963.

About the Author

The Very Rev. Alexander Schmemann is Dean of St. Vladimir's Orthodox Theological Seminary in Tuckahoe, New York, as well as adjunct professor in the Slavic Department of Columbia University. An official observer at the Second Vatican Council, he has also worked closely with the World Council of Churches and has been a leader in the Student Christian Movement. Father Schmemann is widely regarded as a leading spokesman of Russian Orthodoxy in this generation. In addition to his leading role in the Fellowship of St. Alban and St. Sergius, the principal vehicle for dialogue between the Russian Orthodox and the Anglican communion, he has contributed key statements of the Orthodox position in such publications as *The Handbook of Christian Theology*, *The Theology of Missions*, and *The Primacy of Peter and the Orthodox Church*. He is the author of several books, including *The Historical Road of Eastern Orthodoxy*, *For the Life of the World*, and *Sacraments and Orthodoxy*.

Born May 13, 1921, in Reval, Estonia, Alexander Schmemann emigrated to France and received his theological training at St. Sergius Academy in Paris. After his graduation in 1945 he served there for six years as lecturer in church history. He is a graduate of the Sorbonne and an archpriest of the Russian Orthodox Church. In 1951 he came to New York as a professor at St. Vladimir's and was later appointed Dean. Articles by him have appeared in the leading Orthodox journals as well as in *Cross Currents*, *The Ecumenical Review*, and elsewhere.